DEAR ZARI

The Secret Lives of the Women of Afghanistan

ZARGHUNA KARGAR

sourcebooks

This book is a memoir. It reflects the author's present recollections of her experiences over a period of years. Some names and characteristics have been changed, some events have been compressed, and some dialogue has been re-created.

Published by Sourcebooks, Inc.
P.O. Box 4410, Naperville, Illinois 60567-4410
(630) 961-3900
Fax: (630) 961-2168
www.sourcebooks.com

Originally published in Great Britain in 2011 by Chatto & Windus.

Library of Congress Cataloging-in-Publication Data

Kargar, Zarghuna.
  Dear Zari : the secret lives of the women of Afghanistan / Zarghuna Kargar ; edited by Naomi Goldsmith.
    p. cm.
  Originally published: London : Chatto & Windus, 2011.
  1. Women—Afghanistan—Social conditions—21st century. 2. Afghanistan—Social conditions—21st century. I. Goldsmith, Naomi. II. Title.
  HQ1735.6.K37 2012
  305.409581—dc23
                                    2011052703

Printed and bound in the United States of America.
BG 10 9 8 7 6 5 4 3 2 1

*To my mother and father, who are always kind, and
have given me my wonderful brother and sisters*

Contents

Introduction

"IT'S IMPORTANT FOR WOMEN TO KNOW THEIR RIGHTS IN A COUNTRY like Afghanistan," one female listener of *Afghan Woman's Hour* wrote to us.

Another told one of our reporters in Mazar-i-Sharif, "I heard the interview on *Afghan Woman's Hour* about how Afghan women have started working and earning money by using their skills by taking up carpet weaving. I realized that other Afghan women were doing so much while I was just doing the housework. I now weave carpets at home to earn my own money and have gained my husband's respect because I'm able to contribute to our living costs."

A listener from the eastern city of Jalalabad said, "I always listen to *Afghan Woman's Hour*. I love it because it features women from all over the country and makes me feel closer to the people of Afghanistan." And a young man got in touch to say, "I'm writing on behalf of my grandmother. Every Monday night she tells us to keep quiet when it's time for her favorite show. She's asked me to let you know that whenever your program comes on the radio she has to sit down quietly and listen to it, and that her favorite part is the stories, as the women featured in them sound so lovely. They make her feel as if they are telling her own life story."

Just as it was for this older woman and for so many others who regularly tuned in to the BBC's *Afghan Woman's Hour*—both male and female—so too was it for me. I loved the program's life stories, and enjoyed them so much that I would sometimes find myself listening to them again and again. By the time I came to be working on the program I had been away from my country for so long that I'd forgotten just how arduous and cruel life in Afghanistan can be, especially for women and girls. And these women—mothers, wives, grandmothers, sisters, and daughters—all have their story to tell.

⟨⁂⟩

WHEN I LEFT AFGHANISTAN in 1994 women were still going to work and girls attending school, so while they may have been limited in what they could do in certain respects, they still enjoyed a great deal of personal freedom. At that point the Mujahedeen were in power. The Mujahedeen were a collection of opposition groups that considered themselves to be engaged in a "jihad"—a holy war—against non-Muslim invaders, and were financially supported by the US, Saudi Arabia, and a handful of Muslim countries. They had begun forming into rebel groups in the 1970s when Russian troops first invaded Afghanistan and made the country—not for the first time—a pawn in the battle between the two superpowers of the Soviet Union and the United States of America.

When the Mujahedeen first took control of Kabul in 1992 they seized power from President Najeebullah's government. Dr. Najeebullah was to be the last president of the communist era in Afghanistan, elected at a time when the Afghan communist party was still responsible for selecting the country's president. It was in the decade of the communist era that I was born, becoming a child of what was to become known as the "revolution generation."

In the late seventies and early eighties, a coalition government backed by the Soviet Union had ruled Afghanistan. There was a treaty dating back to 1978 in place with the USSR that allowed the Afghan government to call on Soviet military force, were it ever needed. On April 14, 1979, the Afghan coalition government called in this favor and asked the USSR to send troops to help in the fight against Mujahedeen rebels. The Soviet government responded to this request by deploying a huge number of forces and heavy arms to Afghanistan on June 16th of that year. And so began the Soviet-backed Afghan government's war against the Mujahedeen.

According to what I've since learned, the Afghan government at that time was very powerful. Its institutions were strong; its control extended to all the country's many different provinces and its army was more than capable of taking on the Mujahedeen, even though the guerrilla war that had first been fought in remote villages near the border with Pakistan was gradually spreading to the rest of the country. On the whole, the Mujahedeen forces were backed by ordinary Afghan people, who saw the Russians as non-Muslim invaders, bringing with them non-Muslim values and ideas. The invading Soviet forces, meanwhile, tended to be supported by those Afghans employed by the government in public services and in the factories.

But the Soviet support wasn't just military, as the USSR also provided social, economic, and educational aid, and since the Soviet-backed Afghan coalition believed in sexual equality, many Afghan women and girls also traveled to the Soviet bloc for educational purposes. Meanwhile factories were built in Afghanistan that women could work in, and those who had lost their husbands in the recent war were given priority when it came to securing jobs. It appeared then that both the law and prevailing social attitudes saw women as equal to men, free to walk by themselves in the street, go to the cinema, enjoy mixed-sex education, appear on television singing and dancing, and even wear miniskirts. But despite the liberal social climate in the cities, many families in rural areas continued to practice more traditional customs that they expected their women and girls to follow. For example, while the Afghan constitution decreed the legal age of marriage to be sixteen for both boys and girls, many families in rural areas were still marrying off their children as young as eleven or twelve.

Of course, my personal experience was predominantly a Kabul-based one—a developed city with more open-minded social attitudes, where the law was enforced by the police and security forces, a public bus service operated, and men and women worked side by side in schools, hospitals, and factories. I even remember going to weddings where men and women danced together to live bands. All around me, Afghanistan's cities were gradually modernizing. Women were no longer forced to wear a head scarf or *burqa*—although some women chose to. Women from different regions of Afghanistan continued to wear traditional clothes: I remember seeing Hazara women in their long, baggy dresses and colorful scarves, Tajik women in their column dresses and loose-fitting white *shalwar* trousers, and Pashtun women with their brightly colored *shalwar* and loose dresses.

Just as Afghan women were becoming active in politics and working as doctors, lawyers, journalists, pilots, senior army officers, and government officials, so too were they appearing in films and being encouraged to perform on national television. Alongside these developments in opportunities for women, the Afghan state media was busy broadcasting Western films and music, Bollywood movies and Russian programs, all of which contributed to the sense of Afghanistan opening up to the outside world. Kabul itself was a great ethnic melting pot of people from all over Afghanistan: Hazaras, Pashtuns, Tajiks, Uzbeks, Sikh minorities, and Kuchi nomads were all given the same access to education, training, and jobs, as the government was committed to ensuring equal opportunities for everyone. I remember my father telling me at the time that Afghanistan was beginning to move closer toward democracy.

Yet in many ways, life in Afghanistan was the same as it had always been, particularly in rural areas. People with strong religious beliefs tended to continue to follow traditional practices, marrying off their children young in defiance of the national law and allowing women to be given away as a means of settling family disputes, and also denying them any share of family inheritance. There may have been a stable government in place capable of creating new legislation and dispensing justice, but the future of young Afghan girls was still seen by many as a family affair and not one in which the government should interfere. The more traditional communities within Afghanistan generally did not embrace the communist values of the Soviet-backed government, and as a result, the Mujahedeen's propaganda enjoyed greater success in the country's more remote areas. This split between urban and rural values resulted in a number of rural girls' schools being burned down, and in some cases their teachers, or women who dared to appear on television, were even murdered. Fortunately, these attacks were rare.

The government of the time was accused by many of adhering only to communist values and neglecting Afghanistan's own laws. But in practice many Afghans—including my father, who was for four years the Minister of National Radio and later the Minister for Printing and the State Committee—believed deeply in traditional Afghan cultural values. In those days, being seen to be active in party politics was a prerequisite for a successful career in politics; my father was in a high-ranking cadre of the ruling People's Democratic Party of Afghanistan. Like many of his peers, he believed in Islam and traditional Afghan cultural ideals but was careful not to do anything that could be seen as defiant of the country's Soviet-backed rule. Yet interestingly, even though the school my sisters and I attended (one of the best and most modern in Kabul) was built by the Russians, staffed by Russian teachers, and had Russian language as part of the curriculum, we were also taught the Quran and learned about Islamic history and studies.

Everyday life for the ordinary Afghan was full of hardship. It was compulsory for every young Afghan man to spend two years in the army during the tumultuous period between 1978 and 1992. These men were conscripted and trained to fight against the Jihadi groups. Many Afghan families lost a son, husband, or father in this war against the Mujahedeen; and many young men returned from the fighting severely disabled. While the government made special provisions for war widows by giving them a monthly income, job opportunities, and special benefits for their children (sufficient to keep them off the streets), girls and women still suffered through the decades of war in Afghanistan.

Regardless of which political faction was in power, women were always affected badly.

Finally, in 1989—after ten long years in Afghanistan—the occupying Soviet forces left and President Najeebullah's government's grip on power became ever more precarious. He tried to make peace deals with different Mujahedeen factions but without much success; some of its leaders weren't interested in brokering partnerships—they were too busy building up their armies as warlords of lawless provinces.

The final death knell for the government came with the breakup of the Soviet Union; the USSR could no longer prop itself up, let alone support Afghanistan. The dissolution of the Soviet Union resulted in the end of all financial aid to the Afghan government. Overnight, Afghan factories closed, shops were empty, and the Afghan people were starving. Afghanistan became a forgotten zone no longer of strategic or political importance to the superpowers. President Najeebullah's government collapsed and the Mujahedeen took control.

We were still living in Kabul when the Mujahedeen took control. Everything changed very quickly: my dad lost his job, his government car, and his status. I remember he used to say: I didn't harm anyone while I was in the government, so no rebel group can have anything against me. But unfortunately it wasn't that simple; my father was branded a communist and forbidden any sort of governmental position. Soon after the Mujahedeen entered Kabul, different factions within the party started fighting over power, and war broke out in the now divided capital. Every group was armed and there was no appearance of law and order—anyone could use a gun, after all.

In the heat of war in 1994, my family decided to leave Afghanistan. My parents were scared for our safety and we worried about my father every time he left the house. Like millions of Afghans we fled to Pakistan, the nearest safe country. Life was very different there. My sisters and I went to school and my dad managed to get a job. Days, months, years passed and hopes of going back to our homeland were fading fast when, in 1996, the Taliban took over Afghanistan.

The Taliban were strongly dependent on the rules of Sharia law, especially in their beliefs about the treatment of women. They were supported by Pakistan and Saudi Arabia and, unofficially, by the United States; the terrorist organization Al-Qaeda and Osama bin Laden also supported the Taliban. The new government introduced strict rules—for example, women had to stay at home, girls were not allowed an education—with harsh punishment for those who dared to disobey. These were dark days—Afghanistan was isolated and poor.

When the Taliban came to power we gave up all hope of returning home. For a family with many daughters, Pakistan seemed the best place to be at that time—there, my sisters and I had access to education, university, jobs. I went to university and studied journalism and started working as a freelance reporter for the BBC. Yet even then my parents were not totally settled in Pakistan, and they decided that for a better and more secure life, it was best move to the West. My uncle and his family lived in the UK already, so we applied for a visa to move to London. In August 2001, my father was granted a permanent visa to come to the UK. After only a few weeks of living in London, the World Trade Center in New York was attacked; the lives of many Afghans were irrevocably changed, and not just those living in Afghanistan—the attacks even changed my life as an Afghan living here in the UK.

❧

AFTER THE ATTACKS ON the World Trade Center in New York on September 11, 2001, and the collapse of the Taliban, the BBC's Afghan section realized it needed more staff. By this time I was working in London and since I had relevant experience, I was offered a short-term contract and began work on the various different news and entertainment programs. During these early years at the BBC I gained more broadcasting experience and my skills were continually improving by working with senior journalists.

Then in 2004, when the Taliban finally lost power, I started work on a new program for Afghan women called *Afghan Woman's Hour* (developed by the BBC World Service Trust with financial assistance from the British Foreign and Commonwealth Office). The remit of this weekly magazine program was simple: to inform, entertain, and celebrate Afghan women through the power of radio. My knowledge of my homeland was key to my being asked to produce and present this program, and reminded me what my father had always said, namely that if I could understand and speak both the main languages of Afghanistan—Dari and Pashtu—I'd be able to connect with the people and understand the culture of my homeland. The idea was that I'd work with an editor who had experience producing BBC Radio 4's Woman's Hour.

Afghan Woman's Hour was launched in January 2005 with the aim of providing women in Afghanistan with a radio show which would cut across all tribal, social, and economic boundaries. The program reached women in both rural and urban areas of Afghanistan and was broadcast in both Dari and Pashtu, which most women in Afghanistan's thirty-four provinces can understand. We chose each slot of the program according to what we believed our target listeners wanted to hear and learn about. Before the program had been set up, Afghan women and girls both in the country itself and in refugee camps in Pakistan had been asked by the BBC World Service Trust what they would expect to hear if they had their own special radio show. Surprisingly enough, the level of interest for such a radio program was similar to what we have here in the UK for *Woman's Hour*.

With the help of senior BBC producers, I learned how to put together different kinds of material relating to Afghan women's lives. The program had a variety of different slots—for example, a discussion section where an important topic like domestic violence or early marriage would be considered—and both experts and ordinary women would be invited to share their knowledge and experience. We also broadcast educational reports on issues like child mortality and contraception, and shone a spotlight on such female high achievers as Habiba Sarabi, who became the first female governor in Afghanistan in 2005. She was invited on to the program as a guest interviewee, as were a variety of female poets, writers, and musicians. Meanwhile the cultural diversity to be found amongst Afghanistan's different regions was celebrated through songs and recipes. Some days we tackled such taboo subjects as rape, divorce, and virginity; on others we exchanged recipes. Each week we featured women from all over Afghanistan cooking healthy meals good to feed a hungry family. The aim of this slot was to draw on and share the vast repository of recipes from the country's different ethnic groups and tribes. The program also covered any newsworthy achievements of Afghan women. The objective was quite simply to cover the wide range of issues that matter to women—our listeners often told us precisely what subjects they wanted the program to cover.

It was this intervention from our listeners that led to the development of our most popular slot: the life stories. Every woman who told us her life story effectively represented hundreds of others from any number of different ethnic backgrounds. Both Afghan women in Afghanistan and those in refugee camps in Pakistan wanted to hear about other women. They wanted to share their life stories, and they wanted to tell others about the hardships they had endured. Some were ready to share the problems they'd experienced in their marriages; others wanted to seek medical advice from doctors or family planning experts here in the UK. Some were keen to know about their legal rights, and others to share their skills and experiences with us. We organized the program as a series of different slots; the first consisted of an interview or discussion with experts mainly on taboo topics relating to gender, the rights of women in a family and society, and the practicalities of dealing with domestic violence. The second slot was all about jobs, and this was where women shared with the audience their skills, the story of how they acquired them, and their experiences of working in Afghanistan.

It wasn't possible to do all this with just a producer and an editor in London. I returned to Afghanistan regularly to do interviews and also communicated with reporters there. It was *Afghan Woman's Hour*'s aim to train Afghan women to make a radio program for themselves, and to this end we'd begun to hire and train women from the country's different provinces, often those who loved the show and were full of new ideas for developing it. The program first started with two reporters in Kabul, but after a couple of months we managed to find young women in provinces across Afghanistan who could send audio material to us via the Internet. Discussions and interviews with guests and experts were mainly conducted by me from London over the phone, or down the line to the Kabul studio.

Radio is the main source of mass communication in war-torn Afghanistan. Most people in the cities and rural areas have access to it. If you travel to even the most remote part of the country, it is very rare to find a home without a radio, and so it was after just a few months of being on the air that I started receiving letters, phone calls, and emails from our listeners. These were mostly from men—some of whom wrote on behalf of the women in their families—but women and girls also started getting in contact with our local Afghan reporters. Then in 2007, we won the BBC's Best Team of the Year Award. And although *Afghan Woman's Hour* was already being repeated twice a week on the BBC, a couple of local radio stations also started rebroadcasting the program several more times a week. Following the success enjoyed by *Afghan Woman's Hour*, other radio and TV stations started their own women's shows. While most media outlets are still run by men in Afghanistan, there are now women working as presenters, producers, and newspaper editors, and there are even women who run their own radio stations. Nongovernmental organizations (NGOs) play an important role in making this possible, by helping train Afghan women to make their own radio programs.

~~~

AFTER ELEVEN YEARS OF absence from my country, I went back in 2005. I touched down at Kabul airport, which I had never seen before. I found the whole experience of returning to my homeland extremely stressful. The city was nothing like I remembered. The Kabul of my childhood was green and calm, and far from crowded; when I got off the plane, I couldn't believe this was the same city. This land of wild mountains and dusty people scared me and I suddenly questioned why I was there. Why had I left my family behind and come to a dangerous place like this? Was my work really so important? It was even difficult for me to identify with my own people, although I wore a large scarf in deference to my culture. As I sat in the car, being driven from the airport to the BBC office in the center of Kabul, I spotted the block of flats where I'd grown up. We even passed my old school, but I found it hard to make a connection to these places. I had to keep asking the driver where we were as the fighting had damaged many of the buildings and roads so badly I no longer recognized them. But it also seemed as if the war had changed the people themselves; sometimes men would stare at me as if I were an animal in a zoo. Yet despite my initial fear, I fell in love with my country all over again and have returned several times since. The energy and commitment of the women who came to the BBC to be trained to make radio programs inspired me. The bravery it took for them to leave their families and homes and come to Kabul gave me strength and hope, and their powerful stories energized me to continue my work with *Afghan Woman's Hour*.

During that period I helped train more than twenty Afghan women from different parts of the country to interview and make reports about women in their provinces. Some of these women were still at school or university, while others had very little education and had to be taught how to use a computer. Take Kamila, for example. She reported for us from Khost province in the southeast of Afghanistan and was only partially educated. She contacted our Kabul office as one of the program's fans and told me she had many interesting stories she could record for us. She lived up to her promise by sending us a number of fascinating stories from her region, which we were able to broadcast from London to all over the world.

As well as presenting the program, I was also its producer, which meant I had to edit the items to fit the length of the program. A reporter like Kamila would send me a life story she had recorded in her province through the Internet, and I would then have to cut it down to fit the four-minute slot. The art of this job was to split the story into four pieces, and then broadcast one of them each week. As with all good storytelling, I had to end each section at a place where it would sound like a cliff-hanger so the listeners would be impatient to know what happened next. Before I'd started this job, I'd assumed that the life stories section would be the hardest to edit, but the sheer brilliance of the stories and the shocking realities of the women's lives made producing the slot an almost effortless process, with each paragraph so full of emotion and drama that every minute or so there would be another natural cliff-hanger.

Through my work I learned about the dark period that the women of my country had endured during the Taliban era, while I was living abroad. I heard just how hard life had been for them, how families had felt pressured into giving away their daughters to older men, how women were treated as if they were no longer of any use because they couldn't work or get an education. For a decade their faces had been hidden behind the walls of their houses and their voices had never been heard, but I decided—with the help of *Afghan Woman's Hour* reporters across the country—to give these women a voice by airing their stories.

These life stories had such an impact on me that I started having dreams about my childhood in Afghanistan during wartime; I also felt closer to these women as the memories of my years in Kabul came flooding back. It didn't matter whether the life story was that of Nangarhar in the east or Balkh in the north, or whether it came from a Hazara or a Pashtun woman, these were all Afghan women who lived amidst similar traditions and values. The women had all gone through a similarly wretched experience, yet back at the BBC office in London, I could somehow identify with them all and, to a certain extent, I shared their feelings.

Their candor and readiness to share their stories gave me, in turn, the confidence to discuss more sensitive and controversial issues on the program. Indeed these women inspired us to the point where I was often spoiled for choice about which life story to choose. When we'd first started *Afghan Woman's Hour* I'd worried about filling this slot every week and wondered what we could replace them with if we'd run out of stories. How wrong I was to be concerned. For six years Afghan women shared their stories with our reporters and listeners. Women would contact us and ask us to come and record their stories. After two years of being on air, an audience survey carried out by an independent research company for the BBC showed that *Afghan Woman's Hour* had become the second most listened to radio program in Afghanistan, and the life stories was its most popular feature.

Now people in Afghanistan were able to hear these amazing stories on their radios—about brave men and women who fought to liberate their country from its darkest hour and bring peace and democracy;

and from women, whose voices have been suppressed for so long. But I believe these stories are so good and so important that they deserve a wider audience. And as I sat on the tube each day going to work I started to wonder whether the woman sitting next to me reading her newspaper might also be interested in discovering these extraordinary stories told by ordinary women. And what about women in the rest of Europe, the United States, and Australia too? They might lead very different lives to most Afghan women but they too understand what it's like to be a mother, a sister, a daughter, to fall in love, and to face disappointment. So I resolved that I would become the channel through which these voices could be heard, and from the hundreds of life stories I have heard, I've chosen a selection that I think are the most fascinating and inspiring to set down here.

Together these stories offer a glimpse into a closed and complex society and give an insight into what it's like to live in one of the world's poorest and most dangerous countries. What, for example, does a young bride pray for on her wedding night? How does it feel to be sold into another family to settle a dispute? And what happens to those who dare to love a man of their choice? What about the women required to dress and act like men in order to protect their families? And what does a young carpet weaver girl dream of when she's shut in a dusty room and expected to complete a rug so vast it's even bigger than her? If an Afghan widow wears makeup, does that mean she's searching for a new husband? And how do the Kuchi nomads live?

I hope, like me, you'll discover that Afghanistan has a beauty and richness all of its own and a character that's revealed in the cultural diversity of its people, from Turkmen and Uzbek carpet weavers, Hazara tailors, to Tajik cooks and Pashtun poets. All these different voices speak in unison of the common desire for the human spirit to be recognized.

1

My Story

*T*HERE WAS A TIME WHEN I BELIEVED THAT ONCE I WAS LIVING IN London, all my problems would be solved and that I would be the happiest person in the world. How naive I was. The combined hardships of living through war, losing my home, and leaving my homeland may all be in the past, yet even now when I hear about war on the news, I realize I've not forgotten any of my experiences but that they are all stored away in my memory, ready to be triggered by an image on the television. The reawakening of past traumas is easier to endure if you're with your family, but when I was unhappily married, I realized that even though I'd escaped the war and was living in London, happiness was far from guaranteed.

Life as an Afghan woman in London isn't always easy and it can still sometimes be surprisingly painful. There are times when I sit in my small room in South London and think about how my life has turned out. I get so many mixed feelings: childhood memories can bring a smile to my face, while some from my teenage years make me feel sorry for myself, then memories of the war make me fearful and anxious. What if it were all to happen again? Would my family and I survive? As I try to suppress these fears, more memories of my adult life surface, reminding me just how much has happened in recent years and leaving me exhausted.

Somehow, though, despite the pain I've endured, I've had many good times too. From living a privileged life as the daughter of a government minister in Afghanistan to being a war refugee and an asylum seeker, life has certainly shown me its many different faces.

⁓

GOING BACK TO THE beginning, I was born into a family of four girls—I was the second eldest—and received an excellent education at a modern Russian-built school in Kabul. My father was a politician, my mother a housewife, and as the family of a government minister we had the luxury of living in a Soviet-built apartment block with electricity, hot and cold running water, central heating, and modern toilets.

Life seemed uncomplicated then. My father was busy with his work as the head of national radio, in charge of all its programs and publications, while my mother and our maid did the household chores and looked after us girls. In the morning I would go to school with two Uzbek girls, Freshta and Zainab, childhood friends and daughters of our neighbors. I sometimes miss those carefree days, playing games with my sisters and school friends, but even then I was aware of the cultural pressures that weighed heavily on my mother. Despite being happy as we were, just the six of us, my sisters and I still felt incomplete as a family because we had no brother. It wasn't enough that we were well-behaved and successful at school; somehow, as girls, we were not considered good enough by our community—something that pained my mother. My father was an educated and open-minded man and it did not bother him that he had no son, but our life was about more than just our immediate family; we were part of a wider community. We still are.

This was in the late 1980s, as the Mujahedeen were getting stronger and the war against the Russian-backed government of President Najeebullah was intensifying. As a young girl I didn't understand what was happening in my country. I didn't care who was fighting whom, which party was in power, or what was happening in the provinces or remote villages. I thought of the Mujahedeen as uncivilized and dangerous, while I'm sure they regarded my family as infidels because we supported a non-Muslim government which was under Russian control. I was the daughter of someone the Mujahedeen considered to be a traitor and whom some probably wanted dead. But apart from being frightened by some of the stories my friends told me about the Ashrar (a name given to the Mujahedeen by the Afghan government and used by ordinary people, meaning "people who bring violence"), I wasn't all that affected by the war then. All I really cared about was going to a good school, wearing nice clothes, and having a secure home life, and it was just the same for the boys and girls who sat next to me in class as, like me, they were the sons and daughters of government ministers or officials. Most of our teachers were similarly connected to the government in some way. And so in many respects we enjoyed a privileged way of life. Or at least we did until the rocket attacks got closer and closer to our homes and schools.

During these years the Mujahedeen fired rockets almost every day in and around Kabul; and because the rebels wanted to take down the government—so they could take control of Afghanistan—they usually aimed at markets, hospitals, schools, government offices, and other public places where it was easy to kill civilians. It became a daily routine at school that whenever we heard the sound of a big explosion we would leave our desks and follow the teacher to the corridor, which was considered a safe haven.

But in the summer of 1989, one of those rockets changed my life. The first missile of the day landed in our school corridor, creating a huge explosion. It was so close by that the bang of the rocket rang in my ears. I can still recall the sound today. There was black smoke and dust everywhere. I could smell burning rubber. Children and teachers were running around in confusion and screaming. I looked down and could see blood and panicked but quickly realized it wasn't coming from my body. It was from another girl. One of my classmates was lying unconscious, her clothes soaked in blood.

That explosion has never left my mind. After seeing a fellow school girl die, I went into shock and became deeply depressed. My father paid for me to see one of the best doctors in Kabul and every Thursday I visited his private clinic. I soon began to dread Thursdays. Beyond the doctor's office there was a treatment room with a bed and an ECT machine where I would be given Electro Convulsive Therapy. I would lie on the bed and a piece of equipment that looked like headphones with cotton wool on the end would be attached to my temples. It felt cold and wet. When the machine was turned on a sharp pain would rip though my body.

For a time I couldn't cope with going to school and for several weeks didn't attend classes. My studies soon suffered and I became isolated from my friends; I stopped seeing them because I was so afraid of losing them, and became quiet and withdrawn. I was no longer the lively and fun person my school friends once knew, and they started to become frightened of me, calling me "dewana," which means *mad* in Dari. I was so nervous there might be another rocket attack—and one that would kill us all this time—that whenever I went outside to play with my sisters, and the other children started to make a noise, I would get scared. I was even afraid of playing in the snow with Freshta and Zainab, although I soon found that my friends didn't want to play with me as they said I was crazy and couldn't control my outbursts.

All I knew was that I was terribly afraid of my feelings and that when I needed my friends and wanted to play with them, they pushed me away. Their rejection hurt me deeply and made me grow up more quickly, but it also made me sad and lonely. I still feel wounded about the way they treated me then, but can also see now that they didn't understand I was suffering from depression.

I spent a lot of this time with my mother and became particularly close to her. We went to weddings and parties together and I soon became used to the company of adults rather than that of children. It was around this time my mother fell pregnant again and gave birth to a boy: my lovely, clever brother. With his arrival things began to improve for my family for a while. I gradually got better and my mother was overjoyed to have a son at long last.

As the civil war raged on, the different Jihadi groups fought each other to gain control of Kabul, with different areas of the city occupied by different rebel ethnic groups. The Pashtuns accounted for the largest of the factions and formed the Hezbi Islami Group led by Gulbudeen Hekmatyar, the Northern Alliance consisted principally of Tajiks (the second biggest ethnic group) and was led by Burahnuldeen Rabani and Ahmad Shah Masood, while the Hazaras formed a group called Hezbi Wahdat led by warlord Abdull Ali Mazari. Meanwhile the Uzbek faction—known as Junbish—was led by warlord Abdul Rashid Dostam. These were the same Jihadi groups who had supported each other in the battle against the Russian-backed communist regime. But when the United States came onto the scene, things changed quickly as each of the groups struggled for dominance. Where I lived, in the Microrayan district of Kabul, the area was divided between the Uzbek rebels and the Northern Alliance. When the Soviet-backed government had fallen apart, so too had any semblance of integration between the different ethnic groups in Afghanistan. Each faction now wanted power for itself, and its leaders would exploit ethnic tensions to their advantage. So the fighting intensified, with rockets increasingly being fired on a daily basis.

When the fighting eventually subsided we went back to school wearing black clothes and head scarves, and were frightened to see bearded men with guns standing outside our school gates. We also noticed that the statues of Lenin, which had stood in our classrooms, were now hanging from the trees. The men with guns would point up at them and indicate that this was to be the fate of communists. And it soon became clear that girls were being raped or killed just for going to school. In fact, it was increasingly common for warlords to abduct any school girl that they took a fancy to. My sisters and I were young enough at the time to avoid this fate, but keenly felt the dangers facing older girls. We were, for example, all aware of what had happened to Naheed, a girl who'd lived only a few blocks away from us. A Mujahedeen gunman had taken a liking to her, gone to her sixth floor apartment, and tried to rape her, and in order to escape she'd jumped from the balcony and fallen to her death. The next day the people in the neighborhood had launched a protest by carrying her body through the streets on a *charpoie* (a daybed), for all to see. The sight of this had terrified me and my sisters, but life went on. Women continued to go out but were always accompanied by a male family member, and girls went to school and some women to work, but far fewer than had before.

And so life gradually changed. Schoolgirls started to wear black clothes, and swapped short skirts and dresses for long baggy ones, and female teachers and older girls had to wear the *hijab* (head scarf), although this was only compulsory once a girl had reached puberty.

The curriculum at school also changed. We began to have Arabic teachers, were schooled in Islam, and learned English instead of Russian. Some girls were already good at reciting the Quran because their parents had organized for them to have private Islamic tutoring at home—I was fortunate in this respect—but others had difficulty learning the verses of the Quran and couldn't pronounce so much as a single Arabic word. We were routinely tested and if anyone didn't know their Kalama (the Islamic testimony of faith) they would be punished and ridiculed as communists who neither knew nor respected their religion. Not only was the whole educational system changing, but the country itself was split amongst the different Jihadi groups.

There was certainly no unity in Kabul, as different ethnic Jihadi groups controlled different parts of the city. While our neighborhood, for example, was under the control of General Rashid Dostam, just across the road, the area was led by the Northern Alliance and Ahmad Shah Masood. Eastern Kabul, meanwhile, was controlled by Hezbi Islami—led by Gulbudeen Hekmatyar—and yet another district was under the influence of Hezbi Wahdat and controlled by Hazaras.

Once again my father's life was seriously in danger because he'd served under the now discredited Communist regime and was, therefore, not liked by any of the rebel groups. Most of his friends had already fled Kabul; he no longer had a job and he was now father to four girls who were fast becoming teenagers. In 1993 my youngest sister had been born at the height of the civil war; although my parents had been hoping for another boy, this time round gender seemed less important.

Nonetheless, at the time, the security situation in Afghanistan for families with girls was far from good. When my youngest sister was only a couple of months old I used to look after her, and my mother would tell me to keep her warm so that she didn't catch a cold, but really she was far more worried about us older girls. We'd all heard about women being raped and kidnapped, so my parents were increasingly concerned for our safety, even though I was only ten years old. All the while the war became steadily worse, and we became steadily poorer. Then when my father could wait no longer to escape to Pakistan—fleeing the country ahead of the rest of us—winter came, and as it grew colder and the snow came, so the fighting intensified.

⌘

IN PEACETIME OUR FIFTH-FLOOR apartment had wonderful views and enjoyed the coolest breezes during the summer, but in wartime it was considered dangerously exposed to be at the top of the building. And now we were always at home. The war meant that once again there was no more school because the school buildings had been taken over by refugees who'd fled the outskirts of Kabul. War may bring people together, but that doesn't always mean they empathize with each other. The building we lived in housed ten different families, and as there would be intensive rocket firing every day, we would go down to the third floor each morning and join our other neighbors. We children would sit together in the corridor, and all the surrounding doors would be closed so that if a shell hit the building, the blast of broken glass and displaced furniture wouldn't injure anyone. We were taught this survival tactic by the men who bravely ventured out and heard about the experiences of other people in the city, discovering that many of the worst injuries were caused by shattering glass.

Our neighbors also had teenage girls and my sisters and I would often sit with them and swap stories. Muzgan, who lived on the third floor, was both the bravest and the best storyteller among us. She frightened us all with her creepy ghost stories, though I realize now that her storytelling was her way of coping with the fear of being killed in a rocket attack. Like Sheherazade, Muzgan would always tell stories that had no ending. We would hang on her every word and beg her to tell us what happened next but Muzgan would refuse to utter another word, relishing the attention.

While we children listened to Muzgan's stories, every evening the men would huddle around the radio and listen intently to the BBC World Service. Since there was no electricity and we had only one small battery-run radio between us, everyone had to keep quiet during the news. The men listened solemnly as the BBC informed them how many rockets had been fired that day, where they had landed and which group of the Mujahedeen was now in control of which area. We would often recognize the names of the roads and blocks of houses where the rockets had landed, because they were in our neighborhood, but we felt like prisoners in our own homes, unable to go out in the streets and actually see what had happened. Then, as the news program came to an end, Muzgan would always grab the radio and turn the dial to another station, one that played cheerful and lively music, and we girls would try to enjoy ourselves. The men, meanwhile, would embark on serious discussions about what the United Nations should be doing and what was to become of Afghanistan. None of them had jobs any more, and both money and food were fast running out.

For my mother this was a time of enormous pressure, as my father had already fled to Pakistan, having seen how some of his former colleagues had been assassinated or abducted. Before he left, though, there was one occasion at around midnight when we'd heard a knock at our door. My mother had looked through the peephole and seen a man with a scarf wrapped around his face carrying an AK-47 rifle. She had asked what he wanted. The man replied, "Open the door. I want to talk to Akbar Kargar." My mother didn't open the door, nor did she let my father speak to the man. We never did find out who he was. He may just have been a thief, but whenever someone came and asked to speak to my father, we would all get frightened. We lived constantly with this fear, never knowing whether he would still be alive from one day to the next.

Once my father had left Kabul he wrote to tell us that he had arrived safely in Peshawar, but after that we didn't hear any more from him for a while. His silence meant that my mother was uncertain about what to do, because she was waiting for my father's instructions. Life was simpler for us children, though: we would just do what Muzgan told us to do—she would play some music, and we would all clap. I realize now we girls listening to happy songs must have annoyed all those adults burdened with anxiety, and remember how Muzgan's mother would reproach her. "Muzgan, you shameless girl! Can't you see we're in terrible trouble? There might be no food for us tomorrow. Any of us could die. You should be teaching the girls to pray for the war to end." But Muzgan was not ashamed. "I don't care and anyway, I don't want to die feeling sad. Who knows? We might all die tonight, but I want to die when I'm dancing. I want to die happy. When you die, Mother, you'll die worrying." Then her mother would snatch the radio from Muzgan, ignoring our pleas to be able to listen to the music and saying, "Your brother doesn't have any more batteries left and we need to save the radio for the BBC news."

As these domestic squabbles continued, the fighting outside became even more intense. In the end, things got so bad we had to leave our home in Microrayan—which had become the stronghold of two different rebel groups—and move to Shahr-e-naw, another district of Kabul. Shahr-e-naw is right in the center of Kabul, and at that time was considered to be a safer neighborhood than Microrayan. We left Microrayan together with three other families, and as there was no time to pack we left with only the clothes we were wearing. We stayed in a friend's house who had already fled the country and had offered his home to refugees like us. Our living conditions there were cramped and squalid. All the women and children had to sleep together in one room, and as there was no hot water we couldn't shower and we didn't have clean clothes either. The food supplies were running low, and we had no idea what had happened to our homes, although we did hear from a neighbor that our apartments had been looted by the Mujahedeen. This news upset my mother greatly, particularly as she had been waiting and waiting for word from my father. My father is a writer and an intellectual, and the collection of books he had amassed at home over the years was his pride and joy. One large room in our apartment had been filled with shelf upon shelf of books—philosophy, history, politics, novels, and poetry—that were mostly written in Persian and Pashtu, but some in Russian. Our friends and neighbors had called it the Kargar library, and would regularly call in to borrow books.

By the end of 1994—just before the Taliban emerged—our life in Shahr-e-naw became harder than ever, the temperature dropped, and it began to snow. In the evenings it was the girls' job to go outside and fetch water, and by then it was so cold that our hands would turn blue and numb. My mother had also noticed that my sisters, the other girls, and I were spending all day scratching our heads, and had talked to Muzgan's mother about what to do about this lice infestation. She had suggested that my mother simply cut our hair, but we had refused to let her anywhere near us with scissors. Meanwhile the infestation only got worse. Every day I was wearing the same pair of old corduroy trousers and a sweater, both of which had become black with dirt. By now we'd been living in Shahr-e-naw for nearly two weeks, but the time had come to leave.

My father had managed to get a message to us through a male relative and had told us to rent some form of transport and go first to Jalalabad, a city in the east of Afghanistan that was seventy miles from Kabul. My mother and a neighbor duly made plans to rent a minibus, but on the day we were due to leave Afghanistan, the Pakistani government closed the border at Torkham (the main crossing between Afghanistan and Pakistan) in an attempt to stop the flood of refugees trying to flee Afghanistan. We would have to change our escape route.

When the time came to leave Kabul, my mother and our neighbor, Aunt Nasfeesa, both wept. I began to cry too, but I was only crying because my mother was. I didn't understand that I was fleeing my homeland to escape the war. My mother told us to say good-bye to the land we'd been born in, which we dutifully did, but at the time I understood neither the significance of what I was doing nor what was actually happening to us. We left Kabul very early in the morning, when it was still cold and dark. We'd packed the minibus with basic things like bread, drinking water, and bottled milk for my baby sister. We didn't reach Jalalabad until nightfall, staying the night at my mother's cousin's house where we all slept in one large room. My mother had two requests for her cousin when we arrived; first, could she help us get to Peshawar where my father was waiting for us? Second, could she offer us anything to get rid of our head lice? Thankfully, her cousin was able to produce a bottle of gray liquid—with a sharp antiseptic smell I can still remember—and my mother got to work with it straightaway. It was the first time any of us had had head lice and we didn't realize that it's considered embarrassing, and so were surprised when my mother's cousin's daughters began laughing and pointing at us. In turn, they were shocked at how openly we talked about the annoying little insects that were laying dozens of eggs in our hair every day. My mother, however, was mortified and apologized to her cousin for bringing us into her home infested with lice.

The next day we were up early again and drove the minibus to the border with Pakistan. As the official crossing at Torkham had been closed, we were going to have to cross the border illegally through the mountains, via the same route that people living in the border area were using to carry refugees between Afghanistan and Pakistan in exchange for money. We had to cross a narrow river at Naw-a-Pass in a wooden long-tail boat, then when we'd reached the other side we traveled in an open-back military truck. There wasn't a lot of space in it so we were all sitting on top of one another. Apart from the driver and his two assistants, we were all females, with no male relatives (other than my three-year-old brother) to protect us.

To add to our difficulties, we had with us my one-year-old baby sister who drank formula milk, so my mother somehow had to find clean, warm water to mix with the powder. We all took turns to hold my baby sister while she slept. I remember clearly being driven a long way through mountains and rocks, and how I screamed because I was only small and was being flung around all over the place. The mountains were so full of dust that we sometimes couldn't see where we were going. Sometimes we couldn't even see each other's eyes. The dust covered everything: the truck, our clothes, our faces. I think even our minds were affected by it.

We had entrusted our lives to a random driver commandeering an old Russian military truck and his two helpers. So while I feared we might crash and fall down the mountainside, my mother was no doubt more worried about being in a truck full of women accompanied only by men we didn't know. She would have been only too aware that we could have been robbed, raped, or killed; we'd even heard stories of Afghan women and girls being sold to Arab Sheiks.

As day turned into night, my mother and the other women got more and more worried. We'd been told that we would arrive in Peshawar before it got dark, yet night had come and we were still in the mountains. We were risking our lives trusting that we would eventually arrive in a better place and hoping we would finally see my father again after so many weeks apart from him. During that cold night, I thought back to those evenings listening to Muzgan's endless stories, craning our necks to catch the BBC news, and being nagged by Muzgan's mother. I missed Muzgan. Before I'd left Kabul I had promised to write to her. I'd told her I wanted to hear the end of the story of the little girl in the red hat whose grandmother had been eaten by a wolf, but she had said it would take too long. We'd told each other we would see one another again if we didn't die in a rocket attack, but that still hasn't happened. I heard from someone that she's married and has children, but I don't know where she's living. That's the strange thing about war, it can bring you so close to people, then it pulls you apart. You have to get used to losing friends, leaving one place, and moving to another.

As it turned out, we were lucky. The driver and his two helpers were not rapists. The sky was becoming lighter and the driver said his dawn prayers—Salat Ul Fajr—and then announced in a loud voice that we were going down the mountain, that this road would be easier, and that we were on our way to Peshawar. "*Inshallah* (God willing), the road will be faster and we will get there by midday." Full of relief that nothing had happened to any of us in that wild mountain range, my mother told us to thank God for keeping us safe. The rest of the journey was much less dusty and we soon reached a small Pakistani tribal village where a streetlamp cast light on the smooth road ahead. I no longer had to cling on to the bar of the truck, and while my skin was dry from the wind and the smell of the hair-lice lotion lingered in my hair, the dust no longer bothered me. I had swallowed so much of it that it almost felt normal. In comparison, the fresh air and tarmac road felt strange. I had been in those mountains for one and a half days and one long night.

We finally came to a bus terminal where some local people were selling bread, but the dust in my mouth had killed my appetite. Here we exchanged our Russian truck for a smaller Japanese one, which would take us on the final leg of our journey to Peshawar. The Pakistani border police knew when they saw us that we were refugees who had crossed the border illegally, but there was an arrangement in place between them and the drivers. Our driver simply handed over some money to them, and we continued on our journey into Peshawar. We had with us the telephone number of a friend of my father's who was living in Peshawar, and he was able to tell us where my father was staying. When we arrived at the house, my father was there waiting for us.

I had always seen my father clean-shaven and in a suit, smelling of aftershave and smiling. Yet here he was now in a dark green *shalwar kamiz* (loose trousers and dress or top) looking older and grayer. My parents cried as they hugged each other, and we girls wept too as we clung to him, but my baby brother behaved as if nothing had happened while my baby sister stayed asleep. My dad ended up holding her in his arms for hours. After a while we became worried that she was showing no sign of waking, but my mother simply said she was tired after all her crying and the long journey, and would wake up later. My father, meanwhile, told the other women how grateful he was to my mother. He said she was his hero because she had managed to bring his family back safely to him.

At last I was able to change out of my old black corduroy trousers and gray sweater, and have a hot shower. Finally, the smell of the head-lice lotion disappeared, and all the lice were dead. I think the journey had been as effective at killing them as the lotion had. In the evening my baby sister woke up, my mum washed her, and she contentedly drank her milk, while we were given a traditional Afghan meal of Kabuli pilaw rice, lamb, and spinach. The food tasted wonderful after so many hours of hunger and it was such a relief to be reunited with my father, but looking back I can see I didn't fully appreciate what a narrow escape we'd all had. I now give thanks to God for keeping us safe in that old Russian truck and for reuniting my family.

After dinner that first night, my father's friend's wife said to my mother, "Sister dear, you do know this is Peshawar, don't you?" My mother replied that, of course, she knew we had come to Peshawar. But the friend continued, "Sister, you must appreciate this is a very differ-ent kind of society to the one you've left behind in Kabul." My mother was now uncertain as to what she meant and asked in what way it was different. "It's very strict, and your daughters are not dressed appropri-ately. They will have to wear a *hijab* and cover their faces." My mother protested that we were still very young, but our hostess insisted that in Peshawar we would be considered women and it would be dangerous for us to go out dressed as we had done in Kabul.

The next day while my father looked for a place for us to rent, my mother went shopping to buy us *shalwar kamiz* and *hijabs*, and for the first time in my life I felt repressed. In Kabul the restrictions on women and girls' clothes hadn't affected us that much; I'd had to wear a head scarf outside and for school a long black *hijab*, but I had also been allowed to wear jeans, corduroy trousers, and blouses or sweaters. I'd been comfortable in trousers all my life, yet now I was expected to wear a *shalwar kamiz*, and even though I didn't actually mind wearing one, I didn't like the fact that I *had* to wear it. I asked if I could wear my jeans with a *kamiz* shirt, but was told I couldn't. Worse still I had to wear a large scarf called a *chador*, which covered my head and face, and left only my eyes showing. For an eleven-year-old child like me, this was too much. The *shalwar kamiz* might have been a traditional piece of clothing for Pakistani women and children, but it wasn't one I had grown up with. During my early childhood the dress code had been relatively relaxed before the Mujahedeen had made women wear the black *hijab* (something they'd enforced even in the refugee camps). I noticed now that some Mujahedeen groups treated Afghan and Pakistani women differently, and that they looked down on Afghan women and called them "Kabulis," meaning they'd come from a liberal country that didn't adhere closely to Islamic laws. And we were instantly recognizable as refugees because we had to wear the black *hijab* while the Pakistani women didn't—instead they could wear colorful clothes as long as their hair was covered.

~≫~

PESHAWAR IS IN KHYBER Pakhtunkhwa, in the northwest of Pakistan and is one of the most traditional areas of the country, so its tribal code of conduct remains very strong. Women and men do not mix outside the family, boys and girls go to separate schools, and men and women socialize in different rooms at parties and weddings. Compared to other cities in Pakistan, like Islamabad, Karachi, and Lahore, Peshawar is conservative, male dominated, and practices a strictly fundamental form of Islam.

My sisters and I found that men in Pakistan looked at us as if we were pieces of meat, and it frightened us enough to make us change our behavior and act like older women. At this time we were sharing a house with another Afghan family, and as our family had only two rooms, I no longer had my own bedroom and comfortable bed with a proper pillow and blanket. Our existence had become far more basic. I was no longer the daughter of a government minister. We were poor, and my father was looking for work. At that age I didn't understand that my parents were doing the best they could for us under difficult circumstances, so my sisters and I would moan about how the food we ate was too plain and how it was uncomfortable to have to sleep on the floor. My mother told us off for complaining, reminding us that we should be thanking God for keeping us all alive. I'm sure that if I were ever in that situation again I'd be far more supportive of my mother, particularly when I think of everything she went through, coping with the war and holding the family together. I see her now both as a strong woman and as a role model.

My sisters and I were soon given places in a school for refugees and even though I missed our house back in Kabul, life was much better than it had been during those long weeks of bombing and shelling, not knowing whether we would live or die. Gradually I adapted to life as an ordinary Peshawar schoolgirl, and my tastes began to change. I tried to make the best of having to wear *shalwar kamiz* by choosing ones made of brightly colored material and searching out those in the most fashionable styles. When I was at school, though, I had no choice but to wear the black *hijab*. Our refugee school was directly funded by Saudi Arabia—a country supportive of the Mujahedeen—and it concentrated heavily on Islamic studies. I found learning Arabic extremely difficult because even though I could read it—as I'd learned to recite the Quran—I had no idea how the grammar worked or what the words actually meant. When it came to Arabic exams, I remember crying because I found them so difficult.

Life improved when my father got a job with an education project at the BBC World Service. He worked as a writer on a radio drama for Afghans and was sufficiently well paid for us to be able to rent our own house in a better area of Peshawar. At this time, my father decided that my sisters and I should all learn English, saying it was vital for our future. So while we were already studying English at school, he also enrolled us in private language classes. They cost a lot of money, but he was adamant we should have a good education.

After completing high school in Peshawar at the age of seventeen, I went to a university for Afghan refugees to study journalism. I chose journalism because I harbored an ambition to sing or speak on either the radio or the television. I was still young to be going to university at this age but had been able to jump ahead because I'd finished my school exams early. My real dream though was to be able go to Kabul

University, not least because my father had studied there and my mother had always said it would be good to follow in his footsteps. My father had proudly told us about his old university's high standard of education and the quality of its teaching, but my ambition to study there remains unfulfilled. The collapse of the Soviet Union, followed by the period of rule by the Mujahedeen and then the Taliban, shattered those dreams.

~

BEFORE THE FIGHTING BROKE out in Afghanistan, my father wouldn't have entertained the idea of arranged marriages for any of his daughters, but war changes every aspect of life. The basics of survival, food, shelter, and safety end up taking priority over education. Our lives—like those of so many other refugee families—had changed forever, and there was no doubt that it was really hard for my father to be responsible for four daughters. He had not only to ensure our safety, but also our moral well-being. Many fathers ended up dealing with these problems by arranging for their daughters to be married to men living in Europe, where they would enjoy a better standard of living than in Pakistan. Meanwhile, Afghan men who had settled in the West were starting to come back to Pakistan in search of Afghan girls to marry. I consider myself lucky to have got an education before getting married.

Once we were properly settled in Pakistan, I was able to think about my future and my ambition to become a journalist. Many years before, I'd dreamt of becoming a professional singer, but as it's not a career choice held in high regard by my culture, I decided to become a radio presenter. While I was studying, the BBC World Service introduced a free five-day course in journalism for young Afghan refugees in Peshawar. Thrilled, I enrolled on it together with two of my university friends. When the course was over, I started work on an educational program for Afghans. The program was an international aid project set up by the BBC World Service Trust. I started to make short radio packages on subjects of interest to Afghan women in the refugee camps. I visited these women regularly and asked them specifically what kind of information they needed to hear about, and they told me they wanted guidance on a variety of health issues and more information about contraception. Some of these women had particular skills—like weaving—and I would interview them about their craft-making. After recording these interviews in the camps, I would add in some material from relevant experts before editing the material into a radio report that was then broadcast on the BBC's Afghan Service from London.

It felt so good to hear my work on the radio. In fact, I loved it, although when I first heard my voice on the radio I was embarrassed, because it sounded so small and young, rather like a bird chirping. That didn't stop my father being proud of me though. My sisters, meanwhile, were all busy studying and my not-so-baby brother was at a private school and doing well. My father also had a good job writing for the BBC's *New Home, New Life* educational drama, similar to Radio 4's soap *The Archers*. The series has been on air for more than ten years and is the most listened-to BBC program in the whole of Afghanistan.

Despite things continuing to get easier and life becoming more comfortable, it still wasn't safe for us to be living in Pakistan. My father was far from secure in a city where both the Taliban and the fundamental Mujahedeen forces were free to pursue their particular agendas, and Pakistan was not a country that gave sanctuary to political exiles. A couple of Afghan politicians from my father's era had already been murdered in Pakistan by fundamentalist Jihadis—those who had a vendetta against politicians from the Soviet era—and with the Taliban in control in Afghanistan, we knew we weren't safe in Peshawar. We worried every morning when my father left for work and would remain anxious until he returned in the evening. In those days mobile phones were few and far between, so he couldn't let us know he was okay during the day. Pakistan was only ever a temporary stopping point for us; we didn't ever expect it to become our home. We'd always imagined we would eventually return to Afghanistan, but had gradually come to realize that going back to our homeland would prove impossible.

When the Taliban came to power, Afghanistan became a state forgotten by the international community. By this time we'd spent more than six years in Pakistan, and many of our relatives were starting to ask my father if they could marry me or one of my sisters. We were now all in our teens, and in Peshawar it's perfectly normal for people to get married at the age of sixteen or seventeen. Such was the prevailing culture then, that my parents accepted offers both for me and for one of my sisters to get engaged. I was just seventeen years old at the time and was happy to do whatever my parents thought was best. In fact, I didn't really stop to think about what I was agreeing to because I was so busy studying and working full time for the BBC as a writer and producer in a children's radio drama.

Toward the end of 1999 my father's brother helped him get to the United Kingdom as an asylum seeker. Meanwhile my mother went back to Afghanistan with her brother to sell our damaged apartment in Kabul, even though it wasn't safe for her to go back there as a former minister's wife. Fortunately, though, my mother was not well-known and my uncle was just an ordinary young man whom the Taliban considered to be my mother's *mahram* (someone who is legally related to the woman, as a brother, husband, father, or uncle) and therefore a suitable companion for her. They went back to Kabul for just four days. At this time property prices were at their very lowest, as people had lost all hope of Afghanistan having a bright future. Unemployment was high, people were poor, and my mother was not able to secure a particularly good price for our property. When she returned to Pakistan, though, we knew we had cut our last physical tie to our old country.

Two years after my father had left us to go and live in England, he was able to get a family reunion visa so we could join him there. The day I knew I was going to London I went back to dressing in the way I had in Kabul. I bought a new pair of jeans and left my big scarf behind in Peshawar. I felt like a bird being let out of its cage as I shed my *hijab* forever. I had always complained about the strict dress code in Pakistan, threatening to throw off my *hijab* and wear a miniskirt, and my older sister had warned me that as an Afghan girl I could never do such a thing, as people would say I had lost all sense of my cultural values. Every time I would argue back: "My culture is not the *shalwar kamiz*, my culture is my clothes."

My mother would get angry with me for my defiance, but really she didn't bother much about how I dressed.

❧

WE ARRIVED AT HEATHROW airport on August 14, 2001—the air was clean and fresh compared to the polluted humidity of Peshawar, but I couldn't enjoy my newfound freedom because my fiancé was waiting to meet me. I had no idea what he looked like, and knew only that he was the son of a family friend. When I saw Javed for the first time, I realized the engagement was real; it wasn't something I could ignore. I was disappointed that he wasn't the tall, handsome man I had imagined, and angry with my parents for arranging the marriage. I didn't like Javed, didn't want to talk to him, and I spent a lot of time crying. Of course I knew that having a handsome husband was no guarantee of happiness, but I couldn't help my naive, idealized expectations. Ultimately, though, it didn't matter how I felt, because in my culture once it has been decided that a girl should marry a particular man, it would cause immense problems if that agreement was not honored. My mother used to tell me stories of families who'd changed their minds about an arranged marriage and then found that a close male relative of theirs had been killed. My mother reminded me that I only have one brother and warned that she didn't want him to inherit a dispute with another family.

I used to believe in marriage. When I was a girl I thought it, and everything it entailed, was simply to be accepted. So when my parents chose a husband for me, I accepted their decision, telling myself, "Zarghuna, you're a Pashtun girl and you should marry the man your family has chosen for you." I remembered the saying that a girl who accepts the wishes of her parents will never be unhappy in her future life. When I voiced any doubts, my parents told me to be a good Afghan girl and marry Javed. If I didn't go through with the marriage, I would have to leave the family and become someone else's daughter and never ask anything of them ever again. No matter how much I cried and told my parents that I couldn't marry Javed because I didn't like him, their response was always the same: "Hush! It's not for a Pashtun girl to say whom she likes or wants to marry. In our family no girl has ever chosen their partner. If anyone in our family finds out you've been talking this way, they'll gossip about us and we'll never be able to show our faces amongst decent people again."

I was too young to make any drastic decisions of my own; new to Great Britain and the whole Western way of life, I was frightened and didn't know what to do. I had a good job but it involved working with Afghans, most of whom knew my family; my social life revolved around going to Afghans' houses where people would routinely curse girls who had rejected their families' wishes and married a man of their choice. I felt like I had no choice and decided it was best if I married Javed. I wasn't to know that years later I would deeply regret this decision, or that I'd eventually find the strength to confront my family and community about my feelings. But it was July 2003 and I was only twenty-one years old.

～

LIKE SO MANY OTHER Afghan brides, my wedding day began in the beauty parlor. At seven o'clock in the morning my hair was curled, my eyebrows threaded, my nails polished, and I had proper makeup put on for the first time. When she had finished, the beautician picked up a mirror and held it in front of me. She told me to stand up and look at myself, said I was a beautiful bride and that the groom was a lucky man. I looked at my reflection and saw the pretty white wedding dress and the way the eyeliner and mascara made my eyes look larger. I was no longer the short, dark-skinned, plain Zarghuna but a taller, more sophisticated-looking person. The beautician insisted I looked beautiful, but I didn't believe her. I had darker skin than any of my sisters, and I had always been considered the least good-looking in my family. After the beautician took the mirror from me, I looked down. "One thing I should say is that even though you're a very beautiful bride, you're a very miserable one. You should cheer up a bit and smile on your wedding day." I said nothing and waited for Javed to arrive and take me to the wedding in the specially decorated car, a *gulposh*.

About two hundred and fifty guests came to the wedding ceremony, and I sat up high on a dais with Javed. It was the most unhappy day of my life. Here I was, perched on a highly decorated sofa for everyone to see, embarking on a marriage that I did not want but had accepted; all because I was an Afghan woman.

2

Sharifa's Story

THE FAMILY OF GIRLS

IN AFGHANISTAN, WOMEN USUALLY BECOME MOTHERS A YEAR OR SO after marriage. It's perfectly normal for Afghan women to have up to four or five children; in fact, even that would be considered a small family. For most Afghan women the purpose of marriage is simply to have a family, but her family is not considered complete until she produces a son. Any woman who manages to give birth to a succession of sons is cherished by her husband, praised by her mother-in-law, and respected by her community. In this way, the mother feels proud of having achieved what she believes she was born to do. If on the other hand a woman is unable to produce a boy, she feels a failure and her life is made miserable.

As a result, Afghan women tend to go on having babies one after another until a son is born; some women will even give birth to more than ten children in order to achieve their goal. Any woman who gives birth to a boy soon after her marriage is considered to be very fortunate, so many women spend much of their pregnancy praying and worrying about whether or not they will have a son. At special occasions, families will ask God to bless them with a son, and it is customary at wedding ceremonies for older Afghans to approach the young bride saying, "May you become the mother of sons." In my Pashtun community, there are even special songs that reinforce the desire for male children, such as "A Son Is Gold" and "God Only Gives Sons to Those Who Are Loved."

Sons are so important in our culture that some mothers will go so far as to neglect their daughters in favor of their sons. I've spoken to girls who've told me that at Eid their parents will buy new clothes for their brothers but not for them, and in some houses I have seen how mothers will serve their sons a large piece of meat while only giving their daughters a bowl of soup. I remember an Afghan relative who once visited us with her two daughters and son. She looked at me and my four sisters and exclaimed, "Oh my God, seeing so many girls together is very frightening. I wouldn't know how to cope with so many of them."

I've lost count of how many times I've wished I'd been born a boy; I know my older sister feels the same. Before my brother was born, when female friends and neighbors asked my mother about her children, she would look sad and they would sympathize with her for not having a son. Some women in our family would deliberately make spiteful comments about her lack of male children. I remember when one relative—who enjoyed none of the social and professional advantages our family did—had just given birth to a baby boy. She said in a cruel way to my mother, "Oh, this is the will of God. Some women have all life's luxuries while others don't. But a wife who is able to give birth to a boy really completes a family, and that makes her a proper woman." At this my mother became very upset; I could see the pain in her eyes and thought that she felt she was to blame for not giving the family a son. We comforted her and wiped away her tears, although she tried to mask her distress.

"Mum, whenever this woman comes to our house she makes you upset," I said. "Why is this? What does she say to hurt you?"

I remember my mother said, "My child, she's lucky. She's given birth to a boy, a son to the family. She's not worried about the future."

When I asked her how it was that boys could safeguard the future, she replied that they would always be able to take care of the family, their sisters and their mother. I told my mother that I could do that just as well as any boy, and that I would take care of her and my sisters, of the whole family. She smiled and stroked my cheek, saying, "I believe that you could do it, but you can't do it in the way that a boy could."

I knew then that as a girl there was only so much I could do to make my mother feel better. The community had spoken and it had made her feel a failure. My older sister felt my mother's pain too and would try to be like a boy—wearing boyish clothes that disguised the fact that her body was becoming womanly—and my mother would praise her and say how like a son she was. But I only truly understood why it was so important for an Afghan woman to give birth to a son when I was older.

⁓

THE TENDENCY FOR PARENTS to place greater value on their sons than on their daughters is common to every ethnic group in Afghanistan. One day Tabasum, one of our reporters at *Afghan Woman's Hour*, rang to say she had interviewed a mother who had given birth to twins, a boy and a girl, and that the way the mother treated them had made her angry. I asked her what had happened to make her feel like this. She said, "I'm used to seeing girls treated differently to boys, but I don't think this mother would even care if her daughter died. Both her babies are six months old and the son is healthy and active, but the daughter thin and listless. I think she's suffering from malnutrition. How can the twins be faring so differently? I've heard that the mother is breast-feeding the baby boy but has stopped breast-feeding the girl." Tabasum said this was because the mother believed the girl would one day be the property of another family, through marriage to someone else's son, whereas the boy would make a family in his own parents' home. He would bring a bride home and together they would one day care for his mother, so he needed to grow up healthy and strong.

Tabasum and I worked on this story together and were keen to know what the mother was feeding the daughter. When we asked her, she said, "I tried to give my daughter bottled milk but she didn't like it, that is why she's suffering from malnutrition. I've even had to take her to the hospital a couple of times." Tabasum was very worried about the baby girl, saying to me "Zarghuna Jan, when I looked at the baby girl she seemed to be pleading with me to help her. She wasn't kicking her arms and legs like a normal healthy six-month-old baby would, and I just didn't know what to do or say. How could I tell her mother that what she was doing to her daughter was wrong when she believes what she's doing is right?"

As part of the program, we interviewed a doctor who explained how important it was for mothers to feed their babies properly, regardless of their sex. The doctor said, "Dear mothers, think about both your sons' and your daughters' future. Would you want your son to marry a weak and unhealthy girl? Of course not! Every daughter will one day end up living in someone else's house, and would you want your future daughter-in-law to be so unhealthy and weak that she couldn't give birth?"

If mothers don't treat their daughters equally then how can we possibly expect men to treat us equally? A number of women spoke to us about how some family members had made them feel inferior simply because they were female, with one mother of four daughters telling us, "Every time I've given birth to a girl, my husband disappears from the house for days. I've even heard of fathers who haven't so much as held their baby girls for a year, or spoken to their wife for months because they believe she was to blame for giving birth to a girl."

~≈~

As someone who grew up in a family of girls, I know just how much my mother suffered before she had my brother, but after listening to the stories of these mothers I felt both proud and lucky to be part of my family. Sharifa was not nearly so fortunate. She was a school friend when I was a teenager in Pakistan, and I've never been able to forget her story. It shows what happens to those girls who don't have a brother and to those mothers who don't have sons.

Sharifa and I were classmates in 1998 at the university for Afghan refugees in Peshawar, and at the time we both lived in a crowded neighborhood populated mainly by Afghan refugees fleeing the Taliban's occupation of Afghanistan. She was the oldest of six daughters who had been born with only one-year gaps between them all. Sharifa was usually full of energy and fun and loved messing around and playing practical jokes, and was popular with both her classmates and teachers. She was short with big green eyes, and I remember how she wore a dark blue *hijab* that was far too big and swamped her. I would meet Sharifa every day at a bus stop on the busy Arbab Road, which was always dusty and full of cars and lorries belching out fumes. This was at a time when very few women ventured out onto the streets, and as refugee students we were required to cover our heads and faces with large scarves. We always joked that we were wearing our *hijabs* to protect our hair and skin from the pollution in Peshawar.

Sharifa and I enjoyed the journey to university each day, and would chat to the driver and talk amongst ourselves about our futures. However, there were days when Sharifa wouldn't speak to anyone, not even me—her best friend. At first, I thought she was being rude and I felt offended. Then if I asked her whether something was wrong, she would reassure me there wasn't before turning away, lost in her thoughts.

One morning I arrived at the bus stop to find Sharifa in one of her silent moods and decided to try to get to the bottom of what was wrong with her. When I asked her she replied, "Before I get married I want to have a checkup with the doctor to find out if I'm able to have a son. If I'm not able to, then I won't get married at all." Neither of us knew at the time how the sex of a baby is determined, so I advised Sharifa to get married first and then worry about whether she had baby boys or girls.

But still she was upset. She would talk about wanting to make her future husband happy, and clearly believed that would only happen if she gave birth to ten sons. The other girls and I would make fun of Sharifa for being so desperate to get a husband, and she would grow angry with us but didn't fight back. She would simply go quiet and retreat into her thoughts, yet we continued to poke fun at her. Then one day we realized we'd gone too far and that Sharifa was very distressed. When we tried to tell her that we were only messing around, she said, "Yes, I know you're only joking but it still upsets me. You don't understand—my mother has given birth to seven girls, and if my father dies, we won't have anyone to look after us. My mother is not able to have a boy; she's not strong enough."

I had met Sharifa's parents and so I was shaken by what she had told me. "Sharifa," I said, "you have six sisters and that means you're strong. You also have a lovely mother and father, so you really shouldn't worry." But whenever I met Sharifa's mother, she always seemed to have just one thing on her mind. First she would ask after my mother, but then she would always ask about my brother. Similarly, the first question she would ask of her daughters' friends would be how many brothers and sisters they had.

One day I found Sharifa in tears, and I knew she was crying about her situation at home and had finally worked out why she was always asking about my brother and mother; she was trying to find someone else in a position vaguely similar to hers. But of course she thought I was far more fortunate than her because I did at least have one brother, and he represented security. I told Sharifa not to think in such a negative way, saying, "You have a big family and when you and your sisters get married it means you will have brothers, and your mother a son."

But my words didn't comfort her. "Zarghuna, you'll never understand because you have a brother. I'm mostly upset for my parents. Because I'm the oldest daughter, I've seen my mother weep every time she gives birth and discovers that it's another girl. Each time it happens my dad won't talk to her for months and life at home is wretched. Even my grandparents ignore my mother. It's truly awful to see what happens to a woman when she's incomplete."

I tried to calm her down. "Listen, Sharifa, of course your mother is complete. Who says she isn't? I've met her. She's a beautiful and kind young woman—"

"What would you know?" she countered angrily. "She's not complete because she hasn't given birth to a boy. It's as simple as that." Sharifa lowered her voice and confessed, "Sometimes I even get cross with her. If she could give birth to a son, then at last we could have a happy life."

"Sharifa," I replied, "happiness doesn't come like that. It comes with what you already have."

I remember we were sitting in the corner of our college grounds, under the shade of a small tree. We would often sit there and chat. I wiped away the tears from Sharifa's face with my scarf and tried to reason with her that it wasn't anyone's fault that she didn't have a brother, or her mother a son. These things were in God's hands, and there was no point in getting so upset about it as life has to go on. But Sharifa insisted that she personally was being blamed for the situation, "My grandmother says it's my fault. I was the firstborn daughter and therefore all the other girls followed me. I brought bad luck on the family."

I desperately wanted to do something to help Sharifa, but the bell went and we had to go to our next class. Sharifa dried her eyes and tidied up her *hijab* while I wiped the dust off my trousers. But after that conversation, I couldn't stop thinking about Sharifa and prayed that her mother would have a baby boy.

⇜

WEEKS PASSED AND SCHOOL broke up for the holidays. A month later the new school term started and I saw Sharifa again. We hugged each other and met in breaktime under our usual tree. I couldn't wait to hear her news; I wanted to know what clothes she'd made, what earrings she had bought and where she had been during the holidays. "Zarghuna, I'm so happy. I think our life is finally going to change for the better. My mother is pregnant again and we're all hoping that this time she'll give birth to a boy." I promised to pray for the outcome they longed for, but then suddenly she became very emotional. She looked down at that dusty floor and then up at me, before saying quietly, "Zarghuna, I really hope God will be kind to my mother this time. I so hope she gives birth to a boy, because if she doesn't something terrible is going to happen." I looked at her for a few moments before asking what she meant. She looked down and then up at me again, and said, "My father is planning to get married again, and the marriage will be in exchange for me."

I was horrified. "No, that can't be right. He can't do that!"

But Sharifa said simply, "If he does decide to take a new wife in exchange for me, I think I will die." Her words filled me with dread. Even at our young age, I knew she was contemplating suicide. We'd both heard of girls who had set fire to themselves to avoid arranged marriages; it was the last resort for those who feel trapped.

Sharifa took a deep breath and continued, "He has even chosen a girl who is the same age as me. In exchange for her, my father will give me to the other family's son."

"You can't just accept this," I said crossly, and reassured myself with the thought that nothing definite had been decided because Sharifa's mother's pregnancy still had some months to go, and she might yet give birth to a boy.

"God will be kind," I said. "He will give your mother a son." Sharifa agreed and tried to be cheerful.

Several months later Sharifa and her sisters were busy choosing names for the brother they so longed for and—as was the custom amongst the Afghan refugees in Pakistan—my mother and I went to visit the family (as it was usual for mothers to befriend the mothers of their daughter's friends). We arrived to find Sharifa's family all getting very excited in anticipation of what they hoped would be the arrival of a baby boy, and both my mother and I prayed that this time God would indeed give them a son.

We sat in Sharifa's house in a small dark room with Afghan mattresses positioned by the walls and a traditional red Afghan carpet in the middle. The weather was unseasonably hot, so Sharifa served *Roh Afza*, a sweet juice that smells of perfume and is famous in Pakistan for its sugariness. As we sat drinking the juice, I could see how confident and hopeful Sharifa's mother was in her heavily pregnant state, and was pleased to see the family so happy. It was one of the most enjoyable days we'd ever spent together.

A couple of weeks later I saw Sharifa at the bus stop where we used to wait for our school bus. As soon as she saw me she started crying, and passersby stopped to stare at her outburst. Some even poked fun at her for crying on the street, making nasty comments—"Why are you crying? Do you need a man?," "Are you crying for a husband? Why don't you come with me?," "What's the matter, can't you get a man? Do you want some cock?"

I hugged her tightly, not caring what these strangers were saying. I wished I'd been able to shout something back at them, but it wouldn't have been safe. I looked closely at Sharifa, and said, "Try to calm down. What's the matter? Has something happened to your mother?"

Sharifa was more upset than I'd ever seen her. She could barely speak without gulping for air. At last, she gasped, "Zarghuna, I'm ruined, my mother is destroyed, everything is lost." Immediately I thought her mother must have had a miscarriage or a serious problem while delivering the baby. Again I calmly asked her what had happened, but by this time Sharifa was crying hysterically and it was clear from her puffy, red eyes that she'd been crying for a long time. "Zarghuna, it's another girl!"

I could see how exhausted she was, as if all the energy had drained from her body, and I decided to take her back to my home. When we arrived back at my house my mother was surprised to see us both, but I explained that Sharifa was upset and my mother accepted this without further question. I made some sweet tea and as we sat down on the carpet, I tried to calm Sharifa down. As I did so, I wondered what kind of society we were living in. How could it make any sense that an innocent baby girl could bring so much pain and suffering to Sharifa and her family?

I could only imagine that Sharifa's mother was even more distressed than her daughter, and struggled to understand how a lovely baby girl could come into the world and not be wanted by anyone. She was being judged for her gender and it seemed bitterly unfair. Struggling to say the right thing to Sharifa, I ended up saying the first thing which sprang to mind, and it was far from helpful. "You should be happy, Sharifa. You have a little sister who will bring laughter and happiness—"

"No," Sharifa shouted, "that baby has brought nothing but pain and sorrow, and my mother's life is a living hell now. My dad is not speaking to her and no one has even congratulated her for bringing a healthy baby into world. My mother is not feeding her and I can't even hold her."

She lowered her voice and mumbled, "My family will be scarred forever by this, and now I have to marry some stranger that my father has chosen for me, because he is marrying a girl from that family in the hope of bringing a son to our family."

I ventured some more useless advice: "Why don't you show your father how upset you are and ask him not to make you go through with this?"

I knew even as I spoke that this would be impossible. In our culture fathers take no notice of what their daughters say, and once their decision is made about a daughter's marriage, it is final.

I knew not only that Sharifa had no choice but to accept her father's decision, but also that Sharifa's mother would have to live with her husband's new wife, a girl half her age. The usual practice was for a man to pay for a wife by giving her family money, but Sharifa's father didn't have enough money to buy a new bride so he had to exchange one of his daughters instead. For Sharifa's father this arrangement would kill two birds with one stone; he would marry off one of his daughters and get a young bride who would give him a son.

After we'd spoken for a while Sharifa calmed down, we drank more tea, and then I walked her home. When I got back it was clear my mother knew what had happened, so I asked what she thought Sharifa should now do. My mother said, "It's a horrid situation, but if she doesn't agree to the marriage exchange then her family will have even worse problems," and with that, she carried on tidying up the kitchen. I knew only too well from my mother's experience the consequences of not having a son in an Afghan family; mothers without sons and sisters without brothers have suffered for many generations. While the father and the head of the family is alive and well, he is a powerful figure and his wife and daughters are secure, but when he dies the women become the property of the men of the extended family.

≫

IT IS COMMON PRACTICE in Afghanistan for a girl to be exchanged for a wife for her brother, or in cases like Sharifa's, a second wife for her father. According to the Afghan constitution, the legal age for a girl to get married is sixteen and for a boy eighteen, but many girls are exchanged or married far younger. Most girls simply do as they are told and honor their parents' choices for them. In poor families, daughters are sometimes kept for exchange later in life so that the family doesn't have to spend much money on the wedding of their son. This form of exchange is known as Badal: one family finds a bride for their son and in exchange they give their daughter to the brother of the bride, or sometimes to an uncle or cousin, instead of payment.

Strictly it is illegal for a girl to be given away to settle a family dispute or for her to be forced into marriage, but that doesn't stop it happening. It is a common occurrence because domestic matters tend to be solved within the family, and as girls are not allowed to go to the courts or seek legal advice, they end up being totally dependent on their families. Regardless of illegality, most women simply obey their family and consider that whatever happens in their lives is God's will. These young brides tend to be uneducated and therefore unaware of their legal rights, and while most men are aware of the law, they simply ignore it. They think the law should have no say in family matters.

I remember my mother once telling me the story of Zulikha, a girl from her village. After the death of her father, Zulikha and her sisters were distributed amongst their male cousins and forced to marry them, while the mother was compelled to marry her dead husband's brother. According to Afghan law, based on Islamic law, forced marriages are not allowed. Both parties need to consent to any marriage. However, many people do not fully understand the teachings of the Quran, so cultural traditions tend to take precedence over the letter of the law, and in Zulikha's case Afghan tradition was followed. She had no brothers so her family was distributed like possessions amongst the male relatives of her dead husband's extended family. The thinking behind this is that if the woman were to marry another man—a stranger—then the widow's land would be lost to someone outside the family. The law states that husbands and wives have an equal share of land and property but in reality all assets are regarded as the man's. So if a married man dies, then his brothers will come and take what they regard as theirs: the widow, her daughters, and all the property.

As it turned out, Zulikha had quite a good life with her husband because he was educated and had enough money to look after her but she never forgot the fact that she was given to him like an ornament or toy of no value. She could never forgive what her uncle's family had done to her sisters and her mother.

I was aware that Sharifa also had cousins and knew what had happened to Zulikha, but at that time she seemed to be fine. A few months later, though, she stopped coming to school and I started to worry about her. No one seemed to know how things were with Sharifa and her family, so I decided to find out for myself and one afternoon I walked over to her house. It was a good half-hour walk from my home, and I was hot and bothered by the time I arrived. I knocked on the old wooden door and waited, but then I noticed it was ajar and tried to peek through it when Sharifa's younger sister opened the door and invited me in. As I went into the garden I noticed there were piles of mud bricks and planks of wood everywhere; there seemed to be some sort of building work going on.

Sharifa came out to greet me. I hadn't seen her for several weeks— she had lost weight and become pale, and as I hugged and kissed her on the cheek as I normally would, I noticed that her lips were dry. I was sure something awful had happened.

"Salam, Sharifa. What's wrong? Where have you been? Why haven't you been coming to class?" I bombarded her with questions but she didn't reply to any of them; then she began to cry. She asked me to come into her bedroom and began to tell me about the building work, but I interrupted her.

"Are you building a new house or something?"

"My dad needs a new room," she said.

I understood immediately what she meant. Sharifa's father needed to have a room separate from the rest of the house for his new bride.

Inside the house everything was as quiet as if there had been a death and the household was in mourning. No one laughed or smiled. Sharifa told me that her family had decided to exchange her for his new bride, a girl who was just seventeen, the same age as Sharifa and me. In return, Sharifa would be marrying a man in his forties whose wife had died. She would have to look after this man's children and in so doing give up any dreams she might have had of a handsome young man of her own. Sharifa's happiness was being sacrificed to secure her family's future.

As I walked home I prayed fervently that there would be some kind of miracle, or that Sharifa and her family would reject this plan. Sharifa was forfeiting her future with no guarantee of the desired outcome. Who could be certain that the new wife would even give birth to a son? Sharifa's extended family kept saying that people who marry again eventually have a son, but who knew whether that was true?

Two months passed and I heard nothing from Sharifa. She wasn't allowed to leave the house and I was busy with school and household chores. I would occasionally wonder what had happened to her but had gradually come to accept that it was her destiny to marry an old man and safeguard her family's future. One afternoon after school, though, when I got off the bus, I saw one of Sharifa's younger sisters in the street. She was out buying medicine from the pharmacy. I stopped her and anxiously asked how Sharifa was. She said that Sharifa had had to get married before her father brought the new bride home because Sharifa's husband needed help with his five children, and that Sharifa was now their stepmother even though some of the children were almost the same age as her.

"But where is she now?" I asked. "Is she here in Peshawar?"

Her sister's eyes filled with tears. "Yes, she's in Peshawar but she's living outside the city, in a remote village. Her husband's house is a long way away and she's not allowed to come and visit us very often."

Sharifa's sister started crying. "We don't really see our sister anymore. She's too busy looking after her husband and his five children."

I was trying to imagine how young the children must have been, seeing as Sharifa herself was not much more than a child, and asked, "What about your dad? Did he bring home the new bride?"

The sister shook her head, and I asked why not.

"My dad is seriously ill. He fell ill the week before he planned to bring home his new wife and was taken into the hospital. I'm going now to take him these tablets that the doctor has prescribed."

Sharifa's eventful life started to occupy my mind once again. I explained to my mother what had happened and she immediately suggested we should go and visit Sharifa's mother to see how she was. The next day my mother and I went to the family's house. As I pushed open the old wooden door, I could see the garden was full of people and assumed they were celebrating Sharifa's father's wedding. Maybe he had gone ahead with it after all. But then I noticed that people were looking serious and that there was not the joyful atmosphere of a wedding. A group of men moved aside to let me and my mother into the house, and it was then that I heard the sound of crying.

We went into a room and found Sharifa's mother weeping. She was sitting on the floor; her scarf lay crumpled by her side. Her daughters sat around her and they too were weeping, but Sharifa wasn't among them. I approached Sharifa's mother and bent down to kiss her. She hugged me and held me tight and I sensed she was thinking that, as Sharifa's friend, I was somehow connected to her daughter.

"My child, Sharifa's sacrifice didn't bring us any happiness."

This wasn't a wedding. It was a funeral. Sharifa's father had died earlier that day, and he had died before bringing his new wife home or securing a son for the family. Sharifa's mother began wailing and slapping her face.

"Oh God, what will happen to us? I have lost two pieces of my heart: my daughter Sharifa and my husband. What will become of me and my daughters?" She was rocking back and forth, calling out Sharifa's name.

"Sharifa, my child, come and see. Your sacrifice didn't bring a son. Why did you have to leave me? Why? Now instead of you, Sharifa, your father's new bride has to come and suffer with us."

I stood there, unsure what to do or say. All the other women were crying and shouting too. Eventually I left the room and walked around the rest of the house and into the garden. I wanted to find Sharifa. I couldn't believe her husband wouldn't even allow her to come to her own father's funeral. I pictured Sharifa's large green eyes full of tears but unable to cry properly for her family, as she was too busy toiling away in her new house burdened down by five young children. Sharifa, the girl whose dreams were shattered and whose youth was sold.

I never saw Sharifa again. I stopped going to her house and I found it hard to accept that Sharifa had given up her education and was the wife of an older man and mother to someone else's children. But her story, and my memories of our friendship, remain with me to this day.

⟡

SHARIFA'S PLIGHT IS NOT an unusual one. Afghan men often marry a second wife if the first one doesn't produce a son. Most of them have no understanding of how the sex of a baby is determined and simply blame their wives for any difficulty either in conceiving or failing to produce a son—men are never to be blamed for such things. Many mothers still constantly tell their daughters to obey their brothers and do things for them because boys are better than girls, and some Afghan mothers even keep their jewelry to give to their son's bride, rather than to their own daughters. I'm happy to be living now in a society where men and women are equally valued and parents are happy to have either a baby daughter or a baby son.

3

Nasreen's Story

THE BOY NEXT DOOR

*A*S A GIRL GROWING UP IN AFGHANISTAN AND THEN PAKISTAN, MY cultural upbringing has been a mix of Afghan, Persian, Indian, and Arabic influences. Most of the books that I have read are in the two main languages of Afghanistan—Pashtu or Dari—and the songs and poems that I've heard and the movies I've watched have all spoken about the love between a man and a woman. These love stories—such as the Pashtu romance of Adam Khan and Durkhany, for example—have been passed on from generation to generation. Durkhany is a beautiful and intelligent woman who falls in love with a handsome musician but she is betrothed to another man. She and Adam Khan pine for each other and can only be together in death. Some of these famous tales have even been made into Bollywood films. These are the love stories I grew up with.

Perhaps it is inevitable then that the idea of real love between a man and a woman that my friends and I believed as children came totally from these over-romanticized stories. I've since realized that these tales do not, of course, match reality. In the romance films I grew up watching, the elders in the local community helped pave the way for the young lovers to come together—they extol the virtue of two young people in love overcoming all obstacles to be together. These stories are a celebration of love.

Like so many love stories, Nasreen's involves the boy next door. They actually lived in the same house, as many Afghan families do. Nasreen was discovered by one of our local reporters in Kabul but she didn't want to speak to her and insisted she would only talk to me, so I interviewed her down the line from a BBC studio on the local reporter's mobile phone.

> My name is Nasreen and I live in Kabul. I'm about forty years old and have spent much of my life crying and suffering, and here's why. Have you ever wondered about those women who are married to a man whom they never loved and were never suited to?

When she asked this question I hesitated. I wanted to shout out, "Of course I know!" I knew just how it felt to pretend to be asleep when my husband came to bed so as to avoid having to talk to him.

> My husband is sixty years old and I haven't seen my parents for a long time. When I was thirteen years old we shared a house in Kabul with another family, and although they were Tajik and we were Pashtun, my mother and father got on with them very well and I really loved that family. They had a son who was about eighteen years old and some daughters too, and sometimes I'd play with them. It was a carefree time. In fact, looking back, it was the happiest time of my life. I would often go to the boy's mother and she would take care of me in a special way. Her son's name was Abdullah and he was in love with me, and I used to flirt with him. We were both young. My heart would beat harder when I heard his voice and I would find any excuse to take something to his room. It was easy to fall in love with Abdullah because he was so handsome and because we were able to spend so much time together.
>
> The afternoon was a special time for us because most people in Kabul—especially older people—take a nap after praying. I would pretend to my mother that I was going to sleep but as soon as I heard her snoring, I would get up and go to meet Abdullah. I would wait for

him under the shade of a tree, and then we would sit leaning against a wall and talk and talk. My love for him was pure, as was his for me.

And do you know, Zarghuna Jan, Abdullah didn't ever spend his pocket money on himself. He liked to see me wearing colorful glass bangles so he spent all his money buying them for me, and I loved every single one of them. They symbolized his love for me and I always took great care of them.

Nasreen's voice sounded choked, and then she started crying.

Zarghuna Jan, our love was so innocent. I would only have to look at him and he would gaze back at me, and we knew just how much we felt for each other. He had already told his mother that if she wanted to marry him off then it would have to be to me, because he was in love with me. His mother had agreed to this and that's why she gave me special treatment, because she had already begun to see me as a future daughter-in-law. It was easy for her, wasn't it?

I didn't understand what she meant.

It was easier for her because it was her son who was in love, not her daughter. For boys to have these feelings is something for a mother to be proud of and celebrate. It shows that a boy is maturing, so mothers would make sure other women heard that their son was in love and becoming a man. And just as Abdullah's mother was full of joy, so too was I blissfully happy. I felt free as a bird and when I imagined Abdullah as my husband it gave me a warm feeling.

We would meet every afternoon, except on Fridays, when my father, who didn't sleep in the afternoons like my mother, wasn't at work. I carried on meeting Abdullah until one day we were spotted by a neighbor's son, Ghulam. He saw Abdullah and I chatting under the shade of the tree and was jealous of our intimacy, and he began gossiping about us. He told my brother that he'd seen Abdullah and me alone together and that I'd been doing bad things with him, and so my brother began to restrict what I was allowed to do. Even when I told him I was only talking to Abdullah, he stopped me from going out in the afternoon. He also told my mother if he saw me again with Abdullah that he would kill me. My brother felt I was causing his honor to be called into doubt and that his standing in the community would be damaged if people thought of him as being a weak man whose sister was having a love affair he was unable to put an end to. Days passed. I was no longer able to meet Abdullah under the tree, but we would still see each other in the house. It was enough for us just occasionally to catch a glimpse of each other.

Even now, whenever Nasreen mentioned Abdullah's name, I could hear an intense desire in her voice and sensed that she still desperately missed him.

I remained happy because I was certain Abdullah's mother still wanted me to marry her son. I was just waiting for the day when she would come to our rooms and ask for my hand. Then one afternoon, the weather was perfect, it was warm but with a fresh breeze, the sky was clear blue, and the birds were singing. It was a perfect day.

I asked Nasreen if she had met Abdullah under the tree that day, but she said she hadn't. Instead it was the day Abdullah's mother had come to her mother and asked for Nasreen's hand in marriage to Abdullah.

My mother wasn't blind. She already knew I had feelings for him but used to try to stop me from going to his family's rooms and talking to his mother and sisters during the day.

"Listen, my girl, I know you're still young but you're also a woman now so be careful not to look at Abdullah. It's forbidden for you to do anything like that. Do you understand me?" One day I had confessed that I liked him and demanded to know what was wrong with feeling that way. In return, she had slapped me hard and told me I was a shameless woman, asking how I could speak like that and saying that women are not allowed to have those kinds of feelings. She then forbade me to see him again. He was a boy, she told me, so he could do whatever he liked and no one would ever gossip about him, but it was different for me because I was a girl and our family could be shamed forever because of me.

That day I wept and longed to see Abdullah, but knew it would be impossible because my mother was afraid of my father. She had told me that if my father got to hear about my feelings for Abdullah, then the shame would force him to resolve the matter by killing me.

I wasn't surprised when Nasreen told me this because I know of several cases where girls have in fact been killed for loving a man that their family didn't approve of. Gossip can sometimes get out of control, becoming completely exaggerated, but some men in the family find this hard to understand and feel compelled to defend the family honor nonetheless and prove that they disapprove of shameful behavior by killing an innocent girl. There have been some instances in which the boy has been killed for having a forbidden love affair, but it's usually the case that the woman ends up being blamed and punished.

Soon Abdullah's mother began asking my mother for my hand on behalf of her son, and I started to get scared because she was becoming insistent. But my mother actually became quite comfortable with the situation because this is the way marriages in Afghanistan are normally arranged. The boy's family comes to the girl's family, they pay their respects, and then ask for the daughter's hand in marriage. My mother had a kind heart and she knew that I loved Abdullah, so she was pleased that his family had begun to pay their respects to us in this way. She mentioned as much to my father when he came home from work one evening, but he didn't like what he heard one bit, and when my mother tried to persuade him that they were a respectable family and that their son and his daughter already knew each other he flew into a rage. "Just how well does our daughter know this bastard?" My mother's voice shook as she told him that although I had obviously seen Abdullah around the house, I'd not actually had any kind of contact with him. But my father was not to be fooled quite so easily.

"Don't you realize, woman, that we are Pashtuns and they are Tajiks. We don't belong together at all, so just forget all about this."

My mother protested, saying she thought marriage would make me—their daughter—happy and that my happiness should count for something.

"Well, it might be the most important thing for you, but people will say that my daughter married the neighbor and probably had an affair with him beforehand. This is what people will say, you silly woman!"

The more my mother insisted, the more angry my father became until finally he slapped her. When I heard the commotion I rushed into the room and clung to my mother who was weeping. I was furious with my father for upsetting her so much when she was only defending me.

The days passed and my love for Abdullah grew. After a week or so, the men in his family came to see my parents and asked for my hand. My father wouldn't talk to them, but nor would he refuse outright to give them what they wanted. Instead, he called on my uncle to join him in the negotiation process, and together they decided to ask for such an unfeasibly large sum of money in return for my hand that Abdullah's family would never be able to afford it. My father and uncle couldn't bear the idea that their daughter, and niece, had decided to love a boy of her own choosing. According to my family I had committed a terrible crime. As Abdullah's family wasn't rich, they asked for some time to consider this. But a few days later they returned and said they were prepared to pay the price my father and uncle had set, because their son's happiness was more important to them than money.

Nasreen cried throughout telling me her story, and whenever she spoke of her love for Abdullah, I could feel her pain. She told me how lucky Abdullah was that his family respected his love for her enough to be prepared to pay a lot of money to see him happy.

But no one in my family really cared about me or my feelings. I was on my own, and even my mother was unable to help me. Instead, she found herself being blamed for bringing up a daughter who had brought shame on the family: a daughter who had dared to love the man of her choice. Meanwhile, my father continued to make excuses for the fact that he'd refused to allow me to marry Abdullah. If he had let me marry Abdullah it would have meant that he'd accepted our love for one another, but he just wasn't enough of a man to do this. He kept using the excuse that Abdullah was not a Pashtun like us, and in the end I just couldn't bear it anymore and demanded to know why he was behaving so unreasonably. My father almost had a fit when he heard his fourteen-year-old daughter challenge him in this way, and began beating me, calling me a prostitute, and berating me for daring to love "that boy." He hit me so hard I had bruises all over my face and my lips were bleeding. My body ached from the blows.

"You, you are a girl and in our culture girls are not allowed to question their father's authority. Now I am going to make you suffer."

Abdullah's parents must have been able to hear my screams from next door as I was beaten like an animal. My mother wept and pleaded with my father not to hurt me, but father shouted back that it was all her fault. I was her daughter and she had spoiled me.

In between sobs, Nasreen told me that in our culture, fathers are credited with a child's good behavior, but if the child does something he doesn't approve of then the mother will shoulder the blame and also be punished. I tried to hold back my tears as Nasreen continued with her story. I was hoping for a bit of Bollywood magic and a happy ending in which Abdullah would whisk Nasreen away to a place where they could be together forever, far away from those who would judge or criticize them. Nasreen told me how much pain she endured that day and how there had been bruises and scars all over her body. She had even heard Abdullah and his mother crying through the wall.

The next day my father told me we were going to move to another house. I didn't realize this idea had already been discussed with my uncle and that behind my back they had made plans for my new life. The next day, my parents began packing up our house and Abdullah and his family watched and wept at my father's cruelty. To be honest with you, Zarghuna Jan, I will never forgive my father for what he did to me. I don't care what happens to him and don't even know where he is now. Yes, we did move to another house, but it was only later I realized they'd done this to separate me from Abdullah. I was naive. I now know my uncle had advised my parents that they should move unobtrusively so that the neighbors wouldn't know what was happening. Once we'd moved, he said, a decision could then be made about my future.

My father had agreed to this move while my mother had no say whatsoever in the matter. She had given up by this point and no longer told me what was going on. I didn't blame her, though, because she was in a vulnerable position too. The place we eventually moved to was a long way away from Abdullah. I missed him terribly and every day I'd take out one of his bangles from its box and look at it, admiring the colored glass in the light: red, green, blue, yellow. Each bangle carried the memory of him and I cherished each one as a precious token of his love.

A few days after arriving at our new home, I noticed that people kept visiting our house, but I was too miserable at being away from Abdullah and too preoccupied with praying he would come and rescue me to pay much attention. I thought my father's anger with me had subsided and was even hoping he would change his mind and let me marry Abdullah, but this was all just wishful thinking. I had failed to understand my father fully. In his eyes, I had committed a crime by falling in love and he was planning to punish me for it. I should have guessed what was coming because my father had never really spoken to me in the kind way that fathers normally do to their children. He was always angry with me and treated me badly. I don't understand why God allows men who don't care about women and girls to have families. I don't think my father even loved his own mother. He was always cruel to women.

I did eventually ask my mother who all these people that kept calling at our house were and she said, "I don't know, but I'm certain of one thing and that is that something bad is happening. I feel as though there is a dark shadow over us and it frightens me."

The next day my father told my mother to prepare special food for some guests he had coming. My mother appeared to know who they were but wouldn't tell me, and this is the one thing I can't forgive her for. She could at least have told me in secret what was happening. And so the guests—all elders in the Pashtun community—arrived and ate the food my mother had prepared, and I could hear them discussing someone's marriage. When finally they left, my mother asked me to help her wash the dishes, and I helped because there was nothing else to do. From the very day my father had found out about my love for Abdullah he had banned me from going to school and even from leaving the house, so I was effectively a prisoner in my own home. And during this time, with nothing to do, all I did was dream about Abdullah. But of course I heard nothing from him, as it was far too dangerous for him to get in touch; my family would not have hesitated to have him and me killed if he had so much as tried to contact me.

While I was washing the dishes my mother said, "Hurry up with the washing-up. I need to put henna on your hands." I asked why she wanted to do this when it wasn't Eid or any other special occasion, and she replied, "It's because you're getting married. Tomorrow you will be going to a new home." For one wild and happy moment, I thought I was going to be reunited with my love and felt like a bird that has just been released from its cage.

I asked my mother, "Is he going to come for me?" and she shouted at me, "Have you no shame? Haven't I told you to forget Abdullah? Don't ever mention his name in front of your husband or your life will be a living hell."

I began crying, "But I don't want this to happen. Who is this man? Father can't do this to me."

"Your father can certainly do this, and what you want has nothing to do with it. Your father has already taken a lot of money from this family to see you married."

I begged my mother to help me escape, but she began crying and saying that I had committed a sin and must be punished for it. I pleaded with her that I wasn't a criminal and only wanted to be with Abdullah. At the very mention of his name she slapped me and called me shameless.

"You should be thankful your father didn't kill you. If he were like other Afghan fathers he would have disowned you by now. At least he is civil to you." At this I began screaming that I would rather be dead than marry another man, as I loved Abdullah and knew he was waiting for me. My mother scoffed at the mention of love, saying it was nonsense and that Afghan girls didn't love boys and were certainly not allowed to marry someone they loved.

I spent the whole night crying and refused to let my mother paint henna on my hands. I was a wretchedly unhappy bride. At midday, my uncle and one of my brothers came to fetch me. But I was a bride without a wedding, and I didn't even have the traditional new dress usually given to brides or any presents. Above all, though, I couldn't believe the fact that no one in my family had any sympathy for me. I clung to the doorpost as my uncle dragged me away, before bundling me into a car. Waiting for me in that car was my new husband, a forty-year-old drug addict. I kept crying and shouted at the man in the car, "Uncle, please tell them not to take me," but he just laughed and said I was the first bride to call her husband an uncle. He grasped my hand in his large, rough hand and said, "Shut your mouth. I'm your husband now and I've paid a lot of money for you."

He kept repeating that I was his now, and when he smiled, I could see his yellow teeth. He was laughing, happy that he would soon be having sex with a fourteen-year-old virgin. A part of me died then, and my family ceased to exist for me. I'd extinguished any feelings I'd had for them.

Even though I couldn't see Nasreen's face I could tell that she had once been beautiful, but that life and hardship had aged her. A feeling of trust had sprung up between us.

Zari, dear, all the happy times I'd ever had with my family were gone. My relationship with my mother was no more, and I'd left behind my precious bangles. I didn't even have a spare set of clothes. That day, although my soul died, my love for Abdullah lived on and the pain of being separated from him was sharper than ever. It was the start of a lifetime of suffering.

I asked Nasreen if she had ever seen Abdullah again. She said she hadn't and that she hadn't even seen her own parents again.

They thought I was a bad woman because I loved a man. Well, I still love him, and I want them to know that although I can't be with him my feelings for him remain unchanged. I can even still picture his smile.

She then returned to the story of her forced marriage.

I was taken to this man's home—a dark room on the outskirts of Kabul, far away from my parents' home and far away from all the people I knew.

This man, this so-called husband of mine, raped me that night; a forty-year-old man sexually assaulted me, a young girl. But I was already dead inside and my innocence was shattered. I could never forget Abdullah, though, and I really hope he has married someone nice and has a happy family life.

My married life began and I lived like a maid, cooking this man's food, eating the leftovers, and even preparing his hashish. Sometimes he would beat me up as though I were an animal if I was too slow making his tea or preparing his drugs. I just wanted to die. But now I'm an old woman living a pointless, empty life who is simply waiting for God to end it. This is my story.

At this point I stopped recording, my head full of thoughts of Nasreen and her wretched life. I thought too of how she would have been when she was fourteen, fresh, and pretty, and tried to work out how I would edit this material. When Nasreen's story eventually went out on air, I noticed some of my Afghan colleagues here in London made snide comments about her. One said that since she'd fallen in love when she was so young then it wasn't surprising she'd had to face the consequences. I was at a loss to know what to say. To me, Nasreen was just an ordinary girl who'd had a crush on a boy, as many girls do at that age. Her love was innocent, and in my opinion she'd done nothing wrong by simply following her feelings, but she'd paid a terrible price for doing so.

I know in most societies women are not judged simply for liking a man and that relationships are allowed to develop naturally; a woman and man understand each other, their love grows, and they can choose whether to get married. As a result girls and boys learn from what they see and begin to understand how to go about finding the right partner. Yet here I was in the UK having to endure the sneers of some of my male colleagues. I didn't say anything in response, though, but kept quiet. I may have been living in the UK but I was working in a male Afghan environment, so I couldn't defend Nasreen or some of my colleagues would see me as a woman who was using the radio to encourage other women to do shameful things. All I could do was pray that Nasreen would be the last girl to suffer in this way.

One important thing I have learned from Nasreen's story is that no matter where an Afghan woman or girl lives—whether she is brought up in the UK or in Kabul—as long as she is Afghan, she is not allowed to fall in love or express her love for a man openly, and most especially not to her mother or father. To do so would be unacceptable and bring shame on the family. If she were to have an open relationship with a man whom she might one day want to marry, she would be subject to gossip and back-biting from within her community. It wouldn't matter if her parents had brought her up to be a responsible member of society; within her community all her good qualities would be ignored and she'd be branded a slut.

Over the past four years I have met some young Afghan women who have boyfriends, but their relationships are usually kept within a circle of friends, most of whom are not Afghan. They tend to live two very different lives in one city: when they are away from the family home, they are just like any other Western girl, but once they're back home they become a traditional Afghan woman who doesn't talk about men, go out with friends, or enjoy a loving relationship with a man. I personally consider Nasreen to be an immensely brave woman; she at least had the courage to tell her mother about her love for Abdullah, and I can understand just how hard that must have been. If even I—a financially independent Afghan woman living in an open society like the UK—find it hard to talk about my true feelings with my family, then I can fully appreciate just what Nasreen has been through by revealing her love for Abdullah within her closed world.

I often find the attitude of some Afghans here in the UK very upsetting. Some have been living here for more than ten years but they have maintained strong Afghan traditions and cultural values. On my visits to Afghanistan I've met a number of different Afghan men and women, and have been interested to find that some of those who stayed in their own country were much more relaxed about accepting changing values that might have been seen as damaging to their family honor or culture twenty years ago. For example, in some cities families have started letting their daughters and sons go abroad for higher education, taking up the scholarships being offered to young Afghans by Western countries. Yet here in London I have met Afghan parents who strongly oppose the idea of their sons or daughters even living in student halls of residence, as the family's reputation could be damaged. Reputation and the family name is everything. So if a daughter marries the man of her parents' choosing, she will be respected and held up as an example to other girls who dream of falling in love. This is the pressure young Afghan women struggle to live with.

4

Shereenjan's Story

A DAUGHTER'S SACRIFICE

S HE SPOKE IN A SHAKY VOICE, HER HANDS WERE ROUGH AND CALLOUSED, and her face was lined with wrinkles. Each line told the story of her life, and, as Shereenjan herself said, her whole body showed what sort of life she had led.

She was sitting in front of me with her legs tucked round to one side, her large scarf partly draped on the floor. On her feet she wore the plastic shoes older people in Afghanistan so often wear, and her brown dress and *shalwar* were faded. I first met Shereenjan in the summer of 2006 when I was on a work trip to Afghanistan. She lived in the outskirts of Kabul near my grandparents and uncles. I usually spend a day or two with my grandparents and the rest of the family—who all live in one big house—when I visit Kabul, and was one day chatting to my uncle's wife about the life stories on *Afghan Woman's Hour* when she mentioned Shereenjan. I was intrigued by what I heard and asked my uncle's wife to introduce me to her. I wanted to see if I could persuade her to tell us her story.

When I met her, Shereenjan said, "Look, my child, if I tell you my story in detail, you'll have to bring twenty cassettes with you. It's a very long story and most people won't actually believe what has happened to me." At this she laughed. "As you can see I'm alive and well, but I do sometimes wonder how I've survived everything that's happened to me."

I told Shereenjan I would love to hear her story, even if it meant returning with twenty cassettes, and I left her house pleased at having found someone whose life story would relate old Afghan traditions. Back in my room at the BBC guesthouse, I lay on my bed and rested, until suddenly my mobile phone rang. It was my mother calling from England, and I was happy to hear from her. She told me that one of our relatives who lived in Pakistan needed some money to help pay for her wedding, so I took the relative's phone number and promised my mother I would get in touch. That night I slept badly—I couldn't get Shereenjan out of my mind and was really excited about recording her story. In fact, the UN Human Rights Commission says there are hundreds of women in the remote corners of Afghanistan whose terrible stories are never heard, but at least Shereenjan could finally tell hers.

Another phone call woke me early the next morning. I heard a nervous female voice speaking Pashtu but didn't recognize it and asked who it was. The woman on the phone said she was Pana's aunt and began crying. I realized that Pana and her aunt were the relatives my mother had wanted me to get in touch with about money for a wedding. I remembered Pana's mother from childhood memories of when I lived in Kabul. She would often come to our house and, because she was family, would sometimes stay the night, but when the war broke out she had gone to live with her parents in Pakistan. She'd got married, had a boy and a girl, but tragically died when her daughter was only two months old, leaving both her children to be looked after by their grandparents. The grandfather was a traditional village man who believed in following old customs, one of which was the practice of using women to settle disputes, known as *dukhmany*.

I asked the aunt how Pana was, remembering how, after her mother died, my family and I had been very concerned about her, for she was still very young. Her aunt said she was well but that since she was only a child she didn't know what was happening to her. She then told me she was in a hurry and couldn't chat for long.

"Zari dear, I just called really to say that Pana is getting married and we need money to buy her some clothes and a few other things. It would be nice if you could help us out."

I was surprised to hear that Pana was going to be married, since, according to my calculations, she was only eleven years old. I agreed to send some money but asked why Pana was getting married. There was no answer to my question as the phone line suddenly went dead. I was shocked by what I'd heard but still wanted to help them out.

⌘

IT'S NOT UNUSUAL FOR girls in Afghanistan to be married at the age of twelve or thirteen, regardless of their ethnic background or whether they come from rich or poor families. When an Afghan girl reaches puberty her parents begin to worry if no one has yet asked for her hand, and girls are often married when they are far too young to cope with the physical and mental demands of marriage. They are still children who should be living with their mothers—rather than becoming mothers themselves— and tend to be completely ignorant about sex and childbirth, as a well-brought-up girl is not expected to know anything about such matters. So as soon as a girl starts her monthly period, plans for her future married life are put in train: a husband is chosen and new clothes are bought. Overnight her life changes forever as she goes from being a carefree schoolgirl to a dutiful daughter-in-law and wife who must look after her husband. That said, pleasing her in-laws is just as important as keeping her husband happy; some wives have told me how they've been humiliated if they've failed to cook a suitably lavish meal for the whole family.

The legal position on whether a child should be used to settle a dispute is clear: a girl must not get married unless she is sixteen years of age. But in villages where tribal traditions prevail, many families are not aware of the law. If such an arrangement is officially reported it might go to court and be formally dealt with, but if it is a poor, homeless woman who tries to file a complaint, she may find herself being unfairly judged by the police and thereby make herself yet more vulnerable. Terrible things have happened to those women whose cases did get to court. In fact, it's very hard to find a case that has actually been handled in accordance with the law, so most of these marriages simply go unreported.

After talking to a number of human rights and feminist activists I discovered that many premature and forced marriages are arranged as a way of solving a family dispute or problem. Sometimes daughters are exchanged to enable the son of the family to marry, and sometimes disputes are settled by giving a girl away. No matter that the Afghan constitution, which is based on sharia law, says it is illegal. Sadly the government and courts have little power to intervene in such cases, and according to the Ministry of Women's Affairs in Afghanistan, and various nongovernmental organizations, approximately 57 percent of Afghan girls marry before the age of sixteen (though the circumstances of these marriages do vary).

One particular memory stands out. In 2007 in Kabul, I met some family relatives who were very poor. The two older sons were doing building work to earn money, and the two young daughters had just reached puberty. The mother complained to me that her sons and husband struggled to provide enough for the whole family. Then the elder of the two daughters, who seemed very bright, asked me if I had finished school. I told her I had. Then in front of her mother, she told me that she and her sister were no longer allowed to go to school because they were "becoming young" (by this she meant reaching puberty), before going to fetch her schoolbooks and showing me how she had been awarded top marks.

I asked the mother why she'd taken her daughters out of school and tried to explain how important it was for them to have an education, and she replied, "It's just not important as these two girls are going to be given in exchange for my sons. Their brothers have been working hard all their lives to provide for us, and now that they are of a marrying age, the girls can pay them back."

I asked her what she meant.

"We're very poor—too poor to be able to secure brides for our sons—so we'll use our daughters and exchange them as daughters-in-law. In any case, it is better that they stay at home because it's seen as shameful for a young girl to go out by herself. What would other people say? They wouldn't want to marry into our family if they thought we were too liberal."

One of the daughters looked at me and began to cry. "You heard what my mother said; I'm to be given in exchange for my older brother. She says I'm to be married into whichever family is prepared to give my brother a wife."

I realized I wasn't going to be able to persuade the mother to change her mind. As I prepared to leave, the eldest daughter implored me with her eyes to save her, but there was nothing I could do.

⌒⊰⌒

SHEREENJAN LIVED IN A neighborhood of narrow streets and tightly packed buildings on the outskirts of Kabul. When I went to interview her, the driver and I had difficulty finding her house. It was a hot and sunny day and I had my recording equipment in a simple plastic shopping bag. I clutched it tightly as I stood outside Shereenjan's house and knocked at the door, trying to focus on the task in hand while my mind kept drifting back to Pana and how she was going to get married when she was only eleven years old.

Shereenjan's two grandsons answered the door. I told them my name and that I had come to visit their granny and they smiled shyly. One shouted that the woman from the office had arrived and then they both ran away giggling. I went into the house and was greeted by several women who directed me to Shereenjan's room, which was across a courtyard. At the far side of the yard, I could see Shereenjan. She had a stick in her hand and was beating a donkey and it brayed loudly while Shereenjan shouted and cursed, "You useless, lazy donkey, if I don't beat you, you don't move."

Shereenjan then called for Khudai Dad, one of her grandsons, and told him to take the donkey to fetch wood for the household. Khudai Dad ran to her, took the stick, and began beating the donkey himself.

Shereenjan was wearing the same clothes as when I'd last seen her:

baggy, old trousers and a long dress. She greeted me and kissed me on my forehead, as is the custom for older Afghan women with younger women, and invited me to sit by her. Her room was shaded and dark but it still felt hot and humid, and when I sat next to Shereenjan on a thin mattress, it felt damp and oddly cold. I took out my recording machine and plugged in the microphone, and at the sight of it Shereenjan laughed.

"I'm scared I might cough or sneeze. I've never heard my voice recorded. I don't know what to do and I want my voice to sound good, even though my story is sad!" I reassured her that it wouldn't matter if she coughed or sneezed, as I could edit out any unnecessary noises, and told her to relax and just talk normally. Shereenjan giggled like a schoolgirl and pointed to the microphone and asked if it could also take her photo. I replied that it could only record her voice and that for radio we wouldn't need her photo. She sounded so cheerful and normal as she settled down for the interview that I really didn't expect what I was about to hear.

Everything started to go wrong when my father married a second wife. He'd had an argument with another family and wanted to settle it so he paid them a lot of money, but they wanted more. But the disagreement was far more serious than money could settle, as my father had argued about land and the distribution of water in the village and had ended up killing one of their family members. As a result, my father lived in constant fear, and my mother and stepmother seemed worried all the time. Even though I was only a child of nine or ten years old, I knew there was something seriously wrong. Every day men would arrive at our house and intense discussions would take place. I used to carry the water jugs so our guests could wash their hands. I had no clue what everyone was talking about, nor was I that interested either; I just wanted to finish handing out the soap and towels so I could get back to playing with my friends. One day I filled the *koza* (water jug) and took it with the *lagan* (bowl) to the guest room.

One of the guests, who was like an uncle to me, looked closely at me as I poured water over his hands. He then said to my father, "You know, Jabar Khan, there is another way to solve this dispute. We could use Shereenjan."

I looked at my uncle and smiled at the mention of my name; I had no idea what he meant. I giggled and left the room, thinking that he was perhaps praising me for carrying out my duties so well. Of course I now know just what he meant, and these days whenever I think about that man, I have nothing but contempt for him. He put the idea into my father's head, and I sometimes think it would never have happened if it hadn't been for him.

My nightmare began on a lovely sunny day when I wanted to be out playing with my friends. My mother called me into the house and told me to get ready because we were going to a wedding ceremony. I told her I didn't want to go but she handed me my new pink shalwar kamiz. She had made it especially for Eid and I had only worn it once. She tried to comb my hair, but it was sticky and greasy because I hadn't washed it for a while. When I was a little girl, I used to run around like a boy, getting dirty and into all sorts of scrapes, and I didn't much care for washing or looking tidy. I could see tears in my mother's eyes as she struggled to pull the comb through my hair and asked her why she was crying. She said she was sad because I was leaving, so I hugged her and said I didn't want to go to the wedding and would stay behind with her. But she pushed some sweets into my hand and said I had to go to the wedding with my grandmother and two other women. My grandmother held my hand tightly as we walked there, and I asked, "Grandma, why are you not wearing new clothes for the wedding?" She told me there was no need and that I should stop asking so many questions. I could see she was upset too. When we got to the house where the wedding was to take place I was surprised to find there was no music or food.

"Grandma, what sort of wedding is this?" I asked. "There's no music or food. It's stupid. I want to go home and play with Laila and Bassmeena."

My grandmother now became agitated and got angry with me, saying that this was how some weddings were and that I wasn't allowed to leave.

After a while my grandmother and the other two women got up to leave, and I got up to go with them but was told to stay where I was. I started crying, shouting that I wanted to go with my family, and even tried to cling on to my grandmother's dress but she pushed me away saying, "You are this family's property now." I didn't understand what she meant and screamed at being left behind, but no one took any notice. And so began my new life in a house full of strangers.

I was put in a room that I had to share with animals, and I was too small to reach the lock of the door; I had to use a bale of straw to stand on. But when I peered through the keyhole, I discovered they had locked me in. After a few minutes somebody brought me some food, but when I refused to eat it eventually they gave it to the dog. One of the men, now my brother-in-law, said to everyone, "Don't give her any food. Just show it to her. That's as close as she'll come to enjoying the wedding feast. This is her welcome to our family, a family that was torn apart when her father killed my brother."

At first, I didn't understand why they all hated me quite so much. I was scared of everyone. Men, women, and children would beat me whenever they felt like it and my life was no better than that of a dog. In fact, it was worse. Only Allah knows what I went through. Soon, though, I realized that I had been taken from my family so that this family could take their revenge, and at the age of nine I started to understand what *dukhmany* was.

The younger family members would tell the elders that they were looking after me, but in reality I was eating scraps of food left by the dogs, and as the days passed I got weaker and weaker. I missed my family and my friends terribly, and was hungry and miserable. Then one day my grandmother gave a neighbor who was visiting the house some meat wrapped in bread for me. This woman knew all about the terrible conditions I was living in and asked to see me and then slipped me the food. I ate it ravenously, swallowing it as fast as I could, but one of the children spotted me and called out, "Hey, the waste of space is eating meat. Come and look!" My mother-in-law rushed in and snatched the food out of my hand and told the neighbor off for giving it to me. Although I didn't manage to finish it all, the two or three bites I'd had tasted good.

Of course at this stage I didn't know this woman was my mother-in-law. All I knew was that she was cruel; cruel enough to take the food from me and give it to the dog. I wanted to beat the dog but I couldn't, as they would just have beaten me. All I could do was cry. Do you know, my child, they didn't even let me sleep?

I could scarcely believe what I was hearing. How could one person have suffered so much? I told Shereenjan how brave she was, and that her story was extraordinary. She continued.

One day, I was locked in my room, when I heard a man shouting loudly, "Where's the knife?" At this, my heart started beating faster and my legs began to shake; I thought they were going to come and kill me. My brother-in-law used to taunt me by saying one day he would kill me so that my father would know how it feels to lose someone. I stood behind the door, too scared to move, and waited for someone to bring the man his knife. Then I heard one of the boys saying they couldn't find the hen. I was so relieved. The knife was to kill the chicken, not me. Gradually, I calmed down but from then on I would often be afraid that at any time they might come for me.

On a different occasion my in-laws brought wet sticks and wood and put them in my room. I thought they were going to use them to beat me with, but later realized they were just being stored there and they were for the sheep. This is how it is when you are beaten daily. You can't think straight and become paranoid. Nobody was kind to me. Not my own family and certainly not my in-laws; they were my enemies.

In the morning I would be made to go and collect cow dung, even though I could barely walk because I was so weak with hunger. I'd go with some of the older girls in the house and they would make me carry their cow dung all the way back, but then when we got nearer the house they would hit me and take my basket from me. They would tell my mother-in-law that I'd done no work all morning and that I had fallen asleep. My mother-in-law would shout at me for being lazy and useless and then tell her young grandson to beat me with a stick.

Every day my mother-in-law would give me far harder jobs than she would to her own daughters. They were a big family and quite rich too, and they owned a large area of land and had lots of cows and sheep. We often had to collect hay for the cows, and even though I was the youngest child they would force me to get on with the job by slapping my face and pulling my hair. Sometimes they even punched me until I collapsed. If I'd had any ideas about escaping, I would have been stopped by my sisters-in-law who always kept a close eye on me. They told me not to fall behind when we were out because they were afraid I might run away or that my father might come and rescue me.

When we got back with the hay, they would tell my mother-in-law they had collected it all and that I had done nothing, giving her an excuse to give me yet another beating. They used to beat me day and night. After a while some people in the neighborhood suggested I should be allowed to go home and visit my family, but my in-laws said that I wouldn't be allowed to go back until after the matrimonial ceremony. I had no idea what this "matrimonial ceremony" was, but whatever it was I wanted it to be over quickly so I could see my family again, so I went and asked my father-in-law when it would happen. "You dirty shameless woman, can't you wait for it?" he said, spitting in my face.

Everyone started laughing but I couldn't understand why. There was one occasion, though, when I did manage to escape and go back to my parents' house. My mother cooked me lots of delicious food but I knew my in-laws would guess where I was; I was their property now and they would kill my parents if I didn't go back. When I reappeared they demanded a sheep from my family as compensation for my behavior, and I was beaten and told to go and sleep in the cow's shed.

My suffering continued for about three years. I got used to eating leftovers and stealing what I could from the kitchen. When I got caught I would be beaten, but I didn't care because it was as if my body had turned to stone. I no longer felt any pain and had forgotten what love and kindness were. I was alone. Then when I was about twelve years old my monthly bleeding started. I had no idea what it was when menstrual blood first leaked through my tattered *shalwar*, and was too busy with my early-morning chores of making a fire and heating the water to notice it. As usual I was hurrying so that no one could complain I was slow and use this as an excuse to beat me, but then I began to feel a mild aching in my back and legs. The next thing I knew my father-in-law came striding toward me and slapped me hard across the face. "You filthy slut. How dare you show your shame and blood to everyone like this? Go and clean yourself up." I had no idea what he meant and started crying. One of my sisters-in-law handed me an old cloth and told me that now I'd grown up, I'd soon be getting a husband. Then she laughed. Later my mother-in-law came into the cowshed where I was sleeping.

"Shereenjan, you are an evil girl and you are lucky my husband is a kind Muslim and said that we should wait until you became a woman before giving you to my son. Now, though, you are going to sleep with my son and give him babies. It will be you who brings children into this family instead of my murdered son and they will be of our blood."

In a way she was right. If they had been an even crueler family they would perhaps have forced me to sleep with their son earlier. I think I could have coped with it, though. Someone like me can endure any amount of suffering. Their aim had always been to take revenge on me for the death of their son, and they were very good at it. From the older members of the family down to the very youngest, they would always find some new way to hurt me and take satisfaction from my suffering. My father-in-law was angry all the time and would shout out, "Beat her!" And whenever I heard these words I'd start to shake. I wanted to escape to safety but there was nowhere for me to go, and as they beat me with a stick I would cry out for my mother. How I longed for a soft word, a warm hug, or any form of kindness.

The son who was going to sleep with me was also very young; he was fifteen years old. He would also sometimes beat me while telling me that I was soon going to be his wife, but he didn't beat me as much as the others did. Around this time a couple of neighbors told my family about the terrible conditions I was living under and how my in-laws were taking out their anger at the death of their son on me. Soon after, my father came to visit me at the place where I'd collect cow dung, and I was on my own because my sisters-in-law no longer helped with that job. He had been hiding in one of the sheds and I was surprised to see him and asked him what he was doing there. "I've come to take you away with me, Shereenjan. We'll escape and live far away." I was afraid and began shouting that I didn't want to go with him. He hadn't come for me when I was younger and now I was twelve and had got used to my life with my in-laws. My existence was hellish but I had survived it by getting used to it and couldn't face the idea of it getting any worse so I told him I wouldn't go with him. I started to cry. My father then recited some verses of the Quran before leaving and that was the last time I ever saw him. I wept the whole time I collected that smelly shit in my hands, knowing that my in-laws would kick me because I smelled so foul.

I have never been beautiful or vain, but I would envy my sisters-in-law. They would put colorful plastic clips in their hair and paint henna on their hands, and it seemed as though they always had new clothes and sandals to wear. I would stare at them and wish I too had those things. Instead, my clothes were my mother-in-law's castoffs, and because she was so much bigger than me, her faded, ugly clothes hung loosely on my thin body. I could never have gone to a wedding or funeral dressed like that.

There was one occasion when my mother visited me, and when

she saw how thin I'd become and the terrible conditions I was living under, she went home and vomited up blood. I heard later that her distress had caused her to lose the five-month-old baby she was carrying at the time. After that, no one from my family was allowed to visit me. But, Zari dear, somehow I managed to survive by learning some tricks, and despite all the hardship and beatings I was still quite naughty.

At the mention of this Shereenjan covered her mouth with her hand and giggled like a mischievous schoolgirl.

I got this naughty streak from my grandmother who used to tell me how she would misbehave with her in-laws. I would wait until the afternoon when everyone was asleep and the house was quiet, then I would sneak into the bathroom and steal some soap and quickly wash my hands, face, and hair. I had hidden a piece of broken mirror in the shed where I was living so that I could see myself, then I would tell the cows how beautiful I looked when I was clean.

Shereenjan laughed at the memory.

Of course, they didn't take any notice and just carried on eating and mooing, but those cows kept me company and somehow I felt as though they loved me. I would give them their food regularly and keep their shed clean, and so in a way I had a family that no one else knew about. I was relieved my in-laws weren't aware of my little world, as I feared they might separate me from the animals too.

After seven days of my period, my bleeding stopped and my *Nikkah* day came. In the morning my mother-in-law informed me that I would today become Azam's wife. I said nothing. I knew that a girl usually wore beautiful new clothes and makeup on her wedding day, but my mother-in-law gave me none of those things. I wore the same old clothes and was covered in the same old shit, although on this occasion she did tell me to wash because she said her son wouldn't want to sleep with a smelly girl like me. For the first time in five years I was given shampoo to wash my long, thick hair, and I had to wash it four times because it was so full of dirt. It felt so good to smell fresh, and as I combed my clean hair I remembered the last time my mother had combed it and how she had been crying. I began to cry too. I missed her so much.

A mullah came to perform the *Nikkah* ceremony (the contract between a man and a woman in Islam), although no one bothered to ask whether or not I agreed to the marriage. It was all just a formality to allow my in-laws to show the neighbors that they were good Muslims. Afterward I carried on with my normal house and farm jobs. I didn't know what was going to happen, even when my mother-in-law told me that tonight I would sleep in the house. When I asked her why this was, she said it was because I was now married to her son and that she was waiting for me to give her a grandson. I had no idea what she was talking about, but the prospect of sleeping on a *charpoie* in the house had already begun to frighten me, so I told her I was happy in the cowshed. In response, she shook me and slapped my face before telling me to wash and then go to Azam's room. "Girl, this will be your gift to me to avenge the murder of my son." I ran to the bedroom and found Azam waiting for me. He locked the door and started touching my body and I was shocked and frightened and started crying. He ordered me to pull down my *shalwar*, which I did although I was shaking with fear, and he penetrated me so hard that I started to bleed. Once it was over, he kicked me, told me to collect my clothes and to go back to the cowshed.

"Don't think that because this has happened you'll become my wife. You're only going to be the vessel for my children. They will live in the house but you will only come to my room when I need sex so that you can bear me a son."

This sexual violence became just another part of my life as a woman. I was abused in almost every way possible. Beaten and deprived, my very soul had died. After a month, I fell pregnant and soon gave birth to a baby boy. This baby is now the son who looks after me. His arrival marked the beginning of a better chapter in my life. My in-laws were getting older, and I was happy when my father in-law died. Meanwhile my husband, Azam, married the girl of his choice when he was twenty and it was a great relief because it meant I no longer had to go to his room and be abused by him. My mother-in-law also passed away and her daughters married, one by one, and went to live with their husbands, leaving me with Azam, his brother, his second wife, and their children. But I also had my own dear son with me—the person to whom I was closest—and I took great care of him. And although his mother was a despised servant, his father still loved him.

As the elders in the family passed away, I too grew older. My son grew up but he stayed with me, even when he got married and had children, and those children are very good to me. God save them. But now I'm getting old and ill, and I think the effects of all those years of suffering are starting to take hold. All those beatings made my bones and joints weak and painful, and I'm not very mobile. I was young then, but now I'm old, and one day I will go to Paradise.

I don't think badly of my in-laws, besides they're all dead now. It was my destiny to end up with them and nothing could have been done to change that. If anything, I blame my father. How could I have expected my in-laws to be kind to me when my own parents gave me away? If I curse my in-laws, then I would have to curse my own parents first, and I don't want to disturb their souls. What would it change? My husband became kind for a while before he died and I even pray for him sometimes, because if it hadn't been for him then I wouldn't have the beautiful son who now takes such good care of me. This, my child, is the story of my life.

After I had finished recording Shereenjan's story, her daughter-in-law brought us fresh sour yogurt—we call this *shrombi* in Pashtu. We ate it with flat bread that had been freshly baked in a *tanoor* (oven), and as Shereenjan and I tucked into the food, I thought how privileged I'd been to hear her incredible story. I was honored that she had entrusted it to me. Before I left, I gave Shereenjan's daughter-in-law a BBC time-table so they would know when to listen for their mother on the radio. Everyone seemed pleased with this and wished me a warm good-bye—"*Khuda Hafiz*," "May God be your guardian."

Back at the guesthouse in Kabul, I decided to phone Pana's aunt in Pakistan and ask how Pana was. She told me she was out in the yard playing with some of her friends but that the next day she would be going to her in-laws. It struck me then that nothing much had changed in Afghanistan. The same thing that had happened to Shereenjan all those years ago was about to happen to Pana now. I asked the aunt if there was any other way to solve the dispute; might the family accept money instead? She said that Pana had been promised to them, that this was the arrangement and that nothing could be done to change it. All we could do was pray to God that the family would be kind to her.

I felt helpless. I could do nothing to save this eleven-year-old girl. I asked the aunt how Pana was feeling and she replied, "This is how it is for the daughter of such an unfortunate mother. Pana's still a child and doesn't realize she will be going to this new house forever, and once she's there she'll not enjoy the usual privileges of a bride because she's going there to settle a dispute. The poor child won't have a wedding party like other girls and she won't ever be allowed home to see her brother. She's going there to appease the anger of that family, and they will take satisfaction from treating her like a slave because they will want the daughter of their enemy to suffer."

I pleaded with Pana's aunt to make her niece aware of the situation and explain why she was going to this new house and how she wouldn't ever be allowed to return. But the aunt said that was impossible. If Pana knew the reality of what was going to happen then she might refuse to go, and her grandfather would be very angry. I persuaded the aunt that she must at the very least buy lots of food so Pana didn't go hungry.

That was the last I heard of Pana. No one knows what happened to her. When I first recorded Shereenjan's story I took comfort from the fact that the events described in it happened many years ago, but here I was confronted with just the same story in the present day, and one that was taking place within my own family too. How wrong I was to think that such customs only existed in the last century. Cultural roots run deep in Afghanistan and many people believe in them completely, often even more than they do in the Islamic faith.

5

Samira's Story

THE CARPET WEAVER

QAMAR IS A TURKMEN GIRL WHO COMPOSED A POEM ABOUT CARPET weaving which we broadcast on the program. When our reporter first made contact with her she was sixteen years old and living in Shirbighan in Jawzjan province in the north of Afghanistan. Qamar told us she would rather be at school so she could one day become a doctor or a teacher, but as she was the family's main breadwinner she had no choice but to spend her days at the loom. We broadcast her poem because we wanted our listeners to be aware that Afghan carpets tend to be made by women and girls whose skill and hard work is hardly ever acknowledged. When did someone like Qamar's name ever appear on the small label on the backs of those carpets, which sell for hundreds of dollars?

Much of the story of Afghanistan can be seen in its carpets. The country's ethnic diversity—Turkmen, Uzbek, Tajik, Hazara, Kuchi, and Pashtun—is there in its patterns. The wool comes from the sheep, goats, and camels that graze on our hills, and the traditional dyes from our plants, fruits, and vegetables. Pomegranate peel and walnuts make brown, red comes from the roots of the madder plant, yellow from saffron or chamomile, and blue from the indigo plant. But above and beyond the materials, our carpets are threaded through with the emotions and feelings of the women and girls who weave them.

No one knows when Afghan women first started carpet weaving. Whenever I ask about its history I'm told that it goes back centuries and is a skill that has been passed down from mother to daughter, along with particular carpet designs. One thing is certain, though, and that is that our carpets represent the very finest example of Afghan art. In the past Afghan kings would offer carpets as gifts to foreign dignitaries, and now the president gives them to other national leaders. When there is an official event with top politicians or celebrities, everyone will walk on a red Afghan carpet, and when an Afghan girl marries, she is given a carpet for her bedroom by her parents or relatives.

Setting up a loom in the home is easy and the tools needed to weave are both inexpensive and easy to obtain. For nomads there are even small portable looms—with the threads of wool attached to them—that can be hitched to a donkey. Carpet weaving is mostly something women and children can do without having to leave their homes. During the Taliban period, when women were prevented from going out to work—and girls banned from going to school—they could still earn money by weaving carpets, and women and girls who were not originally from carpet-weaving families acquired the skill. Then when many Afghans became refugees in Pakistan and Iran they took up carpet weaving again, and from there exported their handicraft to the rest of the world.

Through making *Afghan Woman's Hour* I met many female carpet weavers, but up until then I had no idea of the hardship they had to endure to make these works of art, and I was struck by quite how unhappy many of these women were. I discovered that in the north of the country girls are valued according to their capacity to weave. These girls were pouring their hearts into their carpets, but no one cared how they felt; they were only concerned with how much money the carpet could fetch. Some girls told me that they were forced to become carpet-weaving machines by their parents. All they did was knot, tap, tie, and cut for hours every day. They were becoming old and tired behind the looms, their energy, beauty, and health ebbing away. They had no concept of what price their carpets could fetch on the international market and knew only that they were chained to the loom. I now look with fresh eyes at the Afghan carpets in my home and wonder about the women and children who made them.

Samira, like Qamar, is from Shiberghan and is a typical carpet-weaving girl. After reading Qamar's poem I was keen to meet other girls like her, and in north Afghanistan they are not hard to find: almost every house has a wooden loom. The north of the country is predominantly made up of Turkmen and Uzbek people, and they certainly value their girls according to their degree of skill in carpet weaving. If, for example, a girl is able to make beautiful carpets that can fetch a high price then a boy's family will pay a high price for her in marriage, and the girl's family would say, "Her five fingers are five *chiraghs* (lights)."

I am permanently reminded of those five lights when I look at the Afghan carpets I have bought. After hearing the life stories of Samira and Qamar I now value those carpets even more because I recognize the real cost of them in terms of sacrifice and dedication.

⬿

SAMIRA SWIFTLY WOVE THE colorful threads together. Beside her on the floor lay the blade for cutting the threads, and in front of her was a drawing of the carpet pattern. She barely glanced at it, though. She didn't need to because she could weave with her eyes shut. After a while, her small, thin fingers began to ache from all the twisting and turning of the thread. Samira sat on a round cushion in front of the *kargah*, a large wooden loom on which the carpet strings were stretched. It reached to more than six meters long and filled almost the entire length of the room. Samira had to stretch up high to reach where she was sewing.

The room she was sitting in was dark and full of dust from the wool. Samira would start carpet weaving early each morning before her mother joined her. She was the eldest child; her younger brother went to school and her sister was still a baby. By the time her brother left the house for school, Samira was already at work at the *kargah* (loom) that her father had built. Samira and her mother would have to sit in front of the loom all day. This was their job. Samira wore a square scarf tight around her head and sat hunched over her threads as she worked. Sometimes, when she was very tired, she would lean against the *kargah*, resting her body against its frame.

Samira was busy weaving and cutting the threads when her mother called out to her, "Oi! You lazy girl, the minute I turn my back you stop weaving and lean on the *kargah*."

Samira began weaving even faster. "No, Mother, I've been weaving all the time you weren't here. Come and look. See, I've done the first pattern already. Are you happy now?"

Her mother looked closely at the piece she had woven.

"All right, my child. Well done, you've sewn it beautifully, but you'll have to work faster now because your baby sister won't let me do as much work as I need to do, and if we don't finish this carpet in time your father will get angry. And what excuse will he give to the *tojar* (trader)?"

Samira stared at the *kargah* and threaded even faster. With every knot she tied she got even angrier, and with every breath she took she swallowed yet another mouthful of carpet dust. Her mother came to sit near her. She was a large, chubby woman and wore a long, traditional Turkmen dress and a dark green, glittery scarf under which she wore a glittery hat. Mother and daughter looked similar: both had large round faces, small noses, and thick red lips. Samira's cheeks were pinker than her mother's, but otherwise the only difference between them was seventeen years.

Samira always asked her mother lots of questions and her mother would answer without missing a beat of either her own weaving or her checking of Samira's work; she would watch her daughter's work carefully and correct any mistakes, teaching her to weave with precision and style. Samira's mother also had a talent for mixing colors and creating new, elegant designs.

"Mother, when we finish this carpet, do we have to start another one?"

Her mother smiled. "My child, you ask this question every day when we start weaving and my answer is always the same; yes, we will have to do this all again. We will have to carry on weaving for as long as we can, as your father has already taken so many other orders from the *tojar*."

"Yes, Mother," Samira replied, "I know, but I am bored of it, and I want to go to school like Naeem. How come he gets to go to school and I don't? I'm eleven years old and he's ten. There's not much difference in our age, is there?"

"Listen, my child, did I go to school?"

Samira shook her head. "No, I know you didn't go to school."

Her mother waved the large metal needle in front of her daughter.

"So! There's your answer. Your mother didn't go to school, so you won't go either. But your father did go to school when he was a child, so now your brother goes too. Don't forget you only have one brother. One day you and your little sister will go to live in someone else's house and then you will both help your husbands with all the household jobs in just the same way as I help your father now."

Samira wasn't too happy with her mother's response but said nothing for a while and kept on weaving. Her mother tuned the radio to a local station playing music, and the song of the Herati girl came on. Samira immediately went to turn up the volume, and her mother laughed when she heard the song because it was an old favorite of theirs. It was sung by Sitarah the Herat, an old Afghan singer. They continued weaving as they listened to the song.

> I am the Herati girl
> I come from a village
> I am a carpet-weaving girl
> I weave beautifully and colorfully
> I am the new flower of this house.

Samira liked listening to Sitarah's song because it felt as though she was singing just for her. Her mother turned down the volume a bit, and said, "You see, my child, carpet weaving is a great skill, even someone like Sitarah sings about our work!"

But Samira wasn't impressed. "What does Sitarah know? She can enjoy singing about weaving but she doesn't have to do all the hard work like us, does she?"

Samira's mother laughed. "I thought you liked the song, but now you're cross with it."

Samira looked at the *kargah* and said, "I want to be a singer, not a carpet weaver, and how's that ever going to happen?"

Samira's mother shook her head and said, "You'll never give up arguing with me about work, will you? You'll never be a singer because your father wouldn't want our family to be shamed."

Samira paused for a moment. "If father isn't ashamed of showing off the carpets I've woven, then why should he be ashamed of people hearing my voice? Singing is just as much of a talent as carpet weaving."

Samira's mother wondered how her daughter had come to be so clever and realized she couldn't win this argument, so she tried to bring her attention back to their work.

"Let's just get on with the job. You're still young and don't yet understand all our traditions."

With that, mother and daughter carried on weaving, their fingers moving in and out of the threads at great speed. It was soon lunchtime and Samira asked her mother if she could stop and have something to eat. Her mother agreed and Samira went outside. The air was dry and crisp. Autumn had turned the leaves on the trees in the yard to yellow and orange, and a strong breeze was blowing them to the ground. Samira tried to look up at the sky, which despite the cold weather was bright and sunny, but found she couldn't open her eyes because the light hurt them too much, so she covered them with her hands. As she traced her fingers around her face she felt an ache in her joints, and when she tried to stand up straight she felt a stabbing pain in her back. Hours hunched over the *kargah* in a darkened room meant she could no longer stand up properly, and because she had been in the weaving room since early in the morning, this was the first time she had seen daylight.

Samira walked slowly toward the kitchen and headed straight for the breadbasket, which was filled with the round flat bread her mother had baked in the *tanoor* early that morning. She took out a piece and then went to the gas stove and put the kettle on to boil. Every day at about midday she would come back to the kitchen, make some green tea, take two cups, some sugar, and bread, and carry it back to the weaving room. This was their lunch. Her mother would only cook in the evenings when her husband came home; she wouldn't take a break from weaving during the day to make food for the children. Besides, it was cheaper to make only one proper meal a day.

Samira sat by a small window near where her little sister was sleeping in her *gahwara* (cradle). She poured tea for her mother and herself, adding lots of sugar, and bit into the bread. Samira enjoyed every sip of her tea and every bite of her bread. After a while, Samira's mother asked her to check on her baby sister. It had been a long time since the baby had stirred, so Samira knelt down by the *gahwara* and looked at her closely.

"Yes, Mother, she's all right. She's just sleeping."

"I don't understand why she hasn't woken up. She's been sleeping since nine o'clock this morning and now it's almost one."

Samira joked that perhaps her little sister was tired like them, and then asked, "Mother, when she's older will you make her weave carpets too?"

Her mother replied, "Of course, she's no different than you or me. She's a girl and she must learn to weave or no man will marry her."

Samira knew what she meant. She had been told many times by both her mother and the local women that to secure a decent husband, a Turkmen girl must be able to weave carpets. Most girls in the village tended to start carpet weaving at home with their mothers, sisters, aunts, or grandmothers at the age of seven or eight. Meanwhile the men of the family would find traders to buy the carpets or locate markets where they could sell them to customers. Some boys would go to school, but not all of them, and some families would even train their sons to weave. But Samira's brother didn't have to weave carpets. As he was the only male child of the family he was especially valuable and his mother knew that carpet weaving was bad for the health—many women and children contracted lung diseases from working in such a dusty atmosphere day after day. Also, his mother wanted him to go to school and one day become a doctor so he could treat both her and his sister for the pain in their backs and fingers.

As Samira was taking her last bites of bread, she turned to her mother and asked, "Mother, do you think my five fingers are like five lights?"

Her mother smiled, went up to Samira, and took her hand and put it in her own. She looked at Samira's small fingers.

"My dear daughter, your fingers are not yet five lights but they are on their way. Shall I tell you when they become lights?"

"Yes, please, Mother," Samira said enthusiastically. "Tell me how and when they'll be like five *chiragh*?"

Her mother gave her fingers a gentle massage. "My dear little princess, when I tell you to get up early and go straight to the *kargah* and you do it immediately, that will be the day. When you stop complaining that your brother goes to school and you don't, that will be the day. When you stop moaning that your fingers are tired and you don't want to weave carpets, that will be the day. And finally, when you weave a six-meter carpet on your own without complaining, that will be the day your fingers become like five *chiragh*!"

Samira didn't much like the answer to her question, and got up and went to sit in front of the *kargah* where she began weaving again. She wove quickly and then started to cut the strings with the carpet knife. Her mother got up to check on the baby before coming back to sit down next to Samira and look at the section that she had just woven.

"Stop it! Stop, Samira. Look at what you're doing."

Samira stopped immediately. "What have I done? I'm weaving just like you."

Her mother took the blade and cut open the stitches on the piece that Samira had just woven. "If you don't push the thread through enough, and if you don't cut neatly or copy the pattern properly, you'll destroy months of our work."

Samira began to unpick the section she had just woven and let her mother start weaving first, before copying her. They both wove swiftly and without speaking. Occasionally the silence was broken by the sound of their wooden mallets hammering down a row of knots they had just tied. Samira's mother had a fixed target of how much work they should do every day, so Samira wasn't allowed to get up and leave the room, except to go to the toilet or the kitchen. Her mother was well aware that Samira would find any excuse she could to escape, even if only for a short while. Samira was too young and didn't care if the *tojar*, or anyone else, liked her carpets. She was bored of weaving and wanted to be out playing with her friends or making clothes for her dolls. For three years now, Samira had been expected to work constantly and hadn't been allowed to go out and play. Her mother and father considered her grown-up enough to stay at home and perfect her weaving skills.

"Mother, if I weave faster today can I go to Shakila's house later and play with her dolls?" asked Samira.

But her mother said, "Look at me, Samira; since early this morning you've been pestering me with excuses and irritating questions. Why don't you just sit down quietly and get on with your work? Stop talking and concentrate!"

Then Samira's mother glanced anxiously at the baby in her *gahwara*. "I've got you pestering me while your baby sister has still not woken up. She's been asleep for too long now and I'm starting to get worried."

Samira's mother kept looking at the *gahwara*, but she couldn't relax and eventually stopped weaving and went over to it. She untied the straps on the cradle, took the baby in her arms, and touched her face, then told Samira to run and fetch some water. The baby's face was pale and she was breathing very slowly. She looked like she was unconscious and Samira's mother couldn't wake her. Samira brought some water on a small spoon and her mother tried to push a few drops into the baby's mouth. The baby swallowed some water but didn't open her eyes, and now Samira's mother was starting to feel really anxious. She needed help and told Samira to go to the neighbor's house and call Khala Shah Gul. "Ask her to come here. Tell her your sister won't wake up."

Although Samira was worried about her sister she couldn't help but feel a sense of release at being allowed out for a few minutes. As she ran to her neighbor's house she felt excited about calling for Khala Shah Gul. She heard her mother shout after her, "Don't get sidetracked and run off with the other girls. Go straight there and come straight back."

Khala Shah Gul was one of the older women in the neighborhood, and she helped deliver babies. She herself had given birth to twelve children—most of whom were now married with their own children—and lived near Samira's family. Khala Shah Gul was also from a family of carpet weavers, but she was known to give advice to mothers on how to keep babies quiet so they could get on with their weaving. While she waited for Samira to return, her mother cradled the baby in her lap, holding her small hands, but there was no energy in her tiny body. It was as if she was drunk. She began kissing the baby's hands and feet.

"Darling little one, wake up. For the love of your mother, wake up. Why are you still asleep? Mummy is getting worried now." She kept talking to her baby and cuddling her. "I know that when you're screaming then I want you to sleep, but now it's time for you to have your favorite milk. Wake up, my love, wake up!"

The baby kept breathing slowly but otherwise didn't move, and Samira's mother began to get increasingly anxious. She opened the top of her dress, took out her breast, and rubbed it gently against the baby's face. Milk seeped out of her nipple and onto the baby's mouth, but she did not latch on and the milk spilled over her face. After a few minutes Samira came back with Khala Shah Gul, and Samira's mother ran over to her.

"Khala, look, my baby isn't moving, she doesn't cry, and she won't drink milk. She's been sleeping for hours and hours. I'm worried something has happened to her. What should I do?"

"I'll have a look at her, but I'm sure she's fine."

Samira's mother handed the baby to Khala Shah Gul and told Samira to get back to weaving while she went to make tea for their guest. Samira went back to the *kargah* and began pulling the threads together, pleased to have had the chance to go outside. Meanwhile Khala Shah Gul sat with the baby on her lap. She touched the baby's cheeks, checked her pulse, and noticed that her skin was cool and her pulse was slow and steady.

Samira's mother came back into the room with a tray of cups and a teapot, and put the tray on the floor in front of Khala Shah Gul.

"Khala Shah Gul, is my baby all right? Do you know what's wrong with her? Why won't she wake up?"

Khala Shah Gul was completely untroubled. "My child, your baby is fine; she's just in a deep sleep. From what I can see I think you've just given her a bit too much opium."

Samira's mother touched the baby's hair. "But, aunt, I didn't give her that much. I only gave her the amount you suggested. It was just one seed."

Khala Shah Gul passed the baby back to her mother. "Here you go, try now to give her your breast milk and force her to have some water. As soon as the dizziness wears off she'll wake up, don't worry."

Khala Shah Gul took a piece of opium from a pocket in her dress, just under her breasts, and broke off a small amount—the size of a seed of wheat—and held it out in the palm of her hand.

"Tomorrow you should decrease the amount of opium you give your baby because she's obviously one of those who can't take too much. Don't worry, though; she'll get used to it and there will soon come a time when her crying won't let you weave even if you've given her a piece the size of a grape."

Khala Shah Gul began to laugh and sipped her tea noisily. Samira's mother told her to have Khala's shoes ready for her, and Samira immediately put Khala's shoes in front of the door so she could step straight into them. The older woman looked down at Samira.

"Well done, my child. God bless you. In addition to being good at carpet weaving you also know how to respect your elders."

After Khala Shah Gul had left, Samira shut the door and went to kiss her baby sister who was still sleeping on her mother's lap. She kissed her on the cheek and tried to wake her up but she didn't stir. Her mother then asked her to empty the potty, which was under a hole in the *gahwara*, and as usual Samira did as she was told. The mother changed the baby's clothes and tried to breast-feed her, and much to her joy the baby finally started to move her lips and tongue and began to suck on the nipple. Samira's mother kissed her baby's forehead fervently.

"Thank you, God! My baby daughter is alive. I'm a lucky mother."

At the same time as the baby drew milk from her breast, tears began to flow down the mother's face. She was so relieved. It was as if someone had given her a second chance at life. Samira wiped away her mother's tears with her fingers. "Mother, why are you crying? What has happened? Is everything all right?"

Her mother kissed her on the forehead. "My dear daughter, these are tears of happiness. See, your sister is sucking at my breast. I'm so happy that she's all right."

Samira was happy too. She placed the potty back under the *gahwara* and her mother put the baby back into her basket. The baby now had her eyes open. Once the *gahwara* had been placed in a corner far away from the *kargah*, so that it was well away from the dust, Samira got up and poured some tea for her mother.

"God bless you, Samira. Now let's weave as fast as we can to make up for lost time."

Even though Samira had been worried about her baby sister, she felt much more relaxed than usual because she'd had so many breaks from her weaving and because she knew her mother had been paying less attention to her because of the baby.

"Mother, why did my baby sister sleep for so long? What kind of medicine did you give her?"

"It was to do with the amount of opium I'd given her; it was more than usual. Now I will show you the amount I'm going to give her every morning, and you must help me check that it's no bigger than a seed of wheat."

"But, Mother," asked Samira "why do you still have to give it to her if it makes her ill?"

"When you were a baby, I used to give it to you. It's because it makes babies sleep well. Otherwise your baby sister would be waking up constantly and disturbing her poor mother who has to weave a huge carpet with her naughty big sister."

Samira's mother smiled at her eldest daughter and carried on weaving, while Samira took a deep breath and stared ahead at the *kargah*, wondering if she would be spending the rest of her life in front of this loom. She wanted to be free of it but knew she would never escape it. Her future had already been mapped out for her, and it would consist of her weaving, weaving, and then weaving some more. And then when her mother finally declared that her daughter's five fingers were like five flames, Samira would become the bride of a Turkmen boy and be expected to weave for him and look after their children.

Samira got up and turned the radio on, and as it was playing music, she turned the volume up high. She told her mother that if they were going to have to stay in this dark room all their lives then they might as well listen to their favorite songs. Mother and daughter both smiled and carried on weaving.

⌘

Samira's mother isn't unusual in giving opium to her baby. I've discovered that it's an age-old practice among families who weave carpets to silence their children with opium until they are two or three years old. We invited a doctor onto *Afghan Woman's Hour* to talk about the dangers of opium for a baby's health, and he told us that it is harmful for their brain, their growth, and their long-term development. The doctor also said that one of the reasons drug addiction was so widespread in Afghanistan was because as babies people had become addicted to it, and then explained how babies who scream and cry until they are given opium are already addicts. Unfortunately, Samira's mother didn't have access to this information, but a survey carried out on behalf of the BBC World Service Trust about *Afghan Woman's Hour* showed that many female listeners felt sympathy for her circumstances. We also found that listeners were grateful to the program for providing them with this information, and that as a consequence many mothers said they would now stop giving their children opium because they'd understood how harmful it was. I was delighted that the reporter and I had managed to bring this problem to our listeners' attention but knew there was nothing I could do to relieve the pain that so many women endure as they weave the carpets which adorn our houses.

The Afghan drug trade generates billions of dollars every year and the country currently produces around 90 percent of the world's opium, but most of the opium production is confined to just nine provinces in the southern and western regions of Afghanistan. The government and the international community continue to fight the drug trade, thereby freeing many parts of the country from opium cultivation, but with so many high-profile people reported to be on the drug payroll, both inside and outside the government, the ongoing battle is proving very difficult. Opium production currently contributes to around 4 percent of Afghanistan's annual GDP.

According to a United Nations report published in 2010 the number of Afghan households involved in opium cultivation amounts to 248,700, and this figure accounts for 6 percent of the total population of Afghanistan. Many of those who cultivate opium are addicts or become addicts, and while the precise number of addicts is not known, it's predicted that it runs into the millions. There are various reasons why people become involved in opium production; first because it's a valuable commodity, second because people are poor, and third because people want to improve their standard of living.

The skill and dedication of people like Samira and her mother have brought Afghanistan an international reputation for its traditional handicrafts, but at what price? No one acknowledges the hardships women like Samira and her mother endure to turn yarns of wool into works of art. And no one thinks of the babies that are silenced by opium so that their mothers can weave sufficiently fast to meet the demands of the *tojars* and buyers.

6

Ilaha's Story

THE WEDDING NIGHT

*T*HIS IS AN EXTRACT FROM A STORY THAT WAS SENT TO ME BY ONE OF the *Afghan Woman's Hour* reporters. It is about Ilaha, a young bride from Jawzjan, a province in northern Afghanistan. Ilaha's life story was one that touched me—and many other Afghan brides—profoundly. As a newly married bride myself, I recognized the anxious desire to please a new husband combined with the concern to not offend the in-laws. I could imagine just how it was for Ilaha on her wedding night, and the fear and shame she must have felt in the morning when the family members came into the marital bedroom.

Every so often you come across a story that stays with listeners long after the program has been broadcast and comes to influence their way of thinking. This was how it was with Ilaha's story. Seconds after the program ended the phone lines were busy with mothers, daughters, and doctors all phoning in.

A doctor from Afghanistan called me to say, "Zarghuna Jan, I've just heard your program on Ilaha's life story and wanted to congratulate you. Well done to you and your colleagues for highlighting an issue that affects so many girls in my village."

I felt ambivalent about this praise, though. As a program-maker I was pleased to have aired such an important subject, but as a woman I was disappointed that in the twenty-first century some people in my country could still be so ignorant. It also made me realize how Westernized I had become after living in London for almost seven years.

⮰

ILAHA'S HOME TOWN IS Shiberghan, the provincial capital of Jawzjan. It's an agricultural region with a strong tradition of female carpet weaving. Different tribes populate the area, but it is Uzbek dominated and the stronghold of the powerful Uzbek warlord General Abdul Rashid Dostum. Dostum and his faction—known as "Junbish"—have many supporters in the north of Afghanistan, but especially in Jawzjan province. He's currently an Afghan government military official who lives in Turkey. There are allegations of war crimes hanging over him. In some ways his political movement is quite open and liberal—Dostum has his own private television channel with female presenters on it and believes that both boys and girls should have access to education—but it is still underpinned by strong cultural values.

A young reporter called Sowsan used to send us stories from that region, but Sowsan wasn't her real name. When she first began reporting for us she told me, "Zari dear, the BBC has many listeners in my hometown and the stories I'll be sending you are likely to offend many men, so I'll have to conceal my true identity or I'm afraid my children and I could be harmed." The safety of our contributors always comes first.

Most women in Afghanistan, particularly those in the provinces, cannot read or write. In fact, the United Nations estimates that up to 48 percent of Afghan women are illiterate. But despite their lack of education, Afghan women are natural storytellers, so our reporters in the field would record their stories and send them back to me in London via the Internet. I first heard Ilaha's story in early 2007. Each day, when I arrived at the cramped office I used to share with two colleagues at the BBC World Service, the first thing I'd do was check my emails. I would then call our reporters who are based all over Afghanistan. It was the reporter in Shiberghan who told me she had a story about virginity that she wanted to share with me.

Sowsan said, "I've met this bride called Ilaha, and she's living a life of misery and shame. She's in a really bad way and is scared she's going mad. When I first met her she was forgetful and tearful. Sometimes she would just sit there bolt upright and stare at me, and I think her terrible experiences have affected her state of mind. I really want you to listen to her story."

Sowsan then went on to give me examples of relatives and neighbors of hers who had all suffered in similar ways to Ilaha, so I told her that if she thought the material would make a strong story then she should record it and we would consider using it on a program.

Time passed and I had deadlines to meet. Sowsan's passion and certainty had convinced me that this material would make for a good program, but she then told me there was a problem and that we couldn't go ahead. I assumed that there were, as usual, technical problems between Afghanistan and London.

"Zarghuna! There's no technical problem; I'm saying we cannot air this material. I've recorded Ilaha's interview but now she doesn't want it to be broadcast. If her family hears it she says they'll kill her. I've told her that we can alter her voice but she doesn't understand and is very frightened. I have her story but not her permission to broadcast it."

It is drilled into all BBC journalists that it is our duty and responsibility to protect our sources if their lives or welfare are threatened in any way, so I tried to think of a way around this problem. I suggested to Sowsan that she write up Ilaha's story and read it herself, so that Ilaha's identity could be protected, and a few hours later she sent me her recording.

My name is Ilaha and I want to tell you my life story. I'm a newly married bride but when I look into my heart the pain that I feel frightens me. My soul, which is pure and clean, aches from a sin I've never actually committed and I spend my nights weeping and my days suffocated by shame, even though I know I've done nothing wrong. Why? Because society thinks I'm a shameless woman. And what was my crime?

My family arranged for me to be engaged to an engineer who was Afghan, but lived in London. We had an engagement party in Afghanistan and soon afterwards my fiancé went back to England. When I had sex with him for the first time on my wedding night I did not bleed, and at first he did not take this too seriously. But two weeks later my mother-in-law asked me to show her some sign of my virginity.

"When we brought a bride into our home we were full of trust and hope," she said. "We expected to see some sign of her having bled on her wedding night." When I told her I had not bled at all, she got angry and demanded to know how girls can be trusted nowadays. She then told my husband that he was stupid to have trusted me and that I had made a fool of him. From that day onward, there were terrible rows and my life soon became hell. My parents got involved and took me to see various doctors in a bid to try to prove that I had been a virgin. The doctors all said that it was too late for that and told my parents that they should have brought me to them on the morning of my marriage. They did also try to explain that not all women bleed when they first have intercourse.

A few days later the arguing stopped and my husband bade me and my family farewell before returning to London. He told me he would do all the necessary paperwork for my visa and that I would soon be able to join him in Britain. In the meantime, I was to stay with my mother-in-law. Her behavior toward me was odd: she kept reminding me that she was doing me a huge favor just letting me stay with her, and said that because I was not a good woman, I did not deserve a happy life. It was a very difficult time for me—I sometimes wished I was dead, but I lived in hope of being reunited with my husband, the love of my life. He was the first man I had ever been with and I loved him and looked forward to starting a family with him, but all these hopes were shattered when one day he rang me from London.

"I don't want to live with you. I don't trust you," he said. "I'm going to do what my mother thinks is best and divorce you. I'll never be able to come back to Afghanistan because of the shame you've brought on my family."

I moved back home to live with my parents. I knew that my life was ruined. No one can understand my suffering except those brides who have been thrown out of their homes or beaten for not being able to prove their virginity. I have told my story to *Afghan Woman's Hour* so that people who are cruel to innocent women like me can reconsider their behavior. How long will Afghan brides have to go on worrying about whether they bleed on the first night of their marriage?

When I heard Ilaha's words I began to cry, but my colleagues could not see I was upset because their desks all faced the wall, and they were busy working with their headphones on. I listened to the end of the story and cried a little more, but I tried to be calm and retain my objectivity. For many journalists the most painful and tragic stories very often make for the best programs, so we are pleased when sad stories like Ilaha's turn up, but this time it was different. Her story affected me personally and reminded me of a very painful time in my life. I too was an Afghan woman and I too was once an innocent bride. It didn't matter where I lived or how different my circumstances were to Ilaha's; the fact that I was an Afghan woman meant I too was expected to accept what was chosen for me. The opinion of the family matters more than anything. I remember how many times I tried to explain to my parents that my marriage wouldn't make me happy, and how they told me that I would never find a man like my husband however hard I looked. It didn't matter that I was living in the UK—a country with different values—all that mattered was the fact that I was an Afghan girl and should be obedient.

There is a moment in every Afghan bride's life when her mother, or another older woman, slips an embroidered white handkerchief into her handbag and tells her that she must put it under her legs when she goes to bed. "Don't forget!" they whisper. But none of these women wait to answer any questions the bride might have about her wedding night. Most young Afghan brides are completely in the dark about the physical relationship between a husband and wife, so when they're given a handkerchief they have no idea what to do with, and no understanding of what importance is placed on whether they bleed or not when they first have sex. The groom, on the other hand, has usually been given clear instructions that his bride must bleed onto the handkerchief as proof of virginity. A bloodstained handkerchief makes for a proud husband.

Girls in Afghanistan are not taught anything about sex, yet when they marry at the age of fifteen or so, they are suddenly expected to know what to do. There is no formal sex education for either girls or boys, and parents don't openly talk about sex to their children, although boys tend to be a bit more knowledgeable on the subject as they talk about it amongst themselves. But more than that, sex tends to be considered as something that belongs to men.

I remember when girls at school wanted to know about sexual relations between men and women, the information we were given was limited to how we should all make sure we were virgins when we married as it would be important to our future husbands. For girls, the very idea that they might want to talk about sex was considered shameful.

On a recent trip to Afghanistan I asked women whether attitudes about the open discussion of sex had changed, but unfortunately they haven't. Sex just isn't talked about, and because girls are scared about being judged if they do ask about it, it tends to be something they only find out about on their wedding night.

Sowsan and I talked about Ilaha's story at length and decided to do further research into attitudes about virginity. One of my Afghan friends said she had produced a series of programs about sex education, and that the matter of whether a woman bleeds or not when she loses her virginity had been raised with a doctor. I was keen to hear the medical view, and my friend said that according to the doctor a woman won't necessarily bleed the first time she has sex. Some women bleed while others don't, and bleeding is no proof of virginity. I turned to the Internet in search of more information.

The next day I managed to interview a doctor in our Kabul studio down the line. He admitted that he thought the tradition of using a stained handkerchief to prove a woman's virginity was misguided, but that he couldn't talk about the matter openly. He pointed out that the whole subject was still taboo in Afghan society and if he spoke publicly about it he would lose respect in the community and his patients would leave his practice. He then refused to go on the record and so we lost the interview.

Sowsan and I were disappointed but refused to give up because we wanted to do what we could to prevent any more women being trapped in the same miserable situation as Ilaha. We set about finding another doctor who would be prepared to talk on the radio about virginity, and several weeks later we found someone in Kabul. He clarified that bleeding is no proof that a woman has not already had sexual intercourse, and gave some examples of women who had not bled on their wedding nights and had consequently been beaten up by their husbands. Some had even been killed.

We discussed this highly taboo subject on the radio in an open and frank manner, but for some of my male Afghan colleagues in London and Afghanistan, it was too much. They criticized both the program and me for being too Westernized and decadent. Some even made crude jokes about the fact that we had mentioned the word "vagina" on the radio. The curious thing is, though, they kept on listening to the program.

There was a handful of male and female colleagues, however, who congratulated me on the program, saying that it was the first time they had heard this taboo subject being discussed so openly and informatively. When the interview with the doctor was aired I prayed that Ilaha's husband's family might hear it. I never heard anything more about Ilaha, though.

≈

As a journalist, the search for stories is relentless. On *Afghan Woman's Hour* we actively ask listeners to contact our reporters on the ground with their stories, so I sometimes had to make trips to Afghanistan to train the *Afghan Woman's Hour* team there.

One day back in 2008 I was working at the BBC World Service's office in Kabul when a woman came to see me. We were able to speak alone in the newsroom because all the other reporters were out on stories. Let us call her Gulalai. She was about thirty years old and had three children. She had a large frame in which she seemed to carry a burden heavier than her body. Gulalai wore fashionable Western clothes and makeup, and arrived wearing a coat rather than a *burqa*. She was an educated woman who taught in a girls' school; her husband was an engineer. Her family lived in Kabul and was prosperous, but she told me that she had been a breadwinner for longer than her husband because she had found a job sooner than him. For a while, she had been the only one who was employed, whilst also looking after the children and doing all the housework. Despite all her achievements, however, a memory from more than fifteen years ago still hurt her deeply. She had been made to feel as though she had committed a crime, and therefore suffered terribly, for something she hadn't actually done. Gulalai spoke with tears in her large brown eyes.

"I was seventeen when I got married. My husband was a lot older than me and had studied in France and Iran. I remember being very scared on the night of my wedding. I didn't know what sex was, or even what relations between a man and a woman were, but I did remember something that my aunt had told me as I was leaving for my in-laws. She had said that when the night of my marriage came, I should use the handkerchief in my bag that she had made for me. When I asked her what the handkerchief was for, she said, 'You'll know when it's night-time and you're alone with your husband.'

"But I still didn't understand; I was too young. The first night I didn't let my husband touch me. I cried and said that I was scared, and he got angry but said he would wait until the second night of the marriage." Gulalai's tears were flowing fast as a river, full of pain, despite the passage of time. "Dear Zari, it hurts when I talk about it." I comforted her and told her not to worry and that I understood.

I had found my husband to be a kind man, but I felt that he had forgotten his kindness and was thinking only about sleeping with me. I was powerless to resist and so he had sex with me and I bled, but as I wanted to be clean, I then went to the toilet and wiped between my legs with tissue paper. I threw the paper soaked with my blood into the toilet and flushed it away, but when I went back to the bedroom he asked, "What did you do with the handkerchief?" Then when I asked him which one he meant, he said, "Your mother must have told you; you've got to keep the handkerchief with your blood on it as my mother will be asking for it tomorrow." I told him that I had used a tissue to clean the blood away and then flushed it down the toilet, and although he didn't say anything in response I could see he was starting to get worried. At that stage, though, I wasn't too concerned because I was ignorant of the tradition surrounding the bloodied handkerchief. But although my husband seemed pleased that his wife was a virgin—reassuring me he was happy I was a pure woman—he did warn me that I would have some questions to answer. I still didn't get it; I just didn't understand what he meant. I was an innocent, young girl who did not realize that the absence of my virginal blood on a handkerchief would scar me all my married life.

Not long afterwards, though, I understood what my husband meant, as early one morning my mother-in-law came to my room and asked for a sign of my virginity: "Show me where the handkerchief with your blood is?" I told her the truth about what had happened, but she didn't believe me. "What will I tell the women who are waiting to see it? What will I say to the other members of the family?"

I didn't know what to say and my husband remained silent. Then that evening my mother-in-law came to the house again and asked my husband, "What should we do now? It's a disgrace. Your wife has dishonored us."

Luckily my husband replied, "No, she hasn't shamed us. She's proved her purity to me so I don't want anyone to ask either of us about it again."

I don't know what my mother-in-law wanted to do to me—maybe she wanted to send me back to my parents' home or maybe she even wanted to kill me. But after she had left my husband turned on me, saying, "You've made a big mistake. You may have proved yourself to me but you have not done so to my family. People will gossip about you and it won't be easy."

I pleaded with him to help me, but perhaps he had already realized that this was a good way to control me. For years afterwards my mother-in-law would say that her family had bought a bride who was not a virgin, and complain that they had never seen a sign of virginal blood from me. She would call me a liar. I went into a deep depression hearing these accusations hurled at me again and again. I tried to commit suicide twice but was not successful. The third time I stopped when I found out I was pregnant.

I am now the mother of three children, but my husband's family still talk about how I was not a virgin when I married because I was unable to display the "sign." I keep asking my husband, why after fifteen years does his family keep tormenting me with this same question? Will they ever let the subject drop? Was it not enough that I suffered on my wedding night, rather than enjoying becoming a woman? I feel as though I have been taken to court for a serious crime, yet it is a crime that I didn't commit. In response to my anguish my husband tells me to thank God that I found a man who did not kick me out and who was able to accept me as his wife.

My mother-in-law still tells me to keep my distance when socializing with the girls who come to the house to see her other sons. I hear her saying, "We never saw her sign; she never had one. We brought a shameful woman into the family so you girls be careful and don't mess around. You must be virgins when you marry, otherwise you will end up like her."

Gulalai began to cry, shouting that she didn't know what to do and that there were still times when she wished she was dead and even felt such hatred toward her mother-in-law that she wished *her* dead. She had three healthy children yet was still unhappy. But she also said that when she'd heard Ilaha's story she had felt a kind of relief.

"I thought you were talking about my life, not Ilaha's. I hope other people—and particularly women—listen to these stories and become kinder to their own sex."

Gulalai and I then said good-bye to each other, but as she left I felt like shouting after her, "Wait! Gulalai, hear my story! I have a life story too!" I had spent so much time reporting on other women's stories that I suddenly felt the need to share my own, and the pain inside me was bursting to come out. But now was not the time. When Gulalai and I parted my eyes were full of tears and I suspect she thought they were for her. I wanted to tell her, though, that no matter where an Afghan woman lives, Afghan society and its culture will always treat her in the same way.

⤳

Ilaha couldn't escape her predicament because she was a poor, uneducated woman with no job in Afghanistan. Gulalai had an education and a professional job but she couldn't divorce her husband either or she would lose her children, and the stain of divorce would remain on her family's name, her children's name, and her name forever. Ilaha and Gulalai remind me of myself on my wedding night, as I was also very ignorant about what to expect. My parents and teachers had told me very little about it, and all I knew about sex from discussing it with friends was that the man would do something to me, that it would hurt, and I would bleed from my vagina. Meanwhile my older sister had told me that if I wanted to avoid getting pregnant I should go to the doctor and get some "anti-baby" pills. I had also been warned by everyone I knew that if a bride does not bleed after she has sex for the first time with her husband, then her life thereafter will be hell.

One of my school friends had also reminded me of an Afghan tradition which maintains that as a virgin—and therefore a pure and clean woman—whatever I was to ask of God on my wedding day would be given to me.

"It's your *Nikkah* time so you should pray now," she had said, and I had raised both hands with my palms held upward toward God and prayed, "God, please make sure I bleed; that's the only wish I have. I don't want money or a big house to live in—I just want this blood."

I was not able to relax and enjoy the wedding, as I was too worried about when to take the "anti-baby" pills. The doctor had told me it was important to take them at the same time every day, but I wasn't wearing a watch and my husband refused to tell me what time it was (I think he suspected why I wanted to know). In the end I had to ask a small boy, only to find that I was more than two hours late taking the pills. At nine o'clock in the evening, a traditional Afghan meal of rice, kebabs, koftas, and manto was served to everyone and as I was feeling weak and tired by then, I ate the food. After dinner, a singer began a romantic Afghan song and I started crying as I realized what I had got myself into. When my father saw my tears he got angry with me, but I still wept when I said good-bye to the guests. One female guest offered me a tissue with the advice that "every woman goes through this."

My husband and I did not get to bed until five o'clock in the morning. The wedding party had gone on for many hours and then there was some difficulty finding the key to our room at Javed's parents' house. Sitting alone on a chair in the corner of his mother's bedroom wearing my white wedding dress, I gazed at the cream polyester sheets on the bed and was frightened at the prospect of what was going to happen. I took off my makeup and had a shower, as it was July and I was hot and sweaty. I then changed into a white silky nightdress that my mother had bought me especially for my wedding night and went back to the corner of the room. Javed was still downstairs with his male friends. He arrived later smelling of alcohol and cigarettes, took off the black wedding suit my parents had bought for him, and brushed his teeth in his vest and underpants. He asked why I was sitting in the corner of the room, and I told him I was scared. He said I shouldn't be frightened, hugged me, and led me to the bed. Without another word, he started kissing me and caressing my breasts, even though I'd crossed my arms over them because of the hungry way he was coming at me.

After a few minutes he told me to open my legs, but I held them shut with my hands. He pushed them open and told me to relax and said that this was how it happens, before asking where the handkerchief was. I told him I was not sure but that I thought it might be under the pillow, as my elder sister had told me she'd put it there. Javed found it, put it on the bed, and said we had to have sex on the handkerchief to catch the blood. When my husband penetrated me my legs began shaking uncontrollably. He told me not to worry. Despite the pain and fear, I did not bleed that night. We both searched frantically on the handkerchief for blood but there was none. God was not kind to me, even on my wedding night.

I remember him saying, "Oh no, there's no blood!"

I said, "Maybe you haven't done it properly."

He began again and it still hurt. After a while, he groaned. I felt something wet between my legs and a few seconds later he stopped. We both inspected the handkerchief again for blood, but there still wasn't any. He looked at me, expecting an answer.

"Maybe I'm different and I don't bleed," I said.

He said, "You should do if you're a virgin."

I cried and said, "I don't know what has happened. This is my first time and you just have to believe me. There's nothing else I can say." Then I started sobbing and suggested we do it again. He told me to relax and go to sleep, but I lay awake feeling anxious and guilty because I hadn't been able to please him. I was also worried about what his relatives would think. Although he hadn't said anything, I could see he no longer trusted me. I knew I was a virgin when I married him, but I had not been able to prove it by bleeding, and as a result my married life had begun with my husband failing to trust me. Whenever he spoke unkindly to me after that I thought it was because he didn't believe I'd been a virgin on our wedding night.

And so my married life began with me constantly trying to please my husband as a way of making up for not being able to prove my virginity. I worked hard to provide for both of us; I cooked him his favorite meals and washed and ironed all his clothes, yet I received no love or encouragement in return. I soon began to feel old and ugly and started spending less and less time in our flat and more time at my parents' house. Even with my education and the support of my relatively liberal family, I had never thought to question the Afghan traditions surrounding marriage and virginity. I had always heard that Afghan women must be virgins when they marry, but no one had ever said anything about men being virgins, so I had this idea that it was down to women to prove their virginity.

Who should I blame for the nights I have cried myself to sleep? Myself, Javed, or my mother who never told me properly about sexual relations between a husband and wife? I now ask myself why I went through all that pain and worry on my wedding night, and why I didn't once ask of my husband: "I know you've slept with other women before marrying me, so what gives you the right to check up on me?"

≈

I KNOW NOW THAT Afghan women feel the same, whether you are Ilaha in a village, Gulalai in Kabul, or Zarghuna in London. The women who blame you for not bleeding on your wedding night have been told by their mothers and their grandmothers that clean and good women bleed. It is the sign of a woman's purity. I know from my experience that Afghan families do not discuss women's feelings. If their son starts chasing girls—following them home from school, writing them notes—then they are proud because it shows that their son is becoming a man. But no one knows when their daughter becomes a woman and no one helps her. How can a girl who does not even know what a period is understand what sex is? Has any young bride ever dared to ask for information or advice? Can she ask her mother or her mother-in-law? A girl like Ilaha could not ask such questions.

A girl who bleeds on her wedding night is fortunate indeed, and the pride of her mother-in-law, her parents, her husband, and the whole family. Bleeding is not just a sign of virginity, it also guarantees the future family life of the young bride, for a girl who does not bleed is not considered to be a virgin, and she must start married life with the worry that she might be kicked out of her in-laws' home or usurped by a second wife.

Girls are kept like dolls in the corner of the house. If they are sent to school, they are taught to see this as a big favor; if they are given the same food as their brothers, they have the best parents; and if they are bought new clothes, then they have the best family.

7

Anesa's Story

A MARRIAGE OF CONVENIENCE

I N AFGHANISTAN, A WEDDING REPRESENTS THE CREATION OF A NEW family, and the family is the single most important institution in that society, providing economic security in times of hardship in a way that the state is unable to do. For example, wherever they are in the world, Afghans will send money to help their less fortunate relatives. They will even help them get jobs. This is seen as fulfilling family responsibility rather than nepotism. The family unit can be quite large and sometimes includes three or four generations living together. Marriages are often arranged between cousins to keep the kinship intact. Afghan society is held together by families—family loyalties are very strong—and weddings represent that coming together. And the more lavish the wedding the better, since this shows everyone your wealth and status.

Weddings are an even bigger affair in villages where traditional values hold greater sway. Hundreds of people are invited—the whole village must be included—but men and women are entertained separately, which, in effect, doubles the cost. Parents save hard for their sons' weddings. New clothes will be required for all family members, sheep and cows will be kept and then slaughtered especially for the occasion, and gold jewelry will be bought in advance for the bride. The bride's family, on the other hand, has few responsibilities. They are respected if they don't ask for money for their daughter, but it is a common practice to receive a large sum of money, which some Afghan women see as a show of respect for the new in-laws. Sometimes the amount is so large that the groom's family has to borrow the money from relatives and can remain in debt for years.

Weddings are generally celebrated in a similar way throughout Afghanistan but there are some regional differences, and working on *Afghan Woman's Hour* helped me discover the roots of some of these traditions. Every day at work I'd be sent new material from across Afghanistan. I learned that there are many similar customs amongst Pashtuns, Hazaras, Uzbeks, and Tajiks. At the same time, I found that in some regions there are families who won't accept any money for their daughters and will celebrate the wedding in a far simpler style. The reporters and I decided to make a series of special programs about the wedding customs of people around Afghanistan. Why, for example, did brides in the north wear white clothes, while in the south Pashtun areas they wear red?

One day, Salmi Suhili, one of our reporters based in Kabul, came to me with an idea: "Zari dear, I want to introduce our listeners to the wedding customs from my home province of Kunduz. I'm going for a family wedding and, if they agree, I could take my recording equipment and get lots of good material."

I didn't want to miss a great opportunity like this and so readily agreed. After two weeks, Salmi returned from Kunduz, and in one of our regular planning meetings between London and Kabul, where reporters and I would exchange ideas on the phone, she burst into the discussion.

"Zari dear, I must tell you all about my experience in Kunduz. I met lots of women there and have recorded heaps of material, but there is one story in particular that I want to share with you."

We all listened intently as Salmi went on. "I met a woman called Anesa," she said, and even though the sound quality on the phone wasn't very good I could hear some anxiety in her voice. "She was very beautiful—a lovely, kind woman with three children. I can't believe someone facing—" And then she broke down into tears.

"Salmi dear, we're all listening to you," I said, trying to calm her down. "This isn't the first time we've heard a very sad story of an Afghan woman. Please carry on."

Salmi cleared her throat. "I met Anesa at our family wedding and she called me especially to tell her story because she knew I was working for *Afghan Woman's Hour* and she was asking for help. She told me the story of her wedding, how she had married as a young girl but—"

Salmi's voice choked and she was unable to speak. Our meeting was drawing to a close and I still needed to listen to the ideas of four other reporters that day, so I suggested that Salmi send the story to me as an audio file.

Later that day, I received Anesa's story. I was impatient to hear what had made an experienced journalist like Salmi break down. What could be so upsetting and shocking? I downloaded the material onto our editing system and heard Anesa's voice. And I discovered one of the most wonderful storytellers our program had heard. Anesa, with a very quiet voice, began her story.

It was about eight o'clock in the morning and I was wide awake but I stayed in my bed. The sun cast lines of light as it made its way through the dark maroon curtains of my room. It was already very hot. I was still wearing my glittery red dress and bright red *shalwar*. The previous evening most of my cousins and the young girls from our village had gathered in our house for the most special night of my life. I smiled to myself as I remembered how my cousin Fareba had smeared dark green henna on my feet. The girls had all been wearing colorful clothes, dancing, and teasing me about my groom. This was my henna night. I wore clothes that my in-laws had made especially for me. It's a tradition for people in Kunduz to bring new clothes for the bride on her henna night.

I loved all the presents and the attention I was getting from my family and friends. Everyone was treating me like a queen. This was to be my last day in my parents' home. I was so excited that at last I was going to see the man I would be marrying. This was my wedding day!

I admired the *kheena paich* (triangular handkerchief) my mother had made for the day. After the henna, my hand had been covered with some white cotton and then the green glittery *kheena paich*. A flowery smell of henna filled the room. I stretched out my legs on the *charpoie*, forgetting that they were also covered with *kheena paich*.

Fareba came into the room. "Wake up, you lazy girl. People who're getting married can't spend all day in bed!" She pulled back the curtains. "Aunt told me that you have to have a bath, get dressed, and have your makeup done."

I was very excited at the prospect of getting my makeup done. I loved makeup and new clothes. I knew I was lucky. My brothers, sisters, and I always had new clothes for Eid and New Year. My father was a government clerk and my mother used to do some tailoring, so they could afford to buy us nice things.

I told Fareba I couldn't walk because my legs were covered with *kheena paich*. She laughed and asked if I expected her to carry me to the bath.

I said, "Yes, you'll have to. I'm a bride, and in a few hours' time I'll be leaving you all, so today you have to treat me like a princess."

Fareba came toward me as if to pick me up but instead, just kissed me on the cheek. "Of course, you're the bride but I'm not the one who's going to be holding you in their arms. Tonight the man of your dreams will hold you tightly and carry you off."

I got embarrassed and told Fareba to be quiet. I knew she was only teasing me but I was excited and anxious about seeing my future husband. I knew my parents liked him and I'd seen him from a distance when he visited our house during the *dawra-e-namzadi* (period of engagement). His family had sent me lots of gifts, as is the custom: clothes, shoes, bangles, henna, and many glittery scarves.

I also knew that this was the day I would start behaving like a grownup, with proper responsibilities—my mother had constantly been reminding me of that. I had set my heart on becoming a wife, a mother, and a daughter-in-law. I was still day-dreaming about the future when Fareba tugged my arm and ordered me to get up for my bath.

Everything I was using was new. The soap was unwrapped from its packet, the shampoo was in a new bottle. Both were gifts from my in-laws. My mother had also put some cold milk into a pot—it's a tradition in Kunduz to wash the bride with milk as a symbol of her purity and to bring luck and prosperity. I held my towel in front of me and told Fareba that she had to leave because I was too shy to wash in front of her. I sat on the stool and washed myself with the warm water, which Fareba had fetched in a bucket.

After my bath Fareba came in and recited the prayers for a new bride. We have a saying in Kunduz that pure and chaste girls gain the *Noor* (or grace) of Allah on their wedding day. It means God will shine his light on you. Fareba said I looked very beautiful, and I hoped I had gained the spiritual glow that comes from the *Noor* of Allah.

Fareba took out a new white bra and white lacy panties from their packets and handed them to me. Everything I would wear that day would be new. I slipped on the white glittery dress that the tailor in our village had made for me. The neck was in a star design and the sleeves were long and flared. My *shalwar* were white and silky with embroidery at the ankles. I looked at myself in the mirror and thought how grown-up I looked.

Soon all my other cousins and friends surrounded me, laughing and joking. One was painting my fingernails, another my toenails. Fareba was combing my hair, attaching lots of colorful clips to create a pretty design.

Guests had already arrived and were wandering around our house. My mother and older members of my family were busy preparing the food. At noon the groom's family would arrive and take me away, so there was a sense of urgency. I noticed my mother hadn't changed her clothes. It's traditional for the mother to express her sorrow at losing her daughter by not wearing new clothes. I could see my mother was under pressure at having to provide food for so many guests. She also seemed a little sad. I guess she was upset because I was going into someone else's family. She wanted my last day with her to be special.

"Fareba, you have to look after Anesa," my mother instructed her. "She's our guest this morning. Give her everything she needs and make sure she has enough to eat."

Fareba and I had grown up together and were close friends. She did more than my mother asked. While Fareba was making up my hair she gave me some advice.

"When you go to the groom's house today you'll be taking care of many people, not just one man. His mother, father, and family will all want respect and attention from you. Make sure you pay them the proper attention—I don't want anything bad to happen to you. You remember what happened to Shigufa? She lives like a prisoner with her in-laws."

I asked Fareba why they treated her like this. She said it was because she only took care of her husband and didn't look after his family as well, who showed their displeasure by not allowing her to return to visit her own family. I wasn't surprised by this—I had heard that in-laws could be spiteful and make a new bride's life a misery. I told Fareba that I would of course respect my in-laws as they would be my family after the wedding. I laughed and said that I wanted them to respect me too.

Fareba pulled my hair and told me to stop being so naughty. When she finally finished doing my hair I thought it looked very impressive. She had copied the style from a postcard of the Indian Bollywood actress Sri Devi. Fareba and I had promised each other that we would do each other's makeup when we got married. All our dreams were of Bollywood movies, and we would eagerly follow the latest styles and fashions of the beautiful and famous actresses. On Eid days and special occasions we would copy their clothes, hair, and makeup, desperately trying to look like them. We were known throughout our neighborhood for doing this.

Finally, Fareba took my velvet chador and placed it at an angle on my head so it looked like a wedding headdress. She draped a green silky shawl around my shoulders and guided my feet into a pair of extremely high-heeled cream shoes. My mother brought in all the jewelry she was giving me and gave it to Fareba to choose what to adorn me with. There was a heavy golden necklace with matching earrings and several rings. On my left hand I was already wearing my gold engagement ring. When one of my cousins saw me she exclaimed, "Oh my God, Anesa, you look like a donkey with lots of bells around its neck."

Fareba told her off for calling me names, then turned back to me. "Don't worry, Anesa. She's just jealous of you because you have so many things and she doesn't. You're special today and she isn't." Then, with tears in her eyes, she added, "You know, after today, Anesa, I'll have to go to the *tanoor* by myself. I'll be baking bread alone. You won't be there." And she flung her arms around my neck.

I said, "I'll still come to the *tanoor* with you every day. No one can stop me. I'm sure I'll have the right to see my family and my dearest cousin."

Then Fareba smudged dark green eye shadow onto my eyes; she traced kohl around my eyes and brushed black mascara onto my lashes. Bright pink blusher was dabbed onto my cheeks and finally my lips were painted with a vivid red lipstick. Fareba picked a fiery red color for my lips to turn the groom crazy, but I told her it was shameful to speak like this in front of the other girls. My cousin held the mirror in front of me and I stared at my reflection. Now, when I look back, I think I must have looked like an over-painted doll. My lips looked as if I had someone else's lips painted on top of them and there was too much glitter, but at the time it was the height of fashion in my village and I thought the effect was simply wonderful. The other girls told me I looked very pretty, and Fareba said she was sure no one else in the groom's family would have my looks and I would make the in-laws jealous.

Listening to Anesa's story took me back to my own wedding day. How different it had been! I wish I'd had a close friend like Fareba with whom to confide my anger and distress. I remember how I didn't care what I looked like and how I deliberately left behind a white pearl necklace that my mother had bought me to wear with my wedding dress. Later in the evening she asked me why I wasn't wearing my new pearls and I pretended that I'd forgotten them. I was angry with her and with the whole arranged marriage but I had to hide my feelings and suffer in silence. I refused even to look at myself in the mirror at the beauty parlor after they had done my makeup and hair. I thought I was the ugliest woman in the world. The makeup, wedding dress, and flowers didn't mean anything to me. In the wedding hall some of the women told me how beautiful I looked but I didn't believe them. Unlike Anesa, I didn't enjoy all the fuss and attention.

> My mother called for me to be taken to a larger room that had been made ready for the occasion. Two wooden chairs had been placed in front of a small table, which was covered with a red glittery cloth. Mattresses had been put around the edge of the room; the middle was empty except for Afghan carpets. Fareba and another cousin held my hands and slowly led me in. I was followed by a procession of women and children. Wherever I went girls followed me playing the *daira* (tambourine) and singing Afghan wedding songs. The girls were playing the "Ahesta Bero" song:
>
> > *Ahesta bero, Anesa Jan. Ahesta bero.*
> > Go slowly, dear bride. Walk slowly, bride.
>
> This is a traditional song that expresses the sadness of a family at losing a daughter. It's sung when the bride leaves her parents' house for the last time. My mother approached me and began to pour some sweets onto my head. Immediately the children started scrabbling and wrestling on the floor for them. Fareba shouted at them to stop and told their mothers to take them away. She said they had to get out of my way in case they tripped me up. She was quite right: I could barely walk in my high-heeled shoes.
>
> My mother kissed me on the forehead. "Anesa, my child, you look as beautiful as the moon. I hope that your life will be as warm and light as the sun."

My procession finally reached the chairs and my mother ordered the girls to tidy the room because lunchtime was getting close. The groom's family had paid for a cook to help my mother prepare all the food. It's usual in our culture for the groom's family to pay for most things. My father only asked for a small amount of money for me, even though the groom's family was willing to pay more. My father didn't believe in the tradition of taking money for his daughter's hand in marriage, though it is usual practice in Kunduz.

While the room was being cleared and the final preparations were made, I sat on my bridal chair and Fareba sat on the one reserved for the groom. She said if he didn't turn up she would be my husband. I laughed and told her that my fiancé would kick her from the chair and take me from her.

I began to feel hot and sweaty in my clothes so Fareba ordered one of the girls to fan me with a *paka* (paddle-shaped fan). This poor girl was thrilled to do it because it meant she could be close to the bride.

A loud burst of music and dancing signaled the arrival of the groom and his family, and Fareba grabbed my hand. "Oh my God, Anesa. They're here already!" All the women stood up, some went to watch the arrival from the windows, but most stood out in the yard to welcome the guests. My mother gestured for Fareba to cover my face with a shawl. I struggled to see what was going on from two small peepholes. I could just make out the groom's family. They were all dressed in brightly colored clothes and wore lots of gold jewelry. Their song went like this:

Ma dismal Awardem.
We have brought the handkerchief.
Aroos Biadar jana ba sad naz awardem.
We have brought our dear brother's bride with lots of joy.

Two of the groom's sisters danced in front of the other women. They must have been very hot and sweaty, but they wanted to show their happiness for their brother's wedding. I was desperate to see what Jabar, my groom, looked like but he was whisked off to the men's room. Instead, his mother made her way to me. She kissed me on the forehead and dropped some Afghani notes on me. Immediately, the children rushed to grab the money. Two young boys were tugging over the same note until it split in half. Fareba tried to push the children away and suggested that my mother-in-law should not put more money on me.

At this, my mother-in-law spun around to address Fareba. "What business is it of yours, young girl, how I express my happiness at my son's wedding?"

Fareba didn't reply to the older woman but later she whispered in my ear, "God, did you hear your mother-in-law just then? She's a right sergeant major."

I hoped that Fareba was just joking and this wasn't really the case. There are lots of jokes about domineering mothers-in-law in my culture. My mother-in-law lifted the *taj* (crown and veil) so that my face could be seen and I lowered my eyes to the ground, as is the custom. Then the groom's family approached one by one to take a look at me. I hoped desperately that they thought I was pretty, for I knew that afterwards the women would be gossiping about me and how I looked. The women were shouting to one another, some were dancing and others were clapping to celebrate my wedding. After a few minutes I was told I could sit down. Finally my mother came into the room and told my mother-in-law it was time to eat. Then women and girls from my side of the family brought water for the guests to wash their hands, and a *desterkhan* (large plastic tablecloth) was opened out on the floor. The plates of food—large dishes of rice, chips, spinach, kofta, and qurma, and huge slabs of bread freshly baked in the *tanoor*—were spread out upon it. Cans of Coca-Cola, Fanta, and drinking water were offered to the guests. Girls stood by to bring anything else a guest might need.

My mother-in-law got up from the floor and brought me a plate of food. She told me to eat it and I was relieved that she seemed kind. But as I ate, I realized that this would be the last time I would eat in my parents' home as their child, and I started to worry about what my new life would be like. Fareba must have seen me frowning at my food. "His lot look very scary," she whispered, which only made me feel worse.

The women sat around the *desterkhan*, shoveling food into their mouths. I could see my mother fussing over the in-laws, making sure everything was to their satisfaction. She knew that if they were happy then things would be easier for me. I guessed a similar scene was being played out in the men's room. I imagined my father ordering the boys around and making sure the male guests had everything they wanted. Young boys and girls were free to wander around as they liked and could eat with either their mothers or fathers.

My wedding was a grand affair for our small village. Hiring a cook was special. I could see my mother had worked hard to get everything prepared. As guests finished their food, my cousins cleared away the dirty plates and wiped clean the *desterkhan*.

The groom's mother and sisters started to sing and clap again: the *Nikkah* time—the contract between a bride and groom—was approaching. The Mullah began reading and Fareba whispered to me to say my prayers. I asked God for happiness and for a good life for my family and myself. My uncle and one of my cousins came to ask me if I would accept Jabar as my husband. According to my religion, I had to say I accepted him three times. As soon as I had done this, the men fired their rifles into the air. Fareba said this meant I was now legally Jabar's wife.

One by one the women came to kiss me and offer me their good wishes. If the guests stood up, I would have to stand and if they told me to sit, I would have to sit. I wasn't used to wearing such high heels, so by this time my feet were hurting and I was exhausted. I told Fareba that it was all too much for me and I couldn't wait for it to be over. She joked back by asking why I was in such a hurry to be taken by my man.

Then finally the groom was brought in to me by the women of his family for the *Aeena Misaf*—the ceremony when we would see each other for the first time—so I was quickly covered up with my green shawl. I could hear the "Ahesta Bero" song being sung for him. My heart started beating fast. Fareba squeezed my hand. "Oh my God, Anesa, he's a big fat man!"

I could feel someone was standing close to me. Fareba and my mother moved to stand behind me, and my mother whispered in my ear, "If they force you to sit down, don't." Traditionally, whoever sits down in the chair first will have no power in the marriage. I had seen this game played many times at weddings; I knew my mother and Fareba would be behind Jabar ready to push him into his seat. His mother announced that it was time for the bride and groom to sit, and then I felt her hands on my shoulders, trying to force me down. I wouldn't give in—I knew the women would be watching to see who won. Finally, we both sat down, I think together, and chanting and clapping broke out.

A mirror was put onto my knees and my mother told me I could now look. The shawl was lifted from my face and I stared into the mirror. The first thing I noticed was that he had a big moustache; the second thing was that he had a round face and bulging eyes. I felt frightened. I looked again and this time he winked back at me. After that, I was too shy to peek again into the mirror. But that first sight of him stayed in my head and it wasn't a nice one. This fat man wasn't young or handsome; he was no Bollywood hero. Just one look at Jabar had destroyed my dreams.

My mother gave us a small holy Quran to read from. As I recited the verses, I didn't glance at Jabar at all. Then Fareba poured some Fanta into two glasses and Jabar and I offered each other a glass to drink from, neither one of us looking at the other. The ceremony was coming to an end and soon it would be time for me to be taken away. My mother said she wanted to sing "Ahesta Bero" for me. She took the tambourine and began to sing, and the group of women in the room parted, allowing my mother and I to walk together.

The house was full of noise, and the atmosphere was very happy. It was so touching, as everyone was talking about me leaving my parents' house and entering a new life. I felt so special. Quietly, I told Fareba, Jabar was not as I had been expecting. She said that she was disappointed too, as she had been told my groom was a good-looking man.

"Fareba, you know, I was hoping for a dashing young man. Why him?"

But we both knew there was nothing I could do. Besides, the wedding taxi, decorated with flowers, was already waiting outside the house.

My mother stopped singing, she hugged me and my father spoke to Jabar: "Jabar, my son, I'm giving you a piece of my heart, my daughter, Anesa. Please take good care of her."

At this I burst into tears, and my mother, Fareba, and most of my relatives also started crying—Afghan women tend to cry when the bride is leaving. I didn't hear what Jabar said in response to my father but I guess he just nodded. I got into the taxi with Jabar and some members of his family. My groom sat next to me but he didn't say much. My mother-in-law kept singing in the car until we got to their house, which was a large villa made of mud and clay and set in its own garden behind a big iron gate. Suddenly, I realized I was among strangers—it was the loneliest moment in my life.

Anesa, like me, was looking forward to a happy family life. Her father hadn't asked for money, and because of this she would have expected her in-laws to show her respect. I too was still hoping that I could enjoy a happy family life with Javed, despite the disappointment I felt at our marriage. In those early days, I believed that if I was a good Afghan girl and did my duty, accepting what our parents wanted, then I would have a successful family life.

Jabar was the eldest son, so his family had decided to make it a big wedding. When I arrived, family members were waiting, ready to put sweets and money onto Jabar and me. A chicken was sacrificed and splashes of blood were put on my shoes. Then I was taken to a large room where the women and girls were partying. A tent had been put up in the yard for the men to party in, and Jabar joined them there. The sound of a local singer and the music of a *tabla* (percussion instrument) and harmonica could be heard throughout the house.

Jabar's sister said, "Don't worry, he won't leave you alone for long but he's a man and he'll have to party. It's his night to celebrate."

I just sat and said nothing, watching the partying going on around me. Children were running around excitedly and I could hear men shouting and laughing. The women were far quieter. I guess they were tired. Some time later I heard some bells jangling and music playing and asked Jabar's sister what the noise was.

"You mean, you don't know? Jabar's father and brother have paid for some boys to come and dance as part of the celebrations."

I didn't understand why young boys had been invited to dance and asked Jabar's sister to explain.

"They're *bacha be reesh* (boys without beards). They're being paid to entertain the men with their dancing and that noise is the bells they have on their ankles," she said. Then she walked over to the window and pointed. "Anesa, look!"

I knew that women sometimes danced for men and would get paid for it, but I was shocked to hear that boys were being paid to dance at the men's party. I looked out of the window and saw a boy, perhaps sixteen or seventeen years old, in a white *shalwar kamiz*. He had some large bells attached to his ankles, which made a noise when he moved. In the moonlight I could see he was drinking water from the well and was wearing makeup like a woman.

Jabar's sister said, "Poor *bacha be reesh*; he's danced so much and now he's thirsty."

I was surprised by the sight but didn't have time to think too deeply about it because my mother-in-law had arrived to take me to my bedroom. She took my hand and led me to a room with a bed in the corner covered in dark red sheets. Sweets and flowers had been placed on it to show it was a bed for a bride. My mother-in-law kissed me on the forehead and said this was now my room.

"We don't know when Jabar's party will be over but he will come to you. In this house we can never be sure when our men will turn up. You can rest and sleep."

I was grateful for the chance to lie down as my feet were still killing me. I took off my high heels and lay down on the bed without washing or taking off any of my jewelry. I felt lonely and frightened. Jabar's mother's words echoed in my mind: "In this house we can never be sure when our men will turn up." I missed my mother and Fareba and wished one of them was here with me. I desperately wanted to sleep but my mind was spinning with thoughts and feelings. The loneliness was keeping me awake. There was still no sign of Jabar. This wasn't what I expected on my wedding night, but what could I do?

I woke up with a start and looked at my watch: it was four o'clock in the morning; the mullah's call to prayer must have woken me up. I sat up in my bed. I had fallen asleep with my jewelry on, which had left marks on my neck and hands. The house was in silence, but still Jabar wasn't there. I was lost in my thoughts when I saw the door open. Jabar walked slowly into the room. I was scared as he looked at me.

"Why aren't you asleep? Were you waiting for me?"

I didn't know what to say and I didn't have the courage to ask him why he had come in so late. He was dressed in the same white *shalwar kamiz* but he didn't look himself. He didn't smell of alcohol but his eyes were red and I guessed he had been taking some sort of drug. He sat on the bed and looked into my eyes.

"You know, you're a pretty woman but I'm *mast* (high on drugs)."

With that, he slumped down onto the bed and fell asleep. I was shocked and wanted to shout or cry but didn't know how. I was alone in a strange house. I longed for Fareba or my mother, but there was no one to come and take me away. I felt suffocated; I wanted to leave and run back to my home.

Life was showing a very strange face to me, one which I had never seen before. Was Jabar unhappy to be married to me? Was that the reason he had stayed out all night and left me alone? I hoped that soon he would be affectionate toward me. Jabar was now snoring loudly like a big fat sheep, so I got up from the bed and sat on the mattress on the floor. Eventually, I lay my head down on the pillow and tried to sleep.

I woke to feel someone touching my face.

"Anesa, come to bed. You're a bride and you must sleep on your bed."

I told him I was quite all right on the floor. He laughed and said he could see I was a very polite girl.

"You have to sleep with me. You're my so-called wife and I have to be a bit naughty with you."

"What do you mean, you have to be naughty with me?"

"Don't ask questions. Now is not the time for talking. I have to prove to your parents and to my own family that I'm a proper man. I'll have to show them the sign soon. Hurry up, it's getting late."

And he started taking my jewelry from my neck and hands. He seemed in a sort of panic as he tugged me by the hand and pulled me to the bed.

I was like a helpless doll in his hands. He did whatever he wanted and got what he needed: the proof that he had slept with me. There was a drop of blood on the white sheet, the sign of my virginity. I think my body went into shock and I couldn't stop shaking. I put my *shalwar* back on and went to sit on the mattress, sobbing and calling out for my family.

On that dark morning my life changed. I had hoped for a happy family life and a loving husband, but my life and freedom as Anesa had ended. I would never look forward to new clothes for Eid or weddings, and I would never watch another Bollywood movie with Fareba.

That morning Jabar was in a deep sleep, snoring loudly, and I was sitting on the mattress when I heard a knock on the door. I opened it and Jabar's mother came in. She told me to wake Jabar up as he had to go for *Shah Salami* at my parents' house. I knew what this tradition was—Jabar would be expected to show my family the sign of my virginity. In some families the groom would show the bride's blood-stained handkerchief. The family of a bride feels a sense of pride that the groom is paying them respect on the morning after his wedding night. I went up to Jabar and told him his mother was calling him. He didn't move so I had to shake him awake. When Jabar had gone, my mother-in-law brought me breakfast and we ate it together.

"Anesa, my child, I'm proud of you," she said. "You're the honor of this family. Later, I'll show you your house. My son has his own place. We only brought you here for the first day. You'll be living with Jabar and we won't interfere with your life at all."

I was alarmed to hear this. I didn't want to leave, even though I knew it was unusual and prestigious for an Afghan bride to have her own house. I liked being with Jabar's mother.

A few days after my wedding I moved to our small house and my life as Jabar's wife truly began. He used to go to work every day, coming home late or sometimes not at all. It was something I got used to after a while. I didn't dare ask him what he got up to. His attention wasn't directed toward me. During the first year of our marriage he was quiet and distant. I got on with my chores in the home and he never spoke about his outside life. My first son was born in that first year of marriage. I was busy looking after him and for most of the time I was alone. The one good thing in all this was that I was allowed regular contact with my family and also with his. Jabar and I didn't really have a loving relationship but he did look after my son and me. He would provide us with enough food and clothes. Perhaps being a mother made me stronger. One day I asked him why he didn't spend more time with his son.

"Anesa, you're a mouse," he replied angrily. "Where did you get the courage to ask me all these questions? Just eat and drink what I provide and shut your ugly mouth!"

But I couldn't keep quiet and repeated my questions, finally saying, "Look, Jabar, you're the father of my son; we both need you and we have the right to spend family time with you."

He didn't listen and carried on doing whatever he wanted, including not coming home at night. Two years of marriage passed and

I had another son. I don't even remember how it happened as we were rarely intimate. I did tell his mother that we didn't see her son that often and I didn't know what he was up to, but she simply said, "Anesa, my child, remember on your wedding night I told you that in this family women never know when men come home and they don't care. It is better to say nothing." She put her hand on my head. "Sometimes ignorance is kind."

I didn't say anything further then but I couldn't cope with keeping silent and not knowing what was happening. One morning I went to the *tanoor* with one of my neighbors to cook bread. I had good neighbors, we were all friends, and I had told this woman about Jabar and about our relationship. Well, that day as we sat by the *tanoor* she told me she had asked her husband to find out where Jabar spent his time. I got very excited, eager to hear what she had found out. "Does Jabar have another wife?" She looked down and said it was a rather shameful story. I didn't understand: what did she mean by shameful?

"My husband says that only we women are ignorant about Jabar. Apparently, all the men in the village gossip about him and what he does."

The suspense was making me dizzy and I told her to hurry up with her story.

"Anesa, your husband is sinful. He's committing a major crime. Your husband has a wrong relationship with a boy. He's a *kuni* (homosexual)!"

I was so shocked, I nearly burned my hand in the *tanoor*. My neighbor told me to take care, and she pointed to my two young sons who were sitting nearby.

"Anesa, you have to stay strong and live for your sons."

I told her I didn't believe Jabar could do this; if he was a *kuni* then why had he married me? I felt angry and confused. I told the neighbor I had to go home, and picking up the baby and grabbing my young son's hand, I ran back home.

I was crying and the boys had started crying too. I was in a state of shock. I couldn't believe my husband was sleeping with another man.

In our culture this is incredibly shameful. I waited all night for Jabar to come home but he didn't appear, so early the next morning I went to his family home with my children. My mother-in-law came out into the yard to greet me. I said I had heard something about Jabar and I wanted to know whether or not it was true. She told me to calm down and explain what had happened.

I looked deep into her eyes. "Please swear on my children's life if it's true that your son is a—"

Suddenly, she put her hand across my mouth to silence me. "Ssshh, Anesa, you must not speak about such matters. Some things are best left unsaid."

"What do you mean?" I shouted. "I'm going to tell people the truth. I know from people in the village that your son is a *kuni*."

She looked at me angrily. "I can't say anything. You'll have to ask your husband."

I grabbed her by the arm and said, "You chose me for Jabar. You came to our house and boasted about him. Remember, you told me that I brought honor to your family. Admit it! It's your fault that I've suffered all this time."

She began to weep and took hold of my hand. "Anesa, no mother wants her son to die. I thought he would change if he married you. I thought you and the children could save him from the village. Do you realize that if it was proved he was doing these things, he would have been killed by now?" She let go of my hand and, without saying another word, walked back into her house. Now I needed to hear the truth from Jabar.

When I arrived home he was already there. He was clearly surprised that I hadn't been at home waiting for him. He stood up when I entered the room.

"Anesa, where have you been?"

I began to cry and told him I'd been out trying to find out about his real face, his other life, and that I thought his mother was ashamed at having given birth to him. He hit me hard across my cheek and asked what I meant by his real face.

"Don't you have any shame? People in the village know what you're doing with a man."

Then he began to beat me properly, punching my face and body, kicking my legs and stomach as I fell.

"Whatever I do is none of your business," he shouted. "Just keep your ugly mouth shut."

Despite the pain and beating, I still wanted to know the truth: "Jabar, I need to know whether what people are saying is true."

"Do you really want to know?" His eyes were red and bulging. "I love that boy. I'm in love with him and I'm going to bring him here to live. My parents forced me to marry you so that they could save me from the judgment of people in the village. My parents would have disowned me if I hadn't married you and pretended that I like women." And with that he left with the children crying at my feet.

All hope I had was now gone. I felt ashamed, frightened, and embarrassed.

I couldn't cope with the fact that my husband was a homosexual; the shame was too much to bear. All I wanted was to be with my mother and dear Fareba.

My mother was at the well when I arrived. She took one look at me and asked, "What's wrong, Anesa? Is everything all right with you?"

I began to sob hysterically. "No, everything is wrong. I'm living in hell right now."

I heard the bucket drop and my mother's steps coming toward me. She flung her arms around me.

"What's happened, my child? Is Jabar all right?"

"Oh, don't worry about him. He's fine. It's me who's suffering and can't live with this shame."

We sat down on a bench in the yard. I told my mother what had happened and she began to cry. She asked me what I wanted to do now.

"Mother, I've come to you. I want to leave him. I cannot live in a house that God doesn't bless. Jabar is a dirty man. He's having an un-Islamic relationship with a boy. I don't want to be with a *kuni*."

Then my mother burst out angrily. "Do you understand what leaving a husband means? *Talaq* (divorce)! You can never do that."

"What do you expect me to do, then? Live with a shameless man? Do you want your grandchildren to grow up in that kind of house?"

"Keep your voice down, Anesa. Some things are better kept to yourself. Your sister-in-law is in the house and if she hears this she'll spread the news to her family, then everyone will know your business. If you divorce you will not be allowed to keep your children, and they'll be called the children of a *kuni*. What are you thinking? In our culture women are expected to die in the house where they are married."

I realized my personal pain wasn't so important to my mother or to my mother-in-law that they could disregard our customs or traditions. I had gone to them for help because I thought as women they would share my pain. Instead, they had told me to say nothing. I grabbed the children and left my mother's home. She ran after me but I wouldn't stop. I was angry with all of them: Jabar's mother had used me as a camouflage for Jabar and his activities, my own mother wanted me to put the reputation of the family before my suffering, and Jabar himself had betrayed me. All the people closest to me had let me down. I had no choice but to suffer in silence. I didn't realize it at the time but it was the beginning of a new chapter in my life.

Jabar was still there when I got home. He laughed when he saw me. "I told you that keeping your mouth shut is the best thing for you and your children."

I was crushed by the way he referred to the children as being mine. I was pregnant with my third child and felt totally helpless; I even wished God wasn't giving me another baby. Looking into my sons' eyes, I felt such sadness for them; they were so innocent.

When Jabar left the house I tried to decide what to do: whichever way I looked at it there seemed no way out for me. I could only do what countless other Afghan women do: I left it to the will of Allah.

Then, late one night, I heard the front door opening. I went to the window in my bedroom and saw Jabar coming into the house with his arm around another man. For a moment I forgot what I had been told about Jabar and was surprised to see him holding this man's hand and talking to him with such apparent affection. He appeared to be introducing him to the house. Suddenly it dawned on me: this was Jabar's lover. I ran out to the corridor and stood in front of Jabar.

"Please, for God's sake, don't pollute my house with your disgusting and degrading acts."

The man and I recognized each other from the village. I said to him, "Don't you have any shame? Get yourself a wife. You're sleeping with my husband, with the father of my two children. Did you know he has two children and there's another one growing in my womb? For the sake of my children, leave my husband."

The man stared at me as if I had gone mad and then spoke in a thin, high-pitched voice. "Anesa, don't you have any shame sleeping with my man?"

Now it was my turn to look stunned. How could a man say such things?

"God is pouring his anger on you, don't you understand?" I told him. "Having sex with another man is prohibited. Where's your respect for your culture and religion?"

At that Jabar marched across the room and slapped me hard.

"Babrak is my lover. He has every right to be in this house. So if you want food and clothes for yourself and your children, you'd better learn to keep quiet. I'm sick and tired of living a double life, of lying all the time. I hate forcing myself to sleep with you, pretending to everyone that I'm your husband. I love Babrak and I want him to have all the things he deserves. It's just as well you know what the situation is now—that my love is only for Babrak. At least now I won't have to have sex with you anymore."

I wanted to die. I ran out and grabbed some matches and a bottle of petrol to pour over myself. Jabar and Babrak ignored me and went straight into our guest room. But right at that moment, a vision of my children came into my mind—only the thought of their innocence stopped me from taking my life. I began to weep and wished I was still that young girl who didn't know what I now knew. I sat in a corner of the corridor and remembered the sound of ankle bells that I'd heard on my wedding night. Now I understood why Jabar had not come to me that night and why he didn't like to be around me. Now I saw why his mother had told me not to stay up for him and why he was always frustrated around me.

Months passed and I stopped going to my family home because I was getting bigger and bigger with the baby. Jabar brought expensive food and special meat, which he made me cook for him and Babrak. Despite being pregnant, I was only given food if Babrak was in a good mood. My children were gradually becoming his slaves; my eldest son had to clean his shoes and do whatever Babrak ordered him to do. I began to feel like just a cook and cleaner in my own home. This state of affairs showed me the worst of human nature.

After four months I gave birth to a baby girl. My mother came to look after me for a few days, and during this time Jabar didn't come home at all—he didn't take any notice of his daughter. When my mother left, he started coming back home with his boyfriend. They used to laugh and talk all night, having noisy sex in the next room.

I used to pray to God to take me out of this situation. I spent two years just living for the sake of saving his reputation. But slowly more people in the village came to realize the truth of the situation. My children would come home from school crying, telling me that their classmates had called their dad a *kuni*. Their friends wouldn't play with them anymore as they thought we were a family that didn't obey Islam. They were told that if the Taliban were in power their father would have been executed. I knew that even with the new, more liberal Karzai government this sort of relationship wouldn't be accepted. It wasn't just the Taliban; no government in an Islamic country like Afghanistan would accept such a relationship. I felt helpless. I went to Jabar's family and asked them to release me and the children, but Jabar's father warned me that if I left, the children would be taken from me.

My children's fate depended on Babrak's mood. If he was in a good mood he wouldn't say much and would let us be, but my God, if he was angry with my children, especially my eldest son, who hated him, then he would tell Jabar and Jabar would beat the boy like an animal. We often went hungry because all the money was spent on Babrak. Jabar would buy new clothes and the best food for him. He bought him expensive shoes and would pay taxi fares for him when he went out. Meanwhile, the children and I got weaker and weaker. My babies wore old clothes and we had little to eat. We only got something when Babrak told Jabar to buy it. Otherwise, the children and I got no attention or kindness. My parents would sometimes buy things we needed. They saw how we were suffering and went to Jabar's family to ask for justice but his family said I had to stay as his wife to protect him in the village.

"If the villagers have proof that our son is a *kuni*, the mullahs will have him killed," they said. "At least while you and the children are with him, the rumors remain just gossip."

My parents didn't push the matter because they were also scared of the shame of divorce. When I questioned my rights I was told that under Islam my children could be taken away from me if I divorced, and yet when it came to my husband neglecting me and my children and sleeping with a man, Islam didn't apply. Jabar's parents were doing everything in their power to protect their son.

His mother pleaded with me: "Anesa, I beg you to keep him safe. I'll die if they kill my son."

I was crying. "Why can't you ask him to change?"

She told me it would be of no use as he had liked boys since childhood. They had married me to him because he never listened to them and wouldn't give up this awful habit.

I went to the independent Human Rights Commission in Kunduz but they couldn't help either. According to their rules, Jabar would get custody of my children if I got a divorce. How could I accept this? I didn't want my children to grow up in a sinful house. What would happen to them if I left them with two *kunies*? So I had no choice but to stay and protect them.

I have lost count of the number of times I've decided to end my life, but because of the children I've always stopped. Sometimes I think of ending mine and my children's lives altogether. It's now the fourth year of living with them and it's not got any easier. Every morning Jabar goes to the *hamam* (steam bath) and then he has sex with Babrak. Babrak is the commander in our house: he decides what I and the children can do. Their father eats with him, most of his money is spent on him and his family. They know about their son but keep quiet because the money makes it easier for them. Jabar has told me he loves Babrak and will die if he leaves him. I know the children and I are just slaves in an unlawful relationship and our happiness is being sacrificed for the sake of our traditions.

So this was the story that had shocked and upset Salmi. It was shocking for me too, how Anesa was still suffering and couldn't find a way out of her difficult situation. Divorce was too big a shame for her to consider and would have had a negative impact on her life and her children's lives. Even though divorce is accepted in Islam, as the last resort, there is still a stigma attached to it. Even men who divorce are ostracized. There is a saying that a widower should be given a bride but a divorced man a stone. A divorced man is no longer considered trustworthy. However, divorce for a woman brings even harsher judgment. A divorced man will still be able to find another wife, but it is virtually impossible for a divorced woman to marry again. In my unhappy marriage I could, only too well, identify with Anesa's fears and worries. I also saw that in comparison I had a lot of advantages: I wasn't financially dependent on my husband and I didn't have any children; I didn't live in Afghanistan or follow Afghan cultural values. These principles no longer meant any thing to me, but for a woman like Anesa, divorce would have meant losing everything. She would no longer be respected, and her every action would be judged. If she was seen dancing at a party, people would say she had become a slut because she hadn't got a husband; if she got into an argument people would say that now her husband has left her she's angry and desperate. Everything she did or said, her mood and her style of clothes, would be judged in the context of her being a divorced woman.

The only option Anesa had was to stay and suffer. Without support from her or his family and without financial assistance, what else could she do?

I tried to work out why Salmi had been so upset by the story. Initially I thought it might be because she had met Anesa—she had seen her in her old clothes, had witnessed her tears, and felt her helplessness. This was a possibility, but then I remembered that I had been affected by stories of women I hadn't met, just by listening to them.

The more I thought about it, the more I realized that I was less shocked by a story about a homosexual because I live in London. I have friends and colleagues who are gay and for me they are the same as someone who is straight. I guessed that Salmi was shocked by the homosexuality in a way that I was not, although we were both horrified by the way Jabar was using Anesa as a human shield.

Anesa's predicament in Afghanistan was miles away from my life in London. In an Islamic society homosexuality is a sin. If you are homosexual you are considered to have no shame, to be abnormal, even, and you have no right to live as a normal citizen because you are living against human nature and religion. There is no respect or tolerance. Of course, there are homosexuals throughout Afghanistan but, like Jabar, they have to hide their sexuality. If they dare to make it public they will face punishment—they may be disowned by their parents, and they will certainly be judged harshly by their community.

Living in the UK has made me realize how different societies can be. I have learned through my friends that being a gay man or woman in the West is considered a normal thing, and that as far as human feelings between adults are concerned, there should be no boundaries of religion, culture, or society. But in my original country, homosexuality is a big taboo; I know even if I say I hang out with people who are gay I will be judged in a negative way for accepting them as my friends.

When I finished listening to Anesa's story, I called Salmi. I told her I'd heard the story and agreed it was shocking and upsetting, and that

Anesa's life was sad, but that we should not forget that Jabar was also suffering. At this, she got annoyed, "Zari dear, why do we need to think about him? He's cruel."

I agreed that Jabar was treating Anesa and her children unfairly but I suggested that he was a victim too. He was trapped in a situation he didn't want to be in. Salmi couldn't grasp the point I was making. She found it impossible to respect or have sympathy for Jabar. I tried to explain how homosexuals are seen in Western countries. I told her that in London I knew Muslim men who were gay but did not need to use anyone to shield their homosexuality.

I asked Salmi if she had heard of any other married men who were also having relationships with men and she replied that at the wedding she had attended women had told her that this sort of thing was common. I explained to Salmi that it was normal human behavior and that there are gay people everywhere in every culture and society.

I began to wonder if we could use Anesa's story as the starting point for a studio discussion about homosexuality in Afghanistan. As I've said, same-sex relationships are not accepted or even openly acknowledged in Afghanistan. The only sexual relationship that is recognized is that between a man and a woman within marriage. However, it is a relatively common practice for some older more powerful men to have boys who they use for sexual relations, even though it is illegal. These men use their wealth and power to buy sex from poor boys. Like the *bacha be reesh* described by Anesa, the boys dance for men and are often kept as sex slaves. They are sexually abused and then shunned by society for their homosexual activity while their abusers somehow evade the law and any blame. If, however, you are reported to the police for homosexual behavior you can expect to be arrested because it is a crime in Afghanistan.

Salmi and I both realized this was a highly sensitive subject and it was going to be difficult to find the right interviewees. However, we felt it was our job as journalists to try to make this program and so we began researching the topic. We spoke to male and female doctors and found people in the provinces to speak to. Many people told us that they knew examples of gay men, but when we asked them to come on the program, they refused. No one would go on the record. One doctor in Kabul told me that a few men had come to him and said they had difficulty sleeping with their wives because they loved and wanted to have sex with men. I asked the doctor if he would come on to our program and talk about this. "Zarghuna Jan, I respect you and your program," he told me, "but as an Afghan citizen living in this country, I have to bear in mind the sensitivity of the topics I talk about."

He said he needed to watch what he said for his own security. "Homosexuality is a taboo subject in this country, as you know. Some men are gay and do have sex with other men, but it is still an unmentionable topic. No one talks about it. It exists, but people ignore it as it is against our traditions and religion. I'm sorry, but I cannot come on to your program. Please excuse me!"

Salmi and I listened carefully to the doctor's words. How could we try and persuade him when we knew that appearing on the program might put his life in danger? We decided not to go ahead with the program and for years Anesa's story has remained only in my notes. I kept the file so I could write this story and share it with others in a way that will not endanger Anesa, Salmi, or me.

8

Wazma's Story

THE INJURED WIFE

In 2005 I went back to Afghanistan after more than ten years' absence. I had left Kabul as a child and I was now returning as a young woman. I could never have imagined that the city of my childhood could have changed so dramatically. When I left in the mid-1990s Afghanistan was in the middle of a civil war, with different factions fighting one another. Every day we would hear rumors of what was going on, but we have a saying in Dari, "What you hear is nothing like what you see." This saying perfectly matched how I felt on the day I arrived back in Kabul. This was the city where I had been born and spent my childhood. I had nurtured the hope that one day it would be peaceful enough for my family to return and live there once more.

I remember that the day we left had been especially beautiful. It was winter and the high mountains that surround Kabul were dressed in white snow. When it snows in Kabul you can look forward to a clear blue sky the next day. It casts such a brilliant light on the snow that it hurts your eyes to look at it. Despite the bitter wind that day, the streets were full of people rushing about on their business. All the shops were open and doing brisk trade as people hurried to buy all they needed before the firing started up again. Women and girls mingled in the crowds, dressed in winter coats and trousers with scarves tied round their heads to keep out the cold air.

This time when I landed at Kabul International airport—not far from the area where I grew up—the atmosphere was very different. A crowd of unkempt men with long beards unnerved me as they surged toward the passengers at the airport. Some wanted to earn money by carrying bags, others were waiting for other passengers, but they all stared at me because I was an Afghan woman who had arrived on her own. As I waited in the long queue at passport control, I held my head scarf tightly. It seemed to me as if every man was staring at me.

I walked into to the arrivals hall and spotted a BBC colleague waiting for me. It was such a reassuring sight. I got into the car without speaking, as my eyes searched for the Kabul I had left behind. I recognized the roads but so much had changed. The huge green trees had gone, the roads were choked with traffic, everything was chaotic and dirty. I could see only men and boys on the streets, staring through the car window at me as we passed. Everyone appeared to be angry and shouting at each other.

I couldn't stop the tears from falling. My colleague asked me if I was all right but I just carried on crying. He and the driver said nothing as I wept and memories of my childhood flooded back. The city of my childhood had lost its color and freshness; now it was covered with the gray dust of a decade of war.

I also saw how war had changed the people. I had spent ten years living in a country that wasn't shaken by the sounds of rockets or shooting. Returning to Kabul, I realized that I had changed too—I had softened. Now every unexpected noise sounded like a bomb exploding; when someone's mobile phone rang I would jump in fear. I was only in Kabul for a week but I thought I would die there.

A colleague had suggested I meet a young woman called Wazma for *Afghan Woman's Hour* because she had an extraordinary life story. One of the aims of that trip to Kabul was to meet some Afghan women face to face. Wazma was one of my interviewees. "War and fighting turns some hearts to stone," she told me.

As a child, war and fighting had certainly turned my heart to stone. Before I left Kabul I hadn't been frightened of the sounds of war. Back then I had witnessed some horrific scenes—people dying and being mutilated—now I was spooked by the sound of a ringtone. The young women I was working with probably thought I was a total coward.

Progress was being made in some parts of Kabul. Building and renovation work were under way, and some houses had electricity from the city power supply. The security situation was also relatively calm at the time. The BBC guesthouse that I was staying in stood at the foot of some mountains. On my way back from work I loved looking up at all the houses perched on the hillside; it was a comforting sight at night to see the lights in people's homes. These houses now had electricity and would shine over the city below like glistening stars. This was the scene that made me fall in love with Kabul again. I was too frightened to return to the neighborhood I'd grown up in and visit my school. I just couldn't face it. Instead, I would stare up the mountain, counting the lights and imagining the lives of people who lived there.

Wazma had once lived up in the mountain. When I interviewed her, I discovered that life up there was the same as in the valley but just a bit harder. She no longer lived there and now she missed it. Her observation that war and fighting turns some hearts to stone made a big impression on me, and during the interview with her I discovered how she came to believe this.

≈

IN THE EARLY HOURS of the morning the sound of the *Azan*—the mullah's call to prayer—echoed throughout the Deh Afghanan area of Kabul. His singing in Arabic was relayed through a tinny loudspeaker. It was still dark but people were starting to get up. There was a stiff breeze in the air. The lights of the houses on the hillside appeared like tiny stars to those in the valley below. One of those stars belonged to the small house of Wazma and her family.

The *Azan* could be heard from the top of the mountain. It woke Wazma up. She stretched, yawned, and sat up on her mattress. By her side lay her husband, Waheed. She turned to see her baby daughter still fast asleep, oblivious to the sound of the *Azan*. The sight gave Wazma a strong maternal feeling. She leaned over and gently stroked her baby's hair. Wazma got up quietly. The room was small. It provided just enough space for them all to lie down in. You had to squeeze through a narrow door to enter it. It was sparsely furnished but Wazma counted herself fortunate. She had a loving husband and a beautiful daughter. She plugged in the old Russian water boiler and put it in the bucket she had filled from the communal well the night before. She then sat beside it on a large stone which was used as a chair. The mullah was coming to the last sentences of the *Azan*.

> *Allah u Akbar.*
> God is great.
> *La Ilaha Ilala.*
> There is no God but Allah.
> *Mohammad Al Rasool Allah.*
> Mohammad is his prophet.

Wazma waited for the water to warm; the weak electric current wasn't helping. She dipped her hand into the water to make sure it was neither too hot nor too cold. Satisfied it was the right temperature, she stood up and went over to her husband and whispered, "Darling, wake up. It's time for prayer."

Waheed woke up and smiled at his wife. He asked Wazma if the water was ready for him to wash. She brushed his hair with her fingers and replied that it was. Waheed left to wash, in readiness for his early-morning prayer.

When she had finished her prayer, Wazma began her daily routine of making fresh green tea. She boiled the water in an old pot, then she put a teaspoon of green tea and added a pinch of crushed cardamom into the little white china teapot with the small purple flowers on it. She poured the boiled water into the teapot and left it for a few minutes so that the green leaves could infuse in the water. Then she filled two china cups and placed them on a tin tray. She sat and waited for her husband to finish praying. He bowed to the ground, which signaled the end of his prayer and came and sat next to Wazma.

It was getting lighter outside. Wazma and Waheed sipped their tea and talked quietly so as not to wake the baby.

"You know, Wazma, I really hope one day to be able to buy a house further down the mountain so you don't have to do all this tiring work, carrying water up and down every day. I will work hard so our family can live more comfortably."

Wazma smiled at her husband. "Waheed, I'm happy to live anywhere with you. I don't need a big house and things are not important to me. When I've finished studying I'll earn money from my teaching salary and then we'll both be earning money. Then maybe we can afford a house further down the mountain, if that's what you want. For me, your love, my baby, and being healthy are the most important things. Inshallah, everything will be fine. I have faith in God that it will."

Waheed leaned forward and kissed her on her forehead. He had one last sip of his tea and left for the local government office where he worked as a clerk.

Wazma began to tidy the room. She had to be quick so she wasn't late for school. She put on her green uniform and looked at herself in the mirror on the wall next to the door. Her reflection didn't look so clear in the dusty scratched mirror but she knew this wasn't the reality; she realized she was much prettier than her image in the glass. She dabbed some moisturizing cream on her face and traced kohl around her eyes. Wazma looked over at the baby who had just woken up and started to cry. She picked her up and held her in her arms. Wazma explained to her daughter that she was going to school soon. "You'll be spending time with Granny until I come back, and when I return I'll bring you some sweets."

Farah was only thirteen months old and far too young to understand what her mother was saying, but she smiled, contented to hear her mother's voice and to be in her arms. Wazma washed her daughter's face, kissed her, and held her tightly. It was as if Wazma didn't want to leave her baby; she had a strange feeling it was the last time she would be doing this. She continued wiping her daughter's face and kissed her on her cheeks again. She fed the baby with a bottle of milk and dressed her in a red spotty dress she had made for her. Farah was playing with the gold chain that hung from her mother's neck. It was the only present given to her by her husband. She held the baby in her arms, picked up the bottle and her handbag, and headed for the door.

It was now eight o'clock in the morning. Wazma went to the next house where Waheed's family lived. She gave Farah to her mother-in-law and handed over the bottle of milk with instructions that it should be given again at ten o'clock. Wazma said good-bye, kissed her daughter, and left.

Hurrying down the mountain track, Wazma pondered on what to make her family for dinner. The path was dusty and steep. It took her fifteen minutes to reach the bottom and the busy roads of Deh Afghanan. On her way to the bus stop she had to pass the fruit and vegetable market.

The sellers jostled with one another to make sure their stall was on the corner where it could be seen from two sides. It was 8:45 a.m. by the time Wazma arrived at the bus stop and the sun was fully up. Wazma took out some change from her purse in readiness for the bus. The roar of the traffic and the shouts from the market sellers could be heard streets away; the sounds even carried up the mountain. People were fresh with enthusiasm for the start of a new day.

Wazma waited impatiently for the bus. At last she could see it coming in the distance. As it approached the stop, Wazma moved forward, together with the other women, men, and children waiting to get on it. Suddenly there was a whistling sound that got louder and louder. Then there was a huge bang. Wazma turned round to see a ball of fire. The power of the blast was enough to throw her to the ground and shatter the windows of the bus. All that was left of it was a tangle of twisted metal and broken glass. The shouts of the fruit and vegetable sellers gave way to cries of pain and screams of panic. Acrid black smoke slowly filled the air until people could not see more than a few meters in front of them. Bodies and body parts were strewn across the ground. An old woman who had been standing in front of Wazma at the bus stop now lay facedown in the dust. Blood seeped out of her head. A rocket had landed between the bus stop and the marketplace of Deh Afghanan.

Wazma lay on the ground. The breath had been sucked out of her. She didn't know what had happened and she felt nothing. The police began blocking off that part of the city and ambulances arrived to take the injured to hospital. In those few seconds Wazma's life changed forever. There was her life before the rocket attack and her life after it.

❧

DURING THE 1980s A large number of rockets were fired into Kabul on a daily basis and the city's inhabitants lived in fear for their lives—just going to school or to work was risky. As children, we didn't understand all the politics behind the attacks but one name we feared was Gulbudeen Hekmatyar, the leader of the main Mujahedeen group in Afghanistan.

The government would launch Russian rockets called "stingers," sometimes twenty at a time. We got so used to the different sounds of the rockets that when we heard the ones being fired at the Mujahedeen we didn't hide in the corridors. My friends and I might be playing outside and if we heard those bangs, we'd tell each other not to be scared. "Those are our rockets, not Gulbudeen's."

At that time my friends and I didn't stop to think that those powerful rockets were being aimed at human beings. This is what the war did to us. We were just happy that our government was firing twenty rockets in a row at the Mujahedeen. We were frightened and hated whenever a rocket landed in our city but we didn't consider what our side was doing in terms of killing and injuring others.

I do wonder about both sides now. The war brings suffering and grief to families on all fronts. Some of the scars of war run so deep that they last a lifetime and the change is devastating. It was like this for Wazma.

❧

I GOT TO KNOW Wazma in the second part of her life. It was several years since the rocket attack on Deh Afghanan and Wazma was now in her late twenties. I went to interview her at a welfare center in Kabul, which had been set up to help female amputees learn new skills and earn a living. The director led me into a room full of women who sat with their heads bent over various bits of cloth. He gestured toward a pale-faced woman, her eyes focused on a colorful Afghan dress. Although she was only in her twenties, Wazma might pass for a woman twice that age. She worked without much energy and, beside her, I noticed two crutches. I walked over and introduced myself to her. "*Salamalikum* (Peace be with you). I'm Zarghuna Kargar and I present *Afghan Woman's Hour* on the BBC."

Wazma looked up from her sewing. She said hello and gave a wan smile. I told her I had come to record her life story, which the BBC World Service would broadcast on the radio. She asked how I knew she had a story worth telling, and I said that one of my friends in Kabul had told me about a woman she'd heard about who was good at storytelling. She seemed pleased that someone she knew had contacted the BBC and now they wanted to interview her.

We moved to a quieter room. Wazma used her crutches to support her legs. She wore a black skirt and a large white scarf. When we got to the room and sat down, I set up the recording equipment and asked Wazma to tell me her story.

❧

"DEAR ZARI, I REALLY want to explain my life to the listeners of *Afghan Woman's Hour*. I want my daughter to hear it and I want my husband to hear me. It's the first time I have spoken openly about my feelings and I'm hoping that people will understand what I have gone through.

"I'm a twenty-four-year-old woman. I got married when I was seventeen. I had a happy life with my husband Waheed. I think he loved me. He was kind to me. My marriage was arranged but I was contented with it. Sometimes I do wonder if my husband didn't really love me but I'd rather believe that he did care about me. Sometimes we human beings prefer to live under the shade of pleasant memories, don't we?"

She looked at me as if expecting a reply. I told her I didn't understand exactly what she meant. At this her eyes filled with tears and she began again in a low voice.

"I have lost so much that living with some happy memories, believing that my husband did once love me and that once I had a beautiful daughter gives me hope. But to be honest, there are many times when I wish I had died in that rocket attack. Living like this is not easy for a woman."

At this she pointed to her right leg.

"Who will want me like this? I'm a disabled woman with a false leg. I'm not strong enough to be a mother and wife anymore. I knew there was a civil war going on and at any time a rocket could land and kill or injure me, but at the same time I didn't believe it would happen.

"My daughter, Farah, was only a year old at the time." I had one eye on the recording equipment and kept another on Wazma. I saw her wipe her tears away from her face. "I didn't know what had happened at first, but when I woke up in the hospital I looked down and saw that I didn't have my right leg. My leg had been blown off from above my knee by the impact of the rocket. All I can remember is that I felt a lot of pain. I forgot who I was and where I was.

"When I was young my mother told me that when you cut your finger with a knife while cooking it hurts a lot, so you should be kind to people who lose their limbs in war because their pain will be much greater. Of course, then I had no idea what she really meant. It was all beyond my experience or imagination."

Wazma then began to quietly weep. She bent her head down as if she didn't want me to see her tears.

"From the moment I accepted I was a disabled woman, I felt stronger. I realized I had to fight the pain and difficulty. I thought about my dear Farah and Waheed and this gave me hope. I became stronger just thinking about them. So what if I only have one leg? I was still young; I had my little family and my life ahead of me. Once I realized this, things became easier and I coped better."

I FOUND IT HARD to believe Wazma's description of the caring relationship she had shared with Waheed. In my experience, that kind of love doesn't exist in an Afghan marriage. I thought that a happy married life meant you weren't beaten or forced to wear a *hijab*; a happy married life meant that my husband accepted me working outside the house and that I was able to have a conversation with another man. It didn't cross my mind that a happy marriage could simply come from two people loving each other. I guess it was the way I was brought up. I believed I should respect my husband however he behaved. It wasn't that I didn't feel unhappy when he refused to go with me to a close friend's wedding, or when I made plans to go shopping on a weekend and he declined to come with me. I was told so many times that he was a perfect husband, so when I saw other Afghan women talking about their caring and loving husbands, I thought they were just showing off.

It seemed normal to assume that a wife's job was to keep the house clean, iron my husband's clothes, and prepare his meals, even though he always criticized my cooking. I was relieved he allowed me to carry on with my job, but I'm a talkative person, and I longed to have conversations with him, but he just wasn't interested in the programs I was making or the stories I was covering. My voice wasn't good enough for radio, he would say, and he certainly never appreciated what I did for Afghan women. And it felt like I was supposed to just ignore this behavior—it hurt that my husband cared so little about the things that were important to me, but what choice did I have?

On one occasion I tried to complain about these feelings to my family. "Look, Zarghuna! Does he beat you?" When I said no, my relative went on, "Well then, accept this life. He is a good man; it is just his way."

But as time passed, accepting his way became hard for me. For him an easy life was more important than ensuring my happiness. I was earning good money, paying for the mortgage and most of the bills. I never asked him to buy me clothes but I did my own shopping, so why would he prevent me from working?

I remember one day I had had a particularly hard time at work. I was very upset by the behavior of a colleague—it was just office politics but it had hurt me a lot. When I came home, I told him that sometimes I felt like leaving my job and staying at home, that perhaps I would go back to my studies. As an Afghan wife I was expecting him to protect me and tell me not to worry, that he would work hard and find enough money to look after our financial needs. I was hoping for a hint that he would protect me, so that if I ever chose to leave my work, I would still have some security. At the time, I was just angry with people at work and I was unlikely to leave such a good job, but somehow I felt tired and fed up of all the responsibility I had shouldered from such a young age. But he lashed out: "No way are you leaving that job—who would pay the mortgage?" I was very hurt by his attitude and the burden of economic responsibility became heavy on me. Just the thought of not having any money scared me and I felt terribly alone.

Our relationship started to falter, and soon there were long periods where we would hardly see each other. He would leave the house earlier than me and I spent more and more time at my parents'. I would try to be asleep when he came home at night, and those nights that I was awake I would pretend to be asleep so we didn't have to talk. My self-esteem was at an all-time low; my respect for him and any residual love I felt for him was fading fast. Talking to Wazma showed me that this was not the only way to live. You don't have to feel like a prisoner in your own home, even if, like Wazma, your home is on top of a mountain in Kabul with very limited facilities.

I was in hospital for a long time. I was given a lot of morphine because my leg hurt so much. The pain was so bad, I couldn't think clearly. After a while, it did get better but then I started to worry. My parents came to visit me every day. They would bring me food and look after me. Each day I would ask for my husband and daughter but they never came to visit me in hospital. I missed them so much. I couldn't wait to hold my daughter in my arms again. After more than a week, I had heard nothing from them. I kept asking my mother where they were and why they hadn't come. She made all sorts of excuses, saying that they had visited the other day but I was asleep or that Farah was ill so they had had to stay at home. The stronger I became, the more determined I was to see them. Weeks passed and I didn't hear anything from my husband. I became convinced that my parents were hiding something from me but the truth was worse than I could possibly have imagined.

One afternoon, my mother came with cherries on a plate. She had just washed them. She kissed me on the forehead and said, "Wazma, my child. You look so pale, as if you don't have a drop of blood in your body. I've brought you some cherries because the doctors told me they're good for the blood."

I took my mother's hand, placed it on my head, and told her I could see how much she loved me. She reassured me that she did but wanted to know why I was holding her hand so tightly. I replied, "I'm a mother too. I also have a daughter. Can you feel my pain?"

I tightened my grip on her hand.

"Where are Farah and Waheed? Swear on my life that they're safe."

I began to shout and cry. My mother started crying too. She said they were safe and coping well without me. She told me to concentrate on getting well myself. At this point, a doctor came into the room. He took my blood pressure and told me I was ready to be discharged.

"Wazma, you're a strong woman. Your life will be different now. I want to wish you all the best for the future. Don't lose hope or strength. Our country is going though a difficult time."

I thanked the doctor for looking after me. My mind, however, was really on my daughter and husband. I was upset that in all these weeks they hadn't visited me even once but at least now I was being discharged and I would see them again.

My mother packed my things into a bag, helped me into a wheel-chair, and pushed me in it to a taxi. It felt strange to be in the fresh air again, seeing and hearing the sights and sounds of the street. My parents were strangely subdued. I thought they would be pleased that their daughter had recovered enough to go home but perhaps they were upset they had a disabled daughter.

I didn't dwell on this, though, as all I wanted to do was to see my daughter again. In the hospital, I had planned to be angry with Waheed and find out why he hadn't visited me, but now the moment had come to see him again I was just excited and happy. When we got into the taxi I heard my father tell the driver to take us to Khairkhana. I protested. "No, wait. Why are we going to your home? I can come and see you later with Waheed and Farah."

Instead, I told the driver to take us to Deh Afghanan. I informed him it was my home and my husband and daughter would be waiting for me there. My father told me to be quiet in front of the driver and he would explain everything later—for now their home was my home once again. I didn't know what to make of it all.

When we arrived at Khairkhana my father and brother lifted me out of the taxi and into the wheelchair. I expected Waheed and Farah to be waiting for me inside my parents' house. I searched the room full of relatives for the only two people I was desperate to see. I wanted to see Farah in the new dress I had made for her and had sweets in my hand for her. I asked where Waheed was but nobody would tell me. Eventually I lost patience and started shouting and crying.

"Where is Waheed?" I screamed. "Why will no one tell me what is going on?"

At this, people averted their eyes from me. Some even started crying. My mother came up to me and put her arms around me.

"You won't see them again, my darling."

She held me closer to her. "They are not coming back to you."

My heart sank and I began to feel sick and faint. I asked her to repeat what she meant. Why would I not see my daughter?

"You can't see them and you won't be able to live with them."

I began to weep. I couldn't understand what was happening.

My mother was crying now. "Wazma, my child. That bastard husband of yours has said now you're disabled he can't live with you. He's going to marry someone else."

I felt as though my whole world had come crashing down. I couldn't believe that my beloved husband would do or say such things. My baby, my little girl, was being taken away from me. All my dreams were crushed, my feelings torn to shreds. At that moment, the world became dark.

Wazma was crying and said, "Dear Zari, this was the worst thing that happened in my life. The pain in my leg has been nothing compared to this."

I could barely believe the story Wazma was telling me and I could feel tears welling up.

I told everyone that I loved and needed Waheed and Farah. I promised I wouldn't get angry with them or ask why they hadn't come to see me in hospital. All I wanted to do was go back to my own home and see them again.

My relatives looked on helplessly as I cried. My mother was crying with me. Finally she spoke. "All right, Wazma, my child. We will take you to see Waheed but you will have to be strong."

My father objected, calling my mother crazy for entertaining such an idea. He asked her why she wanted to take me to that asshole's house. He didn't want his daughter to see him again because he was not worthy of her. But my mother was calm and firm. She said it would be better for me to see with my own eyes and hear with my own ears. Only then would I believe what kind of person my husband had become.

I still couldn't believe what she was trying to tell me. I couldn't stop crying. My heart was beating furiously. I had difficulty breathing. It was as if someone was suffocating me. My father wasn't convinced by my mother's argument but he still went to find a taxi for us.

I was carried into the car. It took my parents and me up the steep mountain road to my house. I started to feel cold and began shivering. I prayed that everything my mother had told me was a lie. I hoped for a miracle and pictured Waheed holding me in a tight embrace and my daughter welcoming me in her new dress with a beautiful smile.

It was beginning to get dark by the time we arrived at my home. Waheed and I had always sat outside our house in the summer and gazed at the stars. Now I looked up at the sky and examined those same stars for messages. Were they telling me not to go in? Were they giving me news of a happy reunion?

The taxi couldn't make it up the last part of the journey, so my mother and father struggled to push my wheelchair up the narrow stony path. Some of my friends and neighbors came out to greet us. They seemed surprised to see me but still stopped to kiss me. They put sweets into my hand, as is our custom, to show they were happy to see me alive. All this made me feel better but the most important man in my life did not come out to welcome me home.

My mother approached my door. I stopped her and said I wanted to knock on it myself. I felt some strength and anger return. I would knock on my door and find out what lay behind it for myself.

I noticed how dusty it had become. I tried to clean it with my sleeve but the dust wouldn't go. Then the door opened. Waheed appeared. I could see from his eyes that he immediately recognized me, even though I had grown thin and pale. But even though he saw me, he wouldn't look into my eyes. I began to weep.

"Waheed!" I shouted. "Waheed jan. It's your wife here, Wazma. I know I'm not strong and beautiful anymore, but I swear to God and I swear on the life of my daughter that my love for you is as strong as ever. I've come back to you."

Waheed began crying but still he wouldn't look at me. And when I asked to be allowed in to see my daughter he raised his hands as if to bar my entry.

"You can't come into the house. It's not your home anymore."

I begged to be allowed to stay so that I could at least be with my daughter, but Waheed shook his head. "I want to be happy," he said. "How can I live with a wife who has no leg? You can't even look after yourself, so how can you take care of my daughter?"

At that moment, Waheed died for me. He became like a small insect in front of me. I had lost my leg, I had lost my love, and now I realized I had lost my baby girl. I heard his words and yet I didn't hear them.

"I am planning to marry again, so you are free from my side. You can do whatever you want but you can't see my daughter again. Now you are disabled I don't think you can look after my daughter properly."

I asked him why he was being so cruel. It wasn't my fault that a rocket had landed and taken away my leg. I had only lost a leg. Everything else about me was the same, especially my love for my daughter. I pleaded with him, as a mother, to let me see my daughter. But no matter how much I begged, he stood like a stone at the door. After a while, he went back inside the house and closed the door. At this, I fell down weeping and shouting. My parents pulled me away, lifted me into the taxi, and took me back to their home.

What choice did I have but to live with my parents? It wasn't easy for them because they were getting old and I needed a lot of help. My leg also gave me a great deal of pain, which required medicine. My sister-in-law resented my presence because I was eating their food, which was paid for with her husband's earnings. I was becoming a burden on my family and even my parents were starting to blame me. I became depressed. I would cry all the time and not do anything or talk to anyone. I was just wrapped up in my feelings and desperately missed my daughter.

One day a neighbor mentioned that there was a center for disabled people in the Qal-e-Fatih Ullah area of town. I asked my father to take me there. They encouraged me to sew clothes and with their help I became a tailor. I am now earning, which means I can give my parents money and contribute to household expenses. They no longer criticize me or moan about me: having money makes me important!

I was very upset by what had happened to Wazma but I admired her for her determination and hard work and asked if I could ask her a few personal questions. She said that after all the hurt she had suffered, talking about her feelings was easy. I asked her what she would have done if the rocket attack had taken Waheed's leg instead of hers? Wazma smiled and replied that she would have stayed and looked after him. She would never have left him. She said she knows that she was cast out because she is a woman. She could accept this abandonment, but the worst thing is being separated from her only child.

"I miss her! Sometimes she comes to the center to see me. She knows I'm her mother and she's nice to me. I'm happy that I see her sometimes. Life has been unfair to me but at least I'm still alive and able to earn a living sewing."

≈

WAZMA IS NOT ALONE. Hundreds of women in Afghanistan suffer like this. According to the United Nations, the decades of war that have plagued Afghanistan—the rocket attacks, land mines, and bombs—have left more than a million people disabled. Some have lost legs and arms, others their sight, and many their peace of mind. You don't have to walk far in Kabul before you come across a disabled person. There is a special ministry in Afghanistan called "The Martyrs and Disabled Affairs Ministry." This ministry is responsible for providing assistance to those disabled through the war, helping them to find suitable jobs and offering them financial aid. Some of the officials are disabled themselves. I ask myself, would my country have such a ministry if it weren't for the war?

It is not unusual to find a man like Waheed with a heart made of stone, as Wazma puts it; a man who would reject his wife because she had become disable. However, there are many women—young and old—who are married to disabled men and take care of all their needs. It is easier for a disabled man to find a wife because the woman has no say in the marriage, but it is almost impossible for a disabled woman to find a man who will accept her.

I made a special radio program on Wazma's story, dedicated to Wazma herself, in which we invited experts to discuss the lives of women in her situation. As a journalist, I couldn't demand that Waheed return Farah to her mother; I wasn't a judge in court but at least I could tell the world her story. The essence of the program was that disabled people have the same rights to family life as anyone else. I hoped this program would have a deep impact on the audience and especially on Wazma's family.

The next day when I went to the office, I was still thinking about Wazma. Her story had affected me too, and I had spent the night thinking about her. A colleague came up to me and told me that I had to be at my desk in an hour's time because someone was going to call me from the United States. I was surprised because I wasn't expecting a call. I asked who the caller was and my colleague just shrugged and said the person only asked to speak to the presenter of *Afghan Woman's Hour*.

An hour later, I found myself speaking to an Afghan living in America. He told me how he had heard yesterday's program and it had made him cry. He hadn't been able to get the woman who had lost her leg in a rocket attack out of his mind and wanted to help her. He offered to provide Wazma with money on a regular basis. Fortunately, I was going to Afghanistan later that month and was able to hand her the money in person. Wazma's story had touched someone in our audience to the point where they were prepared to do something.

9

Janpary's Story

A MOTHER'S STORY

*D*URING MY TIME AT *AFGHAN WOMAN'S HOUR*, NOT A DAY would pass without a reporter sending us a story about a family or woman living in extreme poverty. The war has deprived so many people of their homes, land, jobs, and income, and they now find themselves trying to survive in plastic tents in Kabul city. If you're on your first visit to the capital and compare it to the provincial cities of Afghanistan, Kabul might appear to be quite developed and wealthy, but look closer and you will be shocked by the number of beggars standing in the road.

Out in the field, whenever I was talking to women and gathering stories, people would run toward me, eager to show me their torn clothing and wretched-looking children. They would assume I belonged to a nongovernmental organization (NGO) or the United Nations, there to distribute food or some other aid. There have been many occasions when I have told these women that I'm from the BBC and not from a charity, and seen their hopeful faces fall with disappointment. Once I met a little girl who was carrying water to her home from a nearby well in a village on the outskirts of Kabul. Her hands were frozen and she was crying with cold. I felt useless and wished God could give me millions of pounds so that I could help these people.

Each time I go back to Afghanistan and am confronted by extreme poverty, I think how grateful I should be to God for everything I have.

When I walk into a supermarket in London I'm faced with a bewildering choice of different types of bread and I'm aware that in Kabul a girl will stand at the roadside and beg all day long just for a crust of bread. When I first started returning to Afghanistan I used to give a few coins to beggars on the street but I found that within seconds I'd be swamped by a crowd of people—men, women, and children—all desperate for money. A colleague soon warned me against doing this; he worried that if I didn't give every one of them money, I might be attacked. It was certainly frightening to be surrounded by a dozen beggars in a busy city like Kabul with all the security risks.

According to a UN report, a third of the Afghan population lives below the official poverty line. In many of the poorest families the breadwinner is disabled, has fallen ill, or even died. And these families do not have a relative in the West who can send them money every month. So those who have no one to care for them starve, their children starve, and they die from the freezing cold in winter or the stifling heat in summer.

On one trip to Afghanistan I encountered a woman begging on the streets. She was carrying her baby daughter who looked only a few months old. I tried to talk to the woman about her life, but she said, "Sister, if you're going to give me some money then it's fine to stand here and talk to me. Otherwise, please don't waste my time." I've found it hard to get this woman out of my head, holding her child in the middle of a chaotic and busy street in the center of Kabul. It was dusty and noisy and bitterly cold. The baby's lips had turned blue and the mother wore plastic shoes with holes in the soles. I looked at the two of them, both stiff with cold, and I urgently wanted to help, but there was so little I could do. I gave the woman some money and left. As I walked back to the office, her words were ringing in my head. She was right. Why would she waste her time being interviewed by me when she could be attracting the attention of passing cars and people and getting money for food?

In January 2008, when I was working on the program in Kabul, one of my colleagues from the BBC's news team came into our office asking for donations. He said his friend had called him from northern Afghanistan to tell him that a family there had sold their newborn baby girl for five hundred dollars because they were so desperate. The father did not have enough money to heat the house or buy food. We all gave some money so the father was able to buy back his daughter and get food and fuel. Can you imagine the hopelessness of a mother who decides to sell her newborn baby to get money to feed the other members of her family?

I asked the other reporters in the office about their experience of other people's poverty. Everyone knew of a family that was so poor they had become beggars, sold their children, or died from lack of food and shelter. Not being able to find a home, food, and health facilities is a problem that millions of Afghans face almost every day and many of them have told us of their worries on the BBC Afghan programs. In some cases bringing a baby into the world and selling it for money has been the only way to feed and care for five or six other children, who might otherwise die in the freezing cold.

It was around this time that Hillai, one of our young reporters from Jalalabad, told us about Janpary. Hillai knew her story because Janpary lived in her neighborhood.

This is what I loved about working on *Afghan Woman's Hour*. Sometimes it felt as though every woman who told us her story was opening up a subject that had previously been hidden, and each story gave a fascinating insight into what it is like to be a woman living in Afghanistan. These stories came from all corners of the country and many highlighted the need for women to know their rights. Janpary's story is no exception. It is about poverty, but it's also the story of a woman who discovers her worth, a woman who dares to try to take what is legally hers.

❧

JANPARY WAS BORN IN Nangarhar Province in the east of Afghanistan, an area famous for its pleasant climate and known as "Hamesha Bahar" or "Eternal Spring." Nangarhar shares a border with Pakistan so there is a large amount of traffic of people and goods in both directions. Most of the province uses Pakistani rather than Afghan currency because of regular trade between the two countries. During the war, it was one of the more secure and prosperous cities in the east of the country, and it is still an important trading route between Afghanistan and Pakistan. Many of its citizens are farmers, merchants, and business people, but during the war a lot of the farmers began to grow poppies. In 1990 a severe drought affected Afghanistan and the only crop that grew was the poppy.

Different tribes live in this province but most of them are Pashtuns. Here strong tribal traditions are followed. Young marriages are common. There is a university in Jalalabad, attended by young men and women, but more men go to the university than women. Girls tend to end their education at puberty, especially if they are from more traditional families. In fact, if a girl reaches eighteen and she is not married, she is considered old and past the age for marriage, and the older women in the family will call her a "very ripe woman."

Many people from Kabul moved to Jalalabad during the war between the Mujahedeen and the Taliban because there was no fighting there, and they ended up settling for good. This has helped make it a lively and thriving city, full of interesting life stories. Janpary is not one of the rich women of the city. She's a poor, hardworking widow struggling to feed her children. Hillai went to Janpary's house to record her story and sent it to me via the Internet.

⟨⟩

JANPARY PEERED INTO THE dusty tin and saw there was only a handful of lentils left. She took a deep breath and tried to work out how this was going to feed five hungry mouths, looking around her kitchen to see if she could find something to make the lentils stretch further. Just then her daughter ran in saying she was hungry.

"My child, once again your mother is at a loss. We don't have enough to eat and I don't have enough money to buy food."

Janpary's youngest child was seven years old.

"But Mummy, I've been hungry since yesterday."

Janpary hugged her daughter.

"If I could, I would cook you and your brothers a wonderful meal of meat and rice. And I would give you fresh fruit to savor. But your mother is helpless. There are so few lentils left that even if I cooked them all there wouldn't be enough for you, let alone your brothers."

Her daughter thought for a moment and then said, "So must I stay hungry?"

"No," said Janpary. "I am going out to find some work and I will bring you some food."

Janpary wrapped the blue material of her *burqa* around her head and left the house. She walked briskly in her plastic sandals in the summer heat. She was upset that her children hadn't eaten for two days and wanted to get to her destination quickly. On the outskirts of the village she arrived at a large house with ornate iron gates. Janpary knocked loudly and after a few minutes a young man approached, opened the gates, and asked who she was.

"I want to see Bibi jan."

"Who are you?"

"My name is Janpary. Please tell Bibi jan that the widow Janpary is here. She has come to offer her services."

The young man slammed the door shut and left Janpary waiting outside the gate in the hot sun. After several minutes, he returned and opened the gates, ushering Janpary inside the house. Janpary followed the young man inside and took off her sandals. The house was big and grand, and her feet felt a welcoming cool sensation as she trod on the marble floor. The young man directed her to go upstairs. She climbed up the stairs, her footsteps leaving a damp and dusty outline, and walked into a room that was laid with expensive carpets. Bibi was sitting on a large wooden bed.

"*Salamalikum*, Bibi jan."

The older woman looked kindly at the younger one. "*Waliakum-u-salam!*" She then inquired after Janpary.

Janpary replied, "Bibi jan, my children haven't eaten for two days and they're hungry." She was embarrassed but went on, "Bibi jan, you know I can cope with not eating for a few days." She smiled. "Maybe it's the extra fat on my body; but my children beg me for food every minute of the day and I've promised that I'll bring them something to eat."

At this, tears fell down Janpary's face and she started to cry. "It hurts so much to see them hungry," she said.

The widow slumped down on the marble floor. "The only way I thought I could earn some money was to come to you. I was wondering whether you had any clothes that needed washing? Or some cleaning that I could do? Perhaps some tailoring I could help with?"

The lady of the house looked at her and said, "Janpary, I have told you so many times that I already have cleaners and women to wash my clothes. Please don't come here again and again. This time I'll give you some food to take home with you, but please don't ask me to give you any kind of work. The people who work for me are poor just like you; if I give you their jobs then what will they do?"

She told Janpary that she only needed extra help when there were lots of guests or for special occasions. Janpary stared at the floor as she took in the disappointing news.

"Since you have come here I won't send you away empty-handed." And she called for a maid and told her to give Janpary the leftovers from the previous night's meal. Janpary took the food and prayed for Bibi to have a good life.

As she was leaving she turned around and said, "Bibi jan, if you know of anyone who might need a servant I'm always ready. I swear on my children's life I'll work hard."

Bibi said she couldn't promise anything but would ask her family and friends. Janpary hurried home. Panting for breath, she pushed through the broken door of her house and called out, "Children, come, I've got food."

Within seconds, Janpary's children had clustered around her like hungry tigers. Janpary opened the bag and took out pieces of cooked meat, rice, and vegetables, which the children devoured. Bibi had shown kindness and given her and her children plenty of food. Janpary grabbed a pot, poured out some water, and warned her children to eat slowly so they didn't get stomachache. She watched fondly as they ate. Janpary's daughter scooped some food into her hand and offered it to her mother but Janpary shook her head.

"You eat first; if there's anything left over I'll eat it."

Janpary picked up her old handmade fan and started to wave it over her children. She tried to think what she could do next. Perhaps she could go to her neighbor's house and ask if they needed a servant. What made Janpary's life still more difficult was that at this time women were not allowed to work or study outside the home according to Taliban laws. They couldn't earn wages from normal jobs like cleaning and cooking in government buildings, schools, and hospitals.

～

JANPARY LIVED WITH HER four children in a small clay house, which her husband had left them when he died. She was young when she married and her husband was already married to another woman. Her brother had lost a bet and didn't have enough money to pay his dues so he had offered his sister as a second wife. In this way she was given away to settle her brother's gambling debt and she started her adult life with no wedding ceremony, the second wife to an inveterate gambler. Life wasn't easy for her. Even though her husband wasn't cruel and didn't beat her, she had to work hard in the house to please the first wife. She didn't feel cared for or loved by anyone. It was a long time before Janpary was allowed to visit her parents—she had to wait until she had produced at least two children, because after this she was considered to be a used woman who wouldn't dare escape or be desired by anyone else. Her husband was usually preoccupied with his gambling but he did at least provide food and shelter for Janpary and her children.

Janpary's life became particularly difficult after her husband was killed. It wasn't quite clear what had happened but his murder was linked to his gambling. In the late 1980s, for a while, Janpary survived because the communist government gave assistance to widows and orphans. Widows and government employees were given monthly coupons, which enabled them to get flour, oil, sugar, soap, and some other household items. Most of these items were imported from Russia but when the Mujahedeen and then the Taliban came to power everything changed. There was no longer government help or support for widows like her.

Janpary found herself a widow with no education, stuck in poverty, and with four young children to feed. The pressures of her current situation made her forget that she had been given away to pay for a lost bet to become the second wife of an old man. By now the first wife had died and the children from the first marriage had grown up.

Her brother had nine sons and a house nearby but he didn't support her in any way. Janpary neither asked him for any help nor dared to point out that she was stuck in this situation thanks to his gambling. She visited him and his family very rarely.

⁂

JANPARY'S DAUGHTER AGAIN OFFERED her some of the leftovers but she told her to keep it safe for when they got hungry later. She asked the children to pass her *burqa* to her. "Don't go out anywhere. I'll be back soon."

Once again, she went out in search of work. She walked briskly until she reached a large bungalow in a wealthy part of Jalalabad. She knocked at the gate and a servant came out. Janpary had her face hidden behind her *burqa*. The man looked her up and down. Even though he couldn't see her properly, he knew she was poor from her torn plastic sandals, which had been repaired with thick black string. He could see her hands were used to hard work and her clothes were full of dust.

"Who are you? What do you want?"

Janpary spoke with a low and uncertain voice. "Brother, I've come in search of work. I'm poor and wanted to know if this house needs someone who can clean, wash, and look after things?"

The guard told her to wait outside. He too was poor and felt sympathetic toward her. Janpary knew it wouldn't be a short wait so she sat herself down on the ground beside the gate and leaned against the wall in the shade. She prayed that she would get work. She was prepared to take any job, no matter how menial—the stress of finding enough food to feed her children was becoming too much.

When she heard the guard's footsteps returning she got up quickly and covered her face with her *burqa*.

"Sister, madam is calling you in. I made sure she asked you in."

Janpary blessed him. "Brother, I wish you lots of happiness for your children; you tried to help me, may God help you."

The guard led her into the house and directed her to a large room where the owner of the house was sitting watching television. Before entering, Janpary removed her sandals and left them outside the door.

"*Assalam-alikum,*" said Janpary.

The woman was wearing a new cotton *shalwar kamiz* and in her hand she held a remote control for the television. She turned the volume down, even though it was already very low as this was a time when people had to watch television secretly. The Taliban had banned television but some families continued to watch it surreptitiously, especially if they were rich. The woman returned the greeting to Janpary and asked her to be seated.

Janpary gazed at her new clothes, her golden bangles, and her soft smooth hands. She thought how beautiful she looked. The woman observed Janpary carefully too. Janpary was the younger woman, yet looked older, paler, and tired. The woman asked Janpary what she could do.

"Bibi Jan, I can do all sorts of cleaning, washing, cooking, guarding and looking after the animals!" Janpary gabbled in her desire to impress her hostess.

The woman smiled and said, "Cooking I do myself. I will need some help washing and cleaning, but only for the next two weeks as my cleaner has gone back to her village. Might you be able to start work from tomorrow? I'll give you clothes to wash and you'll be cleaning the house. In return, I'll pay you and you can take the day's leftover food home with you each day."

She said her husband didn't like to eat the same food twice in a row so she had to make fresh dishes for him every day.

Janpary started praying for the woman. "Bibi jan, God bless you and your family. For me even one day's work is a lot. I have to provide for my children and if I don't work they'll go hungry. My pride won't allow me to beg on the streets. Why should I beg when God has given me a body that is fit for work?"

The woman showed Janpary the work that needed doing and instructed her to come back the following morning. Janpary was delighted and proud; she felt as free as a bird. She thanked the guard again on her way out and wished him and his family a happy life. Then she hurried home, excited about giving the good news to her children. As she entered her house, her youngest daughter ran toward her.

"Mummy, where have you been? I've missed you."

Janpary hugged her and told her that as she had found work she could soon buy her the red sandals she had been asking for. Janpary's eldest son, ten-year-old Naqib, had been playing outside. When he came inside, Janpary reminded him that he should work and study hard so that when he grew up he could look after her and his brothers and sister. When she told him the good news he said, "Mother, you don't have to worry because I'll do everything to provide for you. I want to buy new clothes for my sister and brothers just like my cousins have."

Janpary told Naqib not to compete with his cousins because her brother was rich and could easily afford to buy new clothes, good food, and school books, but her son was dissatisfied with this explanation.

"But, Mother, our cousins always show off their new things to us. They say you're begging! Is that true?"

Janpary looked into her son's eyes and said, "Firstly, your uncle should be ashamed of himself. I have told you that begging is an easy job and I won't do it. I'll work for as long as I have the energy to do it. I can wash and I can clean."

She showed her hands to her son. "Look, my child, your mother's hands are strong. They're not made for begging."

Janpary advised her son to ignore what his cousins had said and instead to study hard. She switched off the lamp, lay down on the floor near her four children, and recited verses of the Quran as mothers do to bless them for safety before going to sleep.

The neighbor's cockerel crowed loudly early in the morning but Janpary was already wide awake. She went to wash in the corner of her clay mud house and as she did she heard the mullah's call for prayer, the *Azan*. After performing her morning prayer she went to wake Naqib for school. School is free for boys and girls until the age of eighteen, but parents like Janpary often cannot afford the uniform, pens, and notebooks. School starts at eight in the morning and ends at around half-past twelve in the afternoon. However, many children don't go because they are needed to work in the home, fields, or family business. Others are forced to sell cigarettes and chewing gum on the street. Girls often don't go to school at all because their parents don't see the point of education for their daughters.

Janpary told Naqib which house she would be working in and promised that she would return at lunchtime with food for the younger children. When she arrived at the woman's house the guard showed her a large pile of dirty laundry and she began to scrub the sheets and then all the clothes. She didn't give in to tiredness; she rubbed hard without thought for her skin. She wanted to show Bibi how well she could clean. By the time the woman had got up, Janpary had hung some of the washing to dry on ropes. Bibi looked at the line of clothes and praised Janpary for her hard work. She advised her to take a break and have something to eat, but Janpary wanted to finish the job and insisted that all the clothes should be washed and dried in the sunlight.

When the washing was completed, Janpary made herself some green tea. She poured lots of sugar in her cup and ate a piece of bread that the guard shared with her. Janpary hadn't eaten for three days and this bread tasted like a meal from a rich man's banquet. Afterwards she set to work on the marble floors. She squatted down and rubbed hard, sweating and panting with the effort.

Bibi came to sit on the sofa and ask Janpary about her life. Janpary looked up from the floor.

"My life is very simple. I have no money. I'm a widow with four children who I need to provide for."

Janpary wiped the sweat away from her forehead with her scarf and laughed. "My head is full of stories, Bibi. If I told you all that's happened in my life you'd get tired. Living with a man who was always gambling— and always losing—wasn't easy. I was the victim of a bet between my brother and my husband. I'm still suffering because of this."

"What's your brother doing now?" she asked. "How's his life?"

"My brother is rich," Janpary replied. "He has nine sons and lives in a villa."

The woman asked how her brother had become so rich, and Janpary explained that when her parents died her brother had inherited everything. "Men are so lucky. He took all the land that my father left and now he lives a comfortable life with his wife and children."

"But, Janpary, listen carefully, you must ask for your part in your family's inheritance!"

Janpary didn't understand what Bibi meant and asked how she could do this. Her mistress was educated and recited the Aayat from the Al-Nisa chapter of the Quran: "Men shall have a share in what their parents and closest relatives leave and women shall have a share in what their parents and closest relatives leave, whether the legacy be small or large: this is ordained by God."

"But Bibi," Janpary said, "you know how it is with daughters; in our culture no one gives them anything from their *meeras* (inheritance). I know my brother will get very angry if I ask."

"If you don't ask for your rights, he'll never give you anything; and he should help you, anyway, because he's the one responsible for your hardship."

She sat down on the floor next to Janpary. "All this cleaning and washing you do in houses like mine won't help you forever. You'll get pains in your hands and legs and after a while you won't be able to do the work. I think you've already suffered enough. You should be proud of yourself for working so hard and for being prepared to do whatever is necessary to look after your children. This strength that I can see in you will make it possible for you to take your share from your brother. It's your right. God, in our holy book the Quran, says you should ask for your right."

Bibi's words gave Janpary strength. Before leaving the house she went to find Bibi.

"I'm so happy to have met you. You've shown me a way out of my situation. I now feel able to ask my brother for the *meeras*. My father left behind things for both of us. You're right, if I don't ask my brother he'll keep his eyes closed and will carry on eating my children's food."

Janpary left with food for her children and money for the work she had done. On her way home, she stopped at a shop to buy oil, flour, sugar, and rice. It was the first time for a month that Janpary was able to buy food. She felt so strong and proud of herself for being able to do this. She hurried back to her home carrying two plastic bags of food. Her daughter saw her in the street and ran toward her calling for her mother.

"My child," Janpary said, handing one of the bags to her daughter, "we're going to cook lots of bread and tasty food for you. You won't have to go to sleep hungry anymore."

Her daughter smiled. "But, Mother, you forgot to buy my red sandals."

Janpary laughed and told her that she would buy them soon but couldn't buy everything with her first day's wages.

That day, Janpary's body didn't know what tiredness was. She was so happy and excited to be able to provide for her children that she went straight to the kitchen and began baking bread and cooking rice and vegetables.

Early the next morning, she got her children up and told them to hurry because she wanted to pay a visit to their cousins' house. Her eldest son asked why they were going to their uncle's house so early.

"Naqib, my son, I want to ask your uncle for what is rightfully ours. We're living in hardship and poverty and he may be able to help us."

Janpary's brother was surprised to see his sister and her children at his house so early.

"Janpary, *salaam*. How are you?"

Janpary greeted her brother and told him that she was there to ask him for help. He sat on the *charpoie* while she and her children sat on the floor. His wife offered them all green tea. She and her husband were impatient to know what Janpary was going to ask.

Janpary began by explaining how poor she was. "Brother, you know how difficult it is for women to earn money. Since my husband died I've been finding bits of work here and there to feed my children—some washing and cleaning—but it's not enough. I was wondering if you…"

She paused. Her brother looked at his sister and her four children and laughed out loud. "Janpary, come, come; you know I have an even larger family than you to look after. How can I possibly help you too?"

Her brother's wife joined in: "We can't feed any more people. Where do you think the extra money will come from?"

"I'm not asking for charity," Janpary replied. "When did I ask for that? You haven't let me finish what I was trying to say."

Her brother and sister-in-law were surprised to hear Janpary sound so confident and became alarmed at what this might mean.

"I think you both know what I'm going to ask."

Janpary still had her *burqa* covering her head but her words were coming out loud and clear. "Brother, I've come to ask for my share of our father's inheritance. He left some land, which at the moment you have. If you give me my share, it would be a great help to me and my children."

Janpary's brother could no longer contain his anger and got up from the *charpoie*. Her words were like bullets shot into the back of his head. His wife was first to respond. "Janpary, where is your shame? How can you ask your brother for the *meeras*?"

Janpary's brother came and sat near her. "Look, my dear sister, you know that in our culture no woman—I mean, no decent woman—asks for *meeras*. What our father left behind belongs only to your brother. You got married a long time ago."

"Oh, I swear to God, I swear on my children's lives, that if I had some money or an income I wouldn't be here. If I was able to feed my children I wouldn't ask you for anything." Janpary began to sob. "Please, brother, have some mercy on my fatherless children; don't force me to beg on the streets. Just give me what you can. I'm not asking for all that I'm due."

The more Janpary pleaded the angrier her brother became. He said he would look into a way to try to help her but that she must now leave his house. By now Janpary and all her children were weeping. They were upset to see their uncle angry and shouting at their mother and their mother's helplessness.

Janpary's sister-in-law came close and whispered in her ear. "Woman, I'm telling you: forget all this nonsense about your *meeras*."

"Have you no shame?" Janpary replied. "You've taken the whole of my family's inheritance. If I ask for my share, you think it's shameful, but when you don't give what is rightfully mine, it's not?"

Her sister-in-law faced her directly. "Woman, I'm telling you to stop dreaming about getting even half a rupee. You're just a shameless widow. Go back to your begging and don't bother my husband anymore."

Even through her tears Janpary found her voice. "Whatever you say about me, I'm not weak. I'm not taking anyone else's right. Yes, I know I'm a widow and I'm well aware that I'm not allowed to live like other women whose husbands are still alive—I lost this right when my husband died. I know widows are not allowed to express their feelings; but I'm also a mother. I realize I embarrass you—I have to think twice before I go out, be careful about what I say, and everything I do is judged. Since I lost my husband I haven't worn new clothes; Eid and festival days are closed and dark occasions for me, but pay attention to who I am. I am your sister. I can't wish anything bad on you because your husband is my brother. I wish my brother every happiness and pray that God will direct you in the right way. I can't even curse you because I don't have the malice in me to wish that you were in my situation. If I did that, I'd be no better than you. I don't know where your sense of justice has gone and I don't understand where my brother's kindness has gone."

Then Janpary took hold of her daughter's hand and walked out of her brother's house followed by the rest of her children.

As they walked away Naqib said, "Mother, I wanted to beat my uncle when he shouted at you like that."

Janpary was shocked. "My child, you're too young; you mustn't talk about beating people up. I'll sort this out and make sure we get our share from my brother."

Janpary took her children home and then left the house for work. She wept as she walked through the streets, her *burqa* like a curtain closing her off from the world. She was anxious to see Bibi and tell her what had happened. Her children had cried with her but they were young and couldn't help. She needed a friend to share her pain with. Janpary marched straight into the kitchen, took off her *burqa*, tightened her scarf around her head, rolled up her sleeves, and began washing a large pile of dirty dishes. Next, she sat on a small wooden stool and began to scrub the dirty pots. She splashed them with water as the tears continued to flow down her face. She blew her nose on her sleeves and tried to stop crying but the pain her brother had caused and the fear of poverty made it impossible. Somehow she found the energy to scrub and give a perfect shine to the black pots. She rubbed sand over the bottom of them where they had been scorched with heat and took them out into the sun to dry. She moved quickly to finish her jobs but her mind was stuck on how her brother had treated her.

When Janpary went upstairs to see Bibi, she was just finishing her late breakfast. She greeted Janpary and noticed her red and puffy eyes. She asked if anything was wrong. This one question was enough to start Janpary crying again.

"Bibi jan, it's nothing much. I knew my brother would say no to my request."

Bibi invited Janpary to sit next to her. Then she said, "Too much crying robs you of your energy. It tears you apart, and after many hours of crying, no help comes. It only comes if you try hard for it."

But Janpary couldn't stop crying and she told Bibi how she felt humiliated by her brother. She said he and his wife had cursed her in front of her children when she made the mistake of asking for her rightful *meeras*.

Bibi said, "Of course, your brother was going to do this. If he were a decent man, if he was a good Muslim, he wouldn't let you be in this situation in the first place. You'll have to plan and fight for your share."

Janpary asked how she could do this.

"We have a law and a government. You must go to the courts and speak to a judge. Don't worry, I'll take you there."

Janpary felt so relieved; it was as though someone was giving her a mountain to lean on. She prayed for a long-lasting and happy life for Bibi before finishing the rest of the jobs in the house.

In the late afternoon Janpary returned home to feed her children. When she saw their faces it was clear they were still upset and worried for their mother. Janpary tried to lighten their mood by telling them that she had brought them something to eat, but her daughter ran up to her mother and said, "Aunt is here." Janpary was surprised and asked which aunt. "Aunt Naseema, uncle's wife."

Janpary guessed that her sister-in-law had come to further insult and humiliate her but the two women greeted each other politely. Janpary told her daughter to bring tea for her aunt but Naseema insisted she didn't want anything apart from a quick word with Janpary. Naseema and Janpary sat opposite each other. Naseema was wearing clean cotton clothes and her face and hands were soft and smooth. Janpary wore a large gray scarf around her body, marked with sweat and grime; her hands were red and calloused after scrubbing pots all morning; her face was dark from the sun and it looked as if it was a long time since her hair had been combed.

Naseema cleared her throat. "I know you're really an honorable woman. You're a Pashtun woman so it doesn't suit you to do shameful things like this. Do you know of any Pashtun woman who has done this sort of thing? You're going to embarrass your brother in front of the whole village, so I'm asking you to change your mind. I'm offering you the opportunity to come and live in our house. We'll give you and your children a room in the corner of the house. In return, you can look after the place, so instead of cleaning strangers' houses you can clean mine. Your children can also help. As you know, my children are at school all day and I'm left at home with too many chores to do."

Janpary could barely believe what she was hearing. She couldn't look at her sister-in-law while she was speaking and had been drawing lines on the floor with her fingers, but now she faced her.

"Naseema! Why don't you have any feeling of kindness toward me? I'm a woman and a mother just like you. The only thing I have is this small house, and now you want me to leave this to come and be your servant?"

"Yes, I want you to be my servant! Do you expect me to treat you like a queen?"

At this, Janpary began crying and shouting. "Naseema, be scared of God's anger. Look at my children. I have hopes for them. I too want to send my children to school but you want them to become your servants?"

Naseema said, "For a young woman who roams around other people's houses all day, surely it's better to stay out of sight in your brother's house. It must be preferable to serve your brother and his children rather than wash a strange man's dirty *shalwar*!"

"The sister of a shameless brother like mine has to wash strangers' *shalwars*. If my brother, who lost his sister in a bet, doesn't feel ashamed then why should I? If my sister-in-law is trampling all over me and my four children then why should I be their servant? It offends me to call you my family. Shame on you, woman, shame on you!"

Naseema seemed so angry it looked as if she was about to tear her own clothes in rage. "You *faihsha* (whore)! Go and sleep with the men you work for because you didn't get enough attention from your gambler husband. You'll do anything to shame your brother in the village."

Janpary's children started wailing. Janpary had to restrain herself from lashing out at her sister-in-law.

"Naseema, I came to you in private to ask your husband for my share but now I'm forced to go to court to claim what is mine. I'm going to take every rupee I'm owed by you and your family. God has given me this right."

At this Naseema stood up. "Listen to you! Who do you think you are? Where have you got all this talk of court from? It's from those men you spend all your time with. They must have filled your head with this nonsense."

Janpary's face went red and then pale. "For God's sake, woman, don't insult me just because I'm poor and a widow! How dare you say these terrible things in front of my children? Have you no fear of God? Islam has given me this right."

Janpary went up to Naseema and grabbed her chin—a sign of pleading. "Please don't insult me. I beg you!"

Naseema pushed Janpary's hands away. "Janpary, I'm not stupid. I know you had no idea about this *meeras* nonsense. You're obviously one of those women who sleep around with men. One of your men must have shown you these kind of shameless things."

Janpary gripped Naseema's hand tightly and told her to leave her house immediately. Naseema shoved her back hard. "I'll be telling your brother what you've done today. Just you wait and see what's going to happen to you."

After her sister-in-law had gone, Janpary sat on the floor in the middle of the room, surrounded by her four children. "God, do you ever listen to a widow like me?" she implored. "What should I do? Please show me a way out." She and the children all sobbed and hugged one another.

Naqib said, "Mother, I'm not going to let Aunt Naseema come here again. I don't like how she talks to you. Is it true what she says about you meeting men?"

Janpary was shocked and upset that her own son now appeared to be questioning her. She told him that he would have to wait until he was grown up before he could understand his mother's situation. "I hope I'm still alive when that day comes," she said, mournfully.

Naqib fell silent. He and his brothers and sister were tired. Janpary too was exhausted but it was a long and lonely night for her as she worried about what to do.

Early next morning Janpary rose to say her prayers and to start cooking the children their breakfast. She went into the room where they were sleeping and gently kissed each one on the forehead. At that moment, Janpary decided to take her *meeras* from her brother no matter the personal cost.

Janpary began her cleaning while Bibi was still asleep, impatient for her mistress to wake up so she could get some more advice. At about nine o'clock Bibi finally surfaced. Janpary made tea for her and began to explain how her sister-in-law had insulted her. Bibi said Janpary should go to the police station in the city and get legal advice, offering to send the guard with her. Janpary was frightened at the prospect of doing this but she daren't refuse because she was determined to fight for her right. She had made that decision and was going to stick to it.

Janpary promised Bibi that she would finish all her work when she returned and got into the car with the guard. They had to pretend that they were brother and sister because if the Taliban had found out she was out of the house with a man she was not related to they would consider it *haram*—something that is forbidden in Islam. The Taliban believe you must have a legal and Islamic relationship with the man you are with on the street; they call that man *mahram*.

This was the first time in her life that Janpary had gone to an official place for legal advice. She was nervous about talking to officials about her *meeras*. She sat on a wooden chair, which had been placed in front of large desk in a dark and dusty room. A Talib with a small black turban, a long beard and with eyes that had been underlined with kohl looked at her, and asked, "What is it you want? Why are you here?"

Janpary's hands were trembling. She had heard stories of how the Taliban had beaten up women on the streets. Her voice could barely be heard since her head was facing the floor and was hidden beneath her *burqa*.

"Mullah Saab, I need to get my *meeras* from my brother. We are Muslim and I have asked him for my share of our inheritance. I'm poor and a widow and have four children. I only have a few more days' work left and after that there'll be no more money so I don't know how I'll feed my children."

The mullah snorted. "So what do you want us to do?" He laughed sarcastically and the two police officers who were standing nearby joined in laughing too.

"What? Do you want me to beat him up?"

"No, Saab, I just want to have my *meeras*."

The mullah took some details down about her brother. He ordered Janpary to go home and told her she must not come to the police station again. He said he would look into her case and if she were legally right, they would take the *meeras* from her brother.

Janpary couldn't wait to leave the suffocating atmosphere of the office. She got into the car and told the guard what had happened.

"Oh, Janpary, I can tell you they won't do a thing. Unless their senior mullah orders them, they completely ignore all calls for help from poor people."

Janpary told the guard how the Taliban had warned her not to return and the guard nodded, as it confirmed his view that they would do nothing.

Back at Bibi's house Janpary told her what the police had promised to do. Bibi said this was as much as could be expected and it might put her brother under pressure. They should hope for the best. And so Janpary went back to her work: cleaning, washing, and brushing. When she was free to go home she walked home slowly, feeling an enormous burden on her shoulders.

As usual her daughter was waiting by the door for her. When she saw her mother, the girl began crying; her face was pale.

"Mummy, Uncle is here and he's very angry. He says he's going to beat you."

Janpary told her daughter not to be frightened because her uncle could not harm either of them, but still the girl tugged at her mother's *burqa* and urged her not to go inside.

When Janpary entered the house she saw her brother sitting together with his eldest son. She greeted him but he did not respond. Instead he stood up, walked across to her, and slapped her hard on the face. Janpary's children immediately began crying and pleading with their uncle to stop. Janpary had no strength to defend herself; she only asked why he was doing this to her: "What sort of weak man are you that you beat a woman? What kind of brother are you?"

At this, he hit her even harder, knocking her to the floor, and shouted, "You shameless woman, you went to the police so now the whole village knows about our affairs. You've brought shame on me and my family."

And he started kicking Janpary as she lay on the floor. Naqib grabbed his uncle's hand and sank his teeth into the flesh, but he in turn was badly beaten by his cousin, who was a lot older and bigger than him. Janpary felt the blows as if they had been inflicted on her body.

Her children screamed for help but no one came. Finally, Janpary's brother took a stick and began to strike her, hitting her as if she were an animal. She tried to shout but nothing would come out. She saw her children crying helplessly and her son bruised and battered. Her brother beat her until he became tired. Her face, hands, back, and legs were swollen and covered in cuts and bruises. As her brother left, he warned her to keep quiet or the next time they would all be killed.

"Janpary, this is your punishment for going to the police. Everywhere you go, I'll find out. Whatever you do, I'll know about it. Remember what happened to Khan's daughter? They killed her. If you don't keep quiet your children will lose another parent. I'll make them orphans if you don't shut your ugly mouth! Girls have no rights to *meeras*. There's no such thing here. The bitches who have got them are wrong. You should remember that you were a married woman. I'm not responsible for your widowhood. If you can't stand it why don't you marry again? This is the last time you mention the word *meeras*."

Janpary couldn't move from the floor. Her children crowded round her.

"I don't want to be killed," her daughter said. "I want you and my brothers to live. Please don't ask for the *meeras* again. I promise not to ask for food. We can go and beg on the streets but don't go to Uncle's house again."

Janpary's eyes were so swollen from the beating that she could barely see her daughter. She tried to stand with difficulty. The children rushed to help her. Once up, she hugged them close to her.

"My children, *toba*! I have said *toba* (never ever again) to the *meeras*. Women like me don't have any rights in this country. We must stay quiet; we cannot speak. Our voices are not heard."

That night, her children lay around her sleeping on the floor but Janpary could not sleep. She sat like a ghost in the middle of the room. She muttered to herself that women must stay silent otherwise they will share the same fate as Khan's daughter.

꩜

In Afghanistan it is taboo for women to talk about inheritance. Some families do consider their daughters when sharing out the inheritance but it is a rare occurrence. Tradition usually overshadows religion. Few people are properly knowledgeable about Islam and so cultural practice becomes confused with religious doctrine. Sometimes this confusion is deliberate. Women are, in the main, dependent on men. An Afghan woman never has her own house. When she is young, it is her father's house, when she is married it is considered her husband's or in-laws' house, and when she is old it is said she lives with her son.

Some families are aware that the Quran says women should also inherit a share of what their parents or closest relatives leave but most women and girls are not included and they suffer like Janpary. They are too frightened to go to the courts and petition for their rights because going to a court is seen as a shameful thing for a woman to do. Women who fight for their share of inheritance usually fail. In a male-dominated society like Afghanistan, it is the men who decide their fate and, of course, they mostly make their decisions to suit themselves rather than the women.

Janpary was left wishing she had never consulted Bibi. Sometimes it pays to remain ignorant, she thought. She told her children that their mother should not have stretched out her legs beyond the duvet; she should not have tried to reach beyond her means. Women like her should stay silent and accept their lot.

The next day, Janpary had bruises all over her body but she returned to Bibi's house. She accepted this experience as part of her fate and continued to work in the big house as a cleaner.

꩜

IF YOU GO TO an Afghan village and ask a woman who has not been to school and has no education about her Islamic rights, she would probably tell you about all the traditional rules that she has followed and that her mother, her grandmother, and her aunts have always followed. Information about Islamic rights and the law of the country is very limited. Some human rights organizations have started to give this kind of information to women in villages, but access to those women in remote areas is very limited.

I remember accompanying my mother to a party at the home of an Afghan family who were marking the birth of their son after four girls. It was a happy atmosphere, and we were all served delicious Afghan food. When the party finished and we were going home, the boy's mother gave gifts to my mother and other older women who had come to the gathering. I asked her why she was giving us gifts when she had already gone to so much effort. She said, "I have given birth to a son!"

"But have you given gifts on the birth of your daughters?" I asked.

"Oh no! If I don't do this on the birth of my son, as my mother says, I will be committing a sin!"

To me this illustrates how mixed up my country's traditions have become with its religion. There is nothing in our religion that says you must give away gifts on the birth of your son or you will be seen as a sinner. But many women justify their behavior by convincing themselves that a custom is in fact religious law or duty, when in fact most religious rules are limited to prayers and fasting. Lack of education is chiefly to blame, but these traditions are also maintained at home in each family, and passed down from mother to mother.

10
Layla's Story
THE WAR WIDOW

*L*AYLA WAS SITTING IN FRONT OF THE *DEGDAAN* (A WOOD-BURNING stove made of clay) cooking a meat stew called *shorba* for her family. As she stirred the pot, she sang quietly to herself.

The light of the fire under the pot of *shorba* gave her face a glow; her eyes were red and bright. She dried her tears with the edge of her scarf and wiped her nose. Layla wasn't paying much attention to the pot or to the *degdaan*. She kept stirring, and with each movement of her right hand she remembered the innocent faces of her children. She wondered what they would be eating, how they were sleeping, and who was looking after them.

Suddenly she heard Shakira, her sister-in-law, shouting at her. "Layla! Layla! What are you doing? Can't you smell the food burning?"

Shakira grabbed the spoon from Layla's hand and waved it in front of her face. "You crazy woman, this meat doesn't come free. My husband has to work hard all day for it. All you have to do is cook it but you can't even do that properly. Move out of the way, you useless woman."

"I'm sorry. I was just thinking about—"

"What were you thinking about?" asked Shakira. "Another man?"

Layla started crying and got up to fetch water for the pot. When she returned Shakira passed her back the spoon.

"When you're asked to cook, cook properly. Concentrate and don't mess up expensive food. Otherwise what will we eat, the poison you bring to our house? Hah!"

Layla didn't look at her sister-in-law. Instead, she examined the stove, moving some of the wood so the fire burned better. Layla was wearing a light blue dress that had lost its original color over time and was covered in dark patches from soot. Her skin was dry and flaky from washing pots every day; it was a long while since she had used any cream on her face or hands, and it was even longer since her face had glowed with happiness. She checked that the *shorba* was ready, lifted the large black pot for boiling water, which she had filled from the well earlier, and put it to stand on the last flames of the fire. Before going back in the house she rearranged the scarf on her head, making sure it covered her chest.

The family was all sitting together. Shakira was talking with her husband and the children were watching the television, powered by the generator. Shakira would only allow the generator to be on for a few hours at dinnertime so she and the children could watch their favorite program. Layla was never allowed to watch the soaps she so enjoyed. She glanced at the TV as she walked into the room. Shakira's eyes were on her.

"Layla! We're hungry; hurry up and bring us the food. Your brother here wants to wash his hands too."

Her brother broke in saying his son could bring the water for washing hands but Shakira said, "No, can't you see the poor child is busy watching television and he's hungry?"

Without any fuss, Layla went to fetch a pail of water and all the family washed their hands as she poured for them. She lay the food out on the *desterkhan* and the family gathered round it. Then Shakira took charge, distributing the meat to her husband and children and selecting the biggest piece for herself.

Layla sat in the corner of the room—she wouldn't touch the food until her sister-in-law gave her permission. Finally, Shakira looked at the bowl of *shorba* and said, "Layla, there's not enough meat for you so you may have what's left of the *shorba*."

As Layla served herself, Shakira turned to her husband. "You know the price of food has gone up; it's become really expensive and it's very difficult for me to feed an extra adult."

Layla stared into her brother's eyes. This wasn't the first time she had felt a burden to her brother and his family. Nor was it the first time she had been humiliated for eating her brother's food. Shakira was always complaining that Layla was an extra mouth to feed and forever instructing the children to tell their aunt to leave.

Layla gathered up the *desterkhan*, then went out to the wood-burning stove, carrying a little oil burner so she could see her way in the dark. She poured hot water onto the green tea in the pot and brought it inside for Shakira and her husband. Shakira told Layla to get the beds ready for the children and said she could sleep too after doing that. Layla just nodded and left the room.

Layla slept in a small room in the corner of the yard. She had spent the whole day doing chores in the house and she was very tired. After taking off her scarf she got under an old and unwashed duvet. She tried to sleep because she knew she would have another exhausting day of housework ahead of her, punctuated by Shakira's nagging, but every time Layla closed her eyes, her thoughts would go back to the circumstances that had led her to be living in these conditions.

She remembered a time when she was a young girl in this same house; she remembered a Layla who was loved and cared for by her father and mother and close to her brothers. At that time she hardly ever came to this room, the one she now slept in. It had been a storage room before destiny had brought her here. As memories of her childhood and teenage years came back, she found herself smiling—but where was the joy and happiness now?

⤨

LAYLA'S LIFE STORY WAS brought to *Afghan Woman's Hour* by Tabasum, one of our reporters, who had been on a trip to Takhar Province. Takhar is one of the most developed provinces in the northeast of Afghanistan. It has twelve districts and the provincial capital is Taloqan; it is connected to Tajikistan by the Amoo River. Before the civil war people were able to cross the border using small boats. The Amoo River makes the land around it green and fertile for growing crops. Someone from Takhar once told me, "My province has such rich land that even the mountains are covered not with stones but soil. We grow wheat, rice, and corn everywhere. We even gather food from our mountains, and in spring they're a beautiful mix of green and yellow colors."

Uzbeks are the main ethnic group in this province, followed by Tajiks, Pashtuns, and Hazaras. Like every other region of Afghanistan, national traditions are followed. Boys are more valued than girls, parents arrange marriages for their daughters, and women and girls are dependent on the men in their family. However, both girls and boys go to school. Families tend to allow girls the opportunity of education but there are still young marriages, and it is common for a girl to stop going to school once she is married. People from Takhar are mainly farmers; the men work on the land and the women do household work and weave *gelims* (carpets).

Layla grew up in a very poor family but she was happy with what she had: her mother, father, and brothers all around her. She used to go to the girls' school in the village every morning, and she was lively and popular with her classmates. Like other girls in her village, Layla had been taught weaving and embroidery by her mother, and her perfect embroideries were much admired. Her delicate stitching would be applied to make clothes for the neighbors' babies, and with the money she was paid Layla could buy herself things she wanted: notebooks, pens, hair clips, bangles, and scarves. But when she was thirteen years old her life changed very abruptly, just as it did for many ordinary Afghan girls in her village.

After school, Layla and the other girls used to rush to the village man who sold iced water from a cart in front of the school. Dressed in black dresses and trousers with white scarves around their heads, hundreds of girls would come streaming out in groups, all hurrying to get to the cart first. They were boisterous and loud. Layla was known as the girl who always made it to the cart first to buy cold, fresh water.

She was popular among the girls and they would follow her everywhere she went.

One hot, sunny day, Layla ran fast in the dust to get to the cart.

"Uncle, I need five glasses of water with ice."

She was breathing heavily from the exertion.

The ice-water man laughed. "Once again, Layla, you have beaten all the other girls to get here first. I'll give free cold water to the winner."

Layla and her friends drank the water and then walked in a line, holding their books on the top of their heads to protect them from the sun's strong rays. At around three o'clock in the afternoon, Layla arrived at the front of her house and said good-bye to her classmates. The chickens were sitting quietly in their cages; the dog ran toward her, barking with excitement. She stroked its head and said hello. Her mother came out smiling and kissed her daughter on her forehead. Layla was happy to see her mother but thought it was unusual that she should greet her in this way. She asked her mother if she had missed her a lot and asked why.

Her mother put some sweets into her mouth and said, "The time has come. You have grown up. This is your own sweet."

Layla understood what her mother meant: another family had come to their house to ask that Layla should marry their son and today her parents had decided to give Layla to them. She ran into the house because she was very shy and only thirteen years old. Getting married at that age was customary among the people of their village. Layla didn't mind about the marriage: she knew the family would give a large amount of money to her father who was poor and badly needed it. But she also knew that she would be paying a high price for this, as she would no longer be allowed to go to school, and this was a bitter disappointment. She suggested her mother could ask her in-laws if she could continue to go to school, but Layla's education meant little to her mother and she didn't want to damage the chances of the marriage taking place by putting conditions on it. Layla had no choice but to accept the marriage and leave school.

Layla's fiancé was a member of the national army. His family wanted to have the wedding soon and Layla's family agreed with them. Layla started family life with her in-laws in Takhar. Her husband was kind and considerate to her. He was a young soldier and Layla was quite happy with her life. He was a softly spoken and caring man and Layla soon came love to him. At the age of fourteen, Layla had her first baby. Her husband, who was usually away on duty, could only come home once or twice a month. Her life now consisted of waiting for her love to return; every time he came back safely she thanked God for her good fortune. During wartime many young soldiers didn't make it home.

⤳

DURING THE CIVIL WAR between the communists and Mujahedeen, the loss of a father, husband, or son was an everyday occurrence. One day my mother stopped to count the war widows in our own family. There were six women who had lost their husbands in the fight with the Mujahedeen in my family alone. One of my mother's cousins, a soldier, was killed in a battle with the Mujahedeen in the east of Afghanistan. My first cousin, Abdul Karim, was killed in a fight with Mujahedeen forces in Kandahar. He was a commando officer during the Soviet era in Afghanistan. I remember my aunt crying for her young son on the day of his funeral. The whole family gathered at my uncle's house in Kabul. My aunt kept hitting herself and calling out the name of her son. I had wished it had been his older brother who had been killed. At the time I thought my aunt loved Abdul Karim the most and that if the other brother had died she wouldn't have been so upset, but these were just the confused thoughts of a nine-year-old girl upset at her aunt's distress.

I remember seeing another Afghan mother who was crying for her two sons who had been killed in the war. She was singing and crying at the same time: "Hey, Revolution, may your house be set on fire. There isn't a single Afghan family which isn't mourning for their handsome young men. They have been sacrificed for you: Revolution, may God set you on fire!"

According to the United Nations, there are over one and a half million war widows in Afghanistan and more than fifty thousand live in Kabul. Of course, this is only an estimate. No one knows the exact number. There are widows from the war between the Mujahedeen and the Soviet Union and from the later war between the Mujahedeen and Taliban.

Losing a much-loved son in a war is obviously difficult for any parent, but for those young women who lost their husbands, fortune dealt them an additional blow. Becoming a widow in a traditional society like Afghanistan means you lose the right to talk freely, you lose the right to put on makeup and dress up. Instead, a good widow takes care of her dignity. She wears black, doesn't comb her hair, or take any pride in her appearance.

During my first year working at *Afghan Woman's Hour* I received so many stories from widows, and each one of them could have filled a program. They told of their hopes and fears of remarrying, of the economic hardship they lived in, and of the uncertainty for their children. Each story was heartbreaking. Sometimes, it was almost impossible to organize the weekly schedule because every story felt so important and they couldn't all be included. It seemed to me as if those women were calling on me to tell their stories to the world: "Please, dear Zari, tell my story!"

On one of my visits to Kabul I organized a prerecorded discussion with two widows who had lost their husbands in the war. These two middle-aged women arrived at our studios with their *burqas*. I asked them to try to describe how a war widow feels.

Tears flowed from their eyes and I found myself crying too. My male colleague, who was recording the interview, was moved by our tears. It was an uncomfortable situation; my questions had hurt them. Their tears told me more than words how an Afghan war widow feels and the dirty and torn *burqas* told me what sort of lives these women were living. Finally, one of them looked up at me.

"Zari dear, first of all I want to thank you for asking us this question."

I said there was no need to thank me, that it was quite normal to ask about someone's feelings.

At that point, the other woman spoke: "Zari dear, you're right. It is a normal question to ask, but do you know why our tears flowed so quickly? In all the years we have been widows, not one person has asked us how it feels to be one."

"I've been a widow for ten years; no one has dared to ask how I feel—not even old friends from my parents' village."

"The listeners of *Afghan Woman's Hour* want to know about your feelings," I said, moved by their words. "We care about how you feel. Please tell us what it's like to be a war widow."

Tears welled up again in one of the widow's eyes.

"I can sum it up in one simple sentence. An Afghan widow is like a pot without a lid. People around her throw things into the pot but they don't put the lid on. They say things and gossip about her, they treat her badly, and when she asks for help they run away. She is helpless and hopeless."

The other woman put it like this: "An Afghan widow feels as if she is being watched all the time. Her actions are observed."

Both women spoke at length and this program was one of the most listened to we've ever made. Afterwards, a male colleague said to me, "Zari dear, with this program you've touched the hearts of mothers, daughters, fathers, brothers, and every family member of these widows. I wish you more success."

The program brought to our attention the life story of a nineteen-year-old war widow. She lived with her extended family of in-laws. She told us that after her husband died, the only single man in his family was his seventeen-year-old brother. She said that when her husband was alive she was like an older sister to his younger brother but a year after her husband died she was expected to marry him. She cried as I spoke to her.

"Zari dear, when I was asked to marry my brother-in-law, I felt as if my in-laws had killed me. They didn't see the dead body, which was standing in front of them. I felt as if they had destroyed all feelings and dignity within me. I wanted to shout and tell them he was like a younger brother or son to me. I used to wash his clothes with my children's clothes; I used to make him food when he did the shopping for me. How could I sleep with him now? But I was given a very limited choice. Either I married my youngest brother-in-law or I left my children with his family and returned to my parents' home. My parents were poor; my brothers were all married and were not in a position to look after me. Anyway, how could I leave my children? A year after my husband's death, I died, my soul died, and my belief in humanity died. I cried out. I shouted at my mother-in-law and to my brothers-in-law who were older and married, I asked them to accept me as their servant but my mother-in-law refused and reissued the ultimatum."

This is a usual tradition in Afghan society. Many families have arranged the marriages of the widows of their brothers-in-law, cousins, or other family members. If the widow decides to marry someone outside the family, she is forced to lose her children. In Afghanistan, the in-laws see the children as belonging to them, as family blood, and feel they have the right to take them from their mother.

This woman told us she felt she had no choice but to marry her younger brother-in-law. In this kind of situation, the men are victims too. The woman told us how the young boy was forced to sleep with her. He was locked in the bedroom with her. She cried and he cried. She said, "He shouted like a little boy to me: 'How can I do this to my brother's wife?'

"He was right, we couldn't do it. For me he was my dead beloved's brother and for him I was his lovely sister-in-law who washed his clothes. But you know, now we are both older, he decided to marry a second wife as he never wanted me. After a few years of marriage we did have sex but I didn't have any children with him. He's lucky, though; he's a man and when he got older, the family accepted his desire for a second wife. I, however, had to become a servant. Now I have to clean, cook, and wash for him and his wife. I am just the servant."

⤙⤚

As AN AFGHAN WOMAN, Layla knew very well about the wretched lives of widows—she had met some and she had a widow in her family. That is why she worried about losing her husband every day. After five years of marriage, she was the mother of four children, still living with her in-laws and waiting for her husband to return from fighting. At nineteen, her worst fears came true. When it was time for his leave, Layla's husband didn't come home. There was a week of anxiety, a week of hope that he might return, but this was crushed when his comrades brought his body to her house. Layla and all of his family were devastated. Her husband had been killed in a war with the Mujahedeen, defending his country. For Layla it wasn't only the pain of losing her husband and coping with looking after four fatherless children that troubled her; the fact that she was still very young and pretty was another huge difficulty. Her husband had been her protection in many ways, apart from providing for her and the children: he was a safeguard for her honor. She was nothing without him.

To be widowed at such a young age meant a loss of freedom. If she dared laugh at something, her in-laws, especially her mother-in-law, would comment that she was shameless and had no respect for the soul of her martyred husband. Her mother-in-law shouted at her whenever she wore clean or colorful clothes. And when her brother-in-law got married, she was viewed as a malevolent force who might affect the bride with what they called "her dark shade." Only her children were allowed to go near the new bride. Layla's mother-in-law warned her that if she went near the girl, she would bring bad luck and her son, the groom, might also die. At weddings and other celebrations, Layla would wear simple black clothing. Her lips were usually dry because she wasn't allowed to put on any makeup.

The mother-in-law was nervous that someone might take advantage of her son's widow and bring dishonor to the family. If Layla ventured to the door to look for her children in the street, the family would accuse her of hunting for a man. She had to watch her every step. Years of living like this ground her down. With all the negative talk against her, Layla became pale, hungry, and tired. She kept herself hidden under a large scarf so her husband's family couldn't see her body. The less visible she was, the happier the family was, but whatever she did, Layla and her four children were still treated as an unwelcome burden on the family.

No one ever bothered to inquire how she was feeling; nobody held her hand or let her weep as she told them how she had lost the closest person in her life. No one ever asked if she needed anything for her four young children.

One night, Layla's mother-in-law entered her room and told Layla that as she was still very young, she must marry her younger son, Layla's brother-in-law. She didn't say it in a caring way; instead, she informed Layla that she would actually prefer it if she didn't marry her other son because she was clearly bad luck.

"You ate one of my sons and now the men of the family have to decide whether or not you should marry his brother. If you refuse to marry him, then you must leave our house."

Layla's tears were flowing. She looked at her four children who were sleeping and said to her mother-in-law, "You know my husband's soul won't let me marry his brother. His brother is like my brother. I don't want to marry him."

In some respects Layla was lucky: many young Afghan widows are given no choice and are forced to marry whoever the family decides they should. At least Layla's mother-in-law didn't force her. Layla told her that she would leave the next day for her parents' home. The mother-in-law reminded Layla that as they had looked after her for so long she had no right to take anything from the house. This meant Layla couldn't take any of the gifts her husband had given her or any household items they had bought together. She and the children could only take the clothes they were wearing.

Layla returned to her parents' home but when she got there she discovered things had changed. She was no longer the pretty, fresh-faced, and pure thirteen-year-old who could be exchanged for a large amount of money. Instead, she was a tired and used woman. Layla felt like a shriveled-up flower. This time, her return home wasn't as a guest; she and her four children were homeless and had to be fed every day. She had no money and had been allowed to take nothing from her marriage.

Sometimes Layla's brother would return home from work with his pockets full of sweets for his own children. Layla's children would wait expectantly in the doorway, hoping their uncle would give them some too, but he never did. Their eyes would follow him in but all they could do was look on helplessly and hopelessly. They had lost their father and their security. All they had was a mother who was unable to provide for them.

Layla's mother and brothers would complain at having to bear the extra cost of her and her children so she would try to make up for it by cleaning the house, washing clothes, and cooking. She became like a slave to her sisters-in-law. Only her father seemed to care and understand her needs but he was a poor, helpless man. He was getting old and could only watch and share the pain his daughter was in.

Since Layla had left school early and had not completed her education, she was unable to get a well-paid job. She earned money by cleaning other people's houses and sewing clothes. She gave everything she earned to her mother for her keep but her mother was still angry with her because she hadn't been able to bring anything with her from her husband's home. Her in-laws had kept everything.

After a year and a half of widowhood, her father couldn't cope with his daughter living under these conditions so he decided to have her married again. At first Layla wasn't in love with her second husband but she respected him because he was kind to her children. It was the time of the civil war during the Soviet Union era. Her second husband was also in the Afghan national army fighting in the civil war under the Soviet-protected government.

By marrying again, Layla freed herself from the nagging of her parents. She started wearing new clothes, washing her hair, and going to weddings. On Eid and at New Year, her children, once again, had new clothes and good food. Time passed, and Layla was pleased to find herself pregnant with her new husband's child. She had got used to him and missed him when he was away. She was impatient for his return from the army.

Layla's life had certainly improved with marriage, but her happiness was short-lived. On the day her husband was due home after three months' absence she got the children up early and told them to wash and dress in clean clothes. They were under strict instructions to keep themselves and the house clean. Her husband was usually home by midday, so she cooked rice and meat, and bought lots of sweets. Layla was desperate to tell him about her pregnancy. She wanted to celebrate his return, the new baby, and, most of all, to show him how much she had missed him and that she now felt she was in love with him.

She put on eyeliner and red lipstick, something she had not done for a very long time. Her face glowed with excitement, but she was also a little fearful because past experience had taught her to expect bad news. Layla waited outside by the door under the heat of the midday sun. She looked down the road but couldn't see anyone coming. She called to her son: "Your father must be busy chatting to the shopkeeper. Go and tell him to hurry home because the food is ready."

Her son ran out and down the street. After a short while he returned and said the shopkeeper hadn't seen his father at all. Layla started to worry that it would be bad news again. She snapped at the children for fussing and making a noise. The food got cold and the children became hungry. She let them eat while she sat by the door until the light of the day faded.

Evening came and it was dark but Layla's husband still hadn't come home. She went back into the house, changed out of her new clothes, and washed her makeup off. Once again, she felt that she had no right to wear such things. Layla tried to stop terrible thoughts from coming into her mind and find a simple explanation for his absence. Perhaps he had missed the bus to the village and would get the early one the following morning. When night came, Layla went to bed praying for his safe return. This was all she could do.

Early the next morning, Layla heard someone knocking on the door. She hurriedly put a scarf on her head and ran to the door. She was smiling as she opened the door, expecting to see her husband there and give him a big hug. Instead, she was confronted with two army officers. Layla knew her worst fears were true. She didn't hear what they said as she collapsed at the door.

In Afghanistan, widows are shunned by society. Those who have been widowed twice, like Layla, are considered a particularly bad omen for men. Other women call them "man eaters."

After a few months her baby was born—a daughter—but she was barely capable of looking after her children. Whenever she walked in the village women would give her vicious looks. She wasn't allowed to go to weddings or go near brides because people said she would bring misfortune. Being widowed for the second time depressed her, and she started to believe the superstitions herself. Even Layla's family made her feel as if she were an evil woman responsible for her husbands' deaths.

It didn't take long for another sad period in her life to start. This time it concerned the fate of her children. People around her were unkind and selfish. Layla went to her parents for the second time. This time she had another baby with her, so she had no choice but to obey her brother's wife and act like a servant. The one bright hope she had was for a better future for her children. She began to take more care of them. She provided for her children by accepting any work she could. She washed people's clothes, cleaned their houses, and fetched water in exchange for money. She saved enough to send her children to school. Almost every night she would tell her eldest son how he should look after his sisters and mother when he got older and how his father had wanted him to become an engineer. She also told him stories of his father's bravery and how he had lost his life fighting for his country. But Layla's hopes for a better life with her children didn't last long. Her in-laws from her first marriage came to her house and said they wanted their grandchildren back. She roared at them with the rage of a wild animal.

"Do you people not have any fear of God? These children are mine!"

She was crying and her children were crying and clinging on to her. "They're my life. I'll die without them. I'm only living for them."

Layla began slapping her own face, screaming, and cursing, but her mother-in-law was unmoved. "When a widow marries a stranger she loses her children. You have no right to them anymore. We'll take them into our custody."

Layla looked desperately for ways to stop this happening. She asked her brother and other family members for help but they weren't keen because the burden on them would be reduced if the children were taken. Her brother listened to his wife Shakira more than anyone else, and she had said that according to Sharia law Layla would not be able to keep her children.

Layla discovered a new strength born from the fear of losing her beloved children. She decided to fight as a mother for her rights and turned to the courts. According to Sharia law the family of the children's father have a claim to the children if the father is dead. The mother's claim to keep her children is weak if she is not in a strong financial position to take care of them. Layla was poor and she lost her case.

The grief of widowhood felt nothing in comparison to the pain of losing her children. Layla lost all hope. She hardly ever saw them. She asked people how they were and friends told her that the grandparents were looking after them well. That did allay some of her fears, but she still missed them terribly and found living away from them the hardest thing to bear.

Layla would tell the other women in her village how she now felt like a stone. She said that nothing else could hurt her after the pain of losing the children from her first marriage. Most of the women in the village felt sorry for her and some gave her food, believing that if they helped a woman suffering like Layla they would be loved by God.

A few years later, when Layla was living with her parents, Mujahedeen fighters came to her village and everything changed again. Layla's brother lost his job, while those who supported the Mujahedeen saw their fortunes rise. They acquired money, guns, and land, but Layla's family saw no such benefit. Then one day, one of the local warlords spotted Layla in the village—Layla was still young and pretty. The warlord visited her parents' home to ask for her hand in marriage. Her family was poor; they had no means by which to fight for her and refuse his offer so they gave in. Layla was given to the warlord in exchange for money and food.

She was used to being married off and letting those around her decide her future, so she saw little point in protesting. She had lost all belief in love and human kindness. Even though she was still in her twenties, she'd been through enough experience for a woman forty years older. She had become like an unloved ornament in a dark corner of the house. With no help given or sympathy offered, she had gradually stopped speaking and spent days and nights in silence. She cooked and cleaned in other people's houses but took no care of herself. She felt like the ugliest and most helpless woman in the world. She just wanted to be left alone with her pain.

Her new husband realized he had married a ghost of a woman and, in frustration, found excuses to beat her. He used to tell her he felt cheated because she didn't respond to him in any way. He would insult her every time he slept with her. Once, he even kicked her off the bed saying, "You've tasted two men already; that's why you're like a stone with me."

His words didn't hurt Layla; she would just stare at him and leave the room. Layla was, at least, content that her warlord husband no longer paid her any attention. He was busy with his own activities and she wasn't interested in finding out what he was really doing. His family's treatment of her baby daughter was neglectful and cruel so she asked the girls' grandparents to look after her. It was during this period that Layla's father died. He was old but he was the only person Layla had felt close to and the only one who had understood her suffering.

With so many losses in her life, when she went to bed at night, she couldn't choose which loss to focus her mind on: her first loving husband; her second husband, whom she had just begun to love; her children, who were taken away from her; or her father, who had seen and felt her pain but had been powerless to help.

Layla's marriage to her warlord husband was very unhappy and turned her into an old woman at a young age. Although her marriage to him lasted longer than either of her first two marriages, he too died in the end, and Layla became a widow for the third time. He was killed by his enemies but no one in his family could find out the exact reason why. Instead, they blamed Layla for bringing about his death. They accused her of "eating him" and for being "a woman of dark steps." The women in his family abused and blamed her: "Your bad steps killed him," they would say.

Layla's response was, "All of you knew I had been married twice before, so why did you want me to marry him? I didn't choose to marry him."

She wrapped her large black scarf around her head and body and left their home that instant. Now that her parents had died, she returned to the only place she had left to take refuge in: her brother's house. Her brother couldn't refuse her without bringing massive shame on the family; and there she remained.

~❧~

LAYLA GOT UP FROM her bed and looked out of the small window. She felt she had lived her life once again by remembering every little detail of it. How tired she was of being humiliated by her sister-in-law Shakira. She looked up at the clear sky and a feeling of energy and power began to fill her. She would get up early and do all the jobs she was supposed to do. Then, when Shakira left the house, Layla would take her chance: she would go to a women's rights office in Takhar.

It was the first time she had found the strength to look for a better life. She was tired of being a burden on others. She was taken aback by the warmth and sympathy of the women she met there—she had lost her belief in kindness from her own sex. The woman listened to her story and, for the first time, Layla felt there was something she could do with her life. She explained how she had once been able to sew delicate and beautiful embroideries, but now all she did was household chores.

The women's rights activist arranged for Layla to get all the help she could. Layla started sewing again, concentrating on the style of embroidery she had done as a teenager. She poured all her energy and emotion into her work. Soon her embroideries were taken to a good market in Kabul, and were sent to exhibitions in the capital and in other cities in Afghanistan by the women's organization. Layla made money from her sales and was able to pay her brother for her food and keep.

In her mind she felt she was sewing for her daughters and sons, now older and busy with their own lives. She never saw her children again but it gave her satisfaction to think that they had at least grown up in a family where they were provided for. Her daughters still live in Takhar but she has heard they have been married into very strict families; her son lives far away in Iran.

Layla feels as if she has never had any control over her life. It is as if she has been thirteen years old three times over, as three times she has been given away to a man. It's not known exactly how many widows there are in Afghanistan at the moment, but many are young women with stories as tragic and shocking as Layla's.

11

Mahgul's Story

A FAMILY OF KITE-MAKERS

*A*FGHAN *WOMAN'S HOUR* WASN'T JUST A FORUM TO PROVIDE information to women about their rights; it was also meant to be a celebration of their achievements and a sharing of experiences. My colleagues and I set about creating a series of interviews with Afghan women who had used their skills and resourcefulness to bring change to their lives.

It was 2004 and Afghanistan was emerging from the political and cultural suppression it had been through during the rule of the Taliban and Mujahedeen. People were beginning to rebuild houses, and millions of Afghan refugees were returning from Iran and Pakistan. The security situation was improving but people were still struggling economically. We arranged interviews with an Afghan female judge, reporter, photographer, cleaner, and teacher. At that time, my editor and I worried that we would struggle to find enough successful women to fill the slots, wrongly assuming that after years of being denied an education and years of war and violence, it would be almost impossible for women to gain skills. How wrong we were! The women we found proved that you don't need a university education to bring about a positive change to your life.

As more women joined the reporting team, we were able to bring a greater variety of voices to the airwaves. We heard from a tailor, beautician, embroiderer, carpet weaver, engineer, baker, leather worker, farmer, and a woman who used to make artificial limbs for disabled war victims. These interviews received such a positive response, and many listeners—male and female—contacted us to say how much they appreciated the hard work of Afghan women.

⸙

MAHGUL IS FROM MAZAR e Sharif in the north of Afghanistan. It is the capital of Balkh Province and the fourth largest city. It is famous for its beautiful blue-tiled mosque in the city center. Some Muslims believe it is on the site of the tomb of Ali ibn Abi Talib, the cousin and son-in-law of the Prophet Muhammad. The name Mazar e Sharif means noble shrine.

Our reporter Mariam Ghamgusar spoke to Mahgul and discovered how she had used her talent and skill to bring hope back to her family, a family that had once lost all hope of a brighter future. Of all the enterprising women we spoke to, listeners told us that they learned the most from Mahgul's life story. One woman wrote that, "in our darkest hours we remembered the example of Mahgul and her words brought us hope and strength."

It was late afternoon and many children in my village in Balkh Province were out playing. It was a moment of relaxation for me too. I took the teapot, my cup, and our local sweet called *kunjed* and went to sit by the window. I massaged my aching hands and pulled on my fingers until they gave a satisfying click. I would do this a lot because the repetitive work I had to do made my hands very tired and stiff.

I opened the window so I could feel the fresh air on my face but it was colder than I expected and felt chilly on my skin. My fingers needed warmth so I wrapped them around the teacup and allowed the heat of the green tea to warm me up. I enjoyed the soothing breeze on my face and the glow of warmth around my fingers. I savored the moment: I felt as if my life was under control and I was creating a better future for my children.

I was thinking I ought to return to work when I heard a group of boys running along the road shouting, *"Azadi, Azadi."* *Azadi* is the kite that has been cut from its string by a rival kite and is now flying free. They were chasing after it and as they ran they kicked up a large dust cloud. I followed the boys' eyes and saw a large blue and yellow kite falling through the air. It was a square kite decorated with stars and a sun.

I watched the village boys run and shout after the kite, every single one of them desperate to possess it. High in the sky it seemed as if the kite was showing off, enjoying the fact that so many children desired it. They were dashing around in all directions but no one could catch hold of the string that was dangling down. The boys kept saying to one and another, "This kite is *chalak* (clever). We don't know which direction it's going in next. Bloody kite, why won't you come down?"

I laughed at the way the boys were talking to the kite and the way the kite sailed higher and higher, away from the boys. Quite a large group of boys had gathered by now, watching the kite fly freely through the air. Some tried to follow its every twist and turn, running to the left and then to the right. Others were content to stand and wait. I watched for several minutes. It seemed to me that the kite was dancing like a beautiful bride sought after by so many boys. Her colors were bright, with a small red star on the edge, and orange flames in the two corners to enhance her beauty. A moon-shape of yellow paper was stuck to the top of the kite, and when the wind blew, it looked as if the bride was smiling to herself while contemplating which lucky boy she would ultimately bestow her favors upon. I was enjoying the spectacle as much as the children, but I soon realized that I had drifted off and wasted precious time away from my work.

The boys had kicked up a lot of dirt when they chased the kite. I closed the window to shut out the dust, but the scene I had enjoyed so much was still in my mind and brought a smile to my face. I hadn't been aware how very tired I was. The sight of those happy children and the excitement that the kite had given them had a profound effect on me.

Just as I was taking my teapot and cup to the small kitchen I heard someone banging on the front door. It sounded familiar so I rushed to answer it, taking care to put on my head scarf as I did, just in case it was a stranger. (I could not open the door and be seen without a head scarf.)

"Who is it?" I asked as I opened the door. My two girls and two boys had just come home from school. Seeing their faces and knowing they had just returned from studying gave me such a feeling of pleasure and satisfaction—I knew that for every day that they went to school their future got brighter. I quickly made some food and we all sat and ate it around the *desterkhan*. I used to make them hearty and healthy food like vegetable soup. I made sure they ate a proper meal because we all had to work hard and as well as helping me they had to study too. We would eat our soup with fresh bread that I had made early in the morning. After we finished eating, each child knew what duty they were expected to carry out. My two daughters collected the dirty dishes and wiped clear the *desterkhan* while my sons and I began our daily work: kite-making.

I would start by cutting the large pieces of colored tissue paper, which were very delicate, whilst my sons concentrated on assembling the sticks to make the kite's frame and my daughters would focus on the decoration. They were good at the small details: from leftover pieces of paper they would cut shapes—hearts, stars, suns, moons, and flames—and stick them on the sides of the kites. My sons were expert at putting together the kites and knowing how to build them so they would fly strong and high. They understood where the string should be attached. I would watch them and be ready to help with the gluing. I didn't want them to use the glue because it can harm their young hands. Mine have already been damaged but I don't care because I've already had my youth. I want to take care of them now so they can lead a happy life when I'm not there to look after them.

After a couple of hours of hard work we would put away the kites and materials in a safe place. My sons love to fly kites themselves, so sometimes after our meal I let them go out and play with other boys, but not every day. I remind them how their situation is different to that of other children. My sons and daughters all go to school. They have to do their homework before it gets dark because there's no electricity and otherwise they cannot see what they're writing. I let them take turns—while one studies the other makes kites and then they swap.

This is my happy family, the family of Mahgul and her four children. What more can an Afghan mother want? I get pleasure from seeing the children in my village get excited playing with the kites that I and my children have made. From our window I can see some boys running after a kite that we have made with our own hands. We are a family of breadwinners. If you were to ask me how we got to this stage my answer would be, "Not easily!" I went through a lot of pain and suffering, starting back in 2001.

My husband was a taxi driver, and he used to take passengers on the main highway between Mazar and Pul-e-Khumri. We were poor but had a good enough life because he was hardworking and kind, and God gave us our four wonderful children. My husband had a small house, which had been left to him a long time ago by his parents. He had no other family members so my children and I were everything to him. He sometimes earned extra money at *Nowrooz* (Afghan New Year) and he would be busy taking people to the shrine of Hazrat Ali, the fourth Imam of Islam.

People would come from other provinces to Pul-e-Khumri and my husband would take the passengers to the shrine in Mazar for prayers. Women, men, boys, girls, elders, everyone wanted to visit Mazar; our city is considered holy because of the shrine and mosque. My husband was softhearted and even if it was getting late he would still take passengers who were ill and wanted to pray.

I used to tell him, "Look, you're getting tired and it's not safe to drive at night. I get worried when you don't come home on time. We don't want you to work any harder. We're content with what you can provide for us. We would rather have you at home."

He would smile at this. "You know, Mahgul, I enjoy working hard and taking passengers to the shrine. Going to those holy places gives me energy. And what's more I can earn extra money for you and our children. I want them to go to school and have books and pens so they can become teachers and doctors and not have to work as a taxi driver like me. My father didn't care if I went to school or not because he was a simple man who didn't understand the value of education, but I do. I can't read or write—that's why I'm just a taxi driver. Our children have me as their father and you as their mother and they know we will do anything to give them a better future."

He held my hand in his and massaged it. "I want my children to have all the things I never had. I love you, Mahgul, because you're such a wonderful wife and mother."

I loved the way he used to talk to me. After years of being married to him he became everything to me. The way he gave such love to me and the children was amazing. He had so much energy and enthusiasm for making the family happy. He took so little from us and gave us so much in return. He became my friend, my soul mate, my everything. On occasions he was even like a sister to me and we would gossip together. He was my support and my teacher in life as well as my husband and lover.

After a couple of years of marriage my mother complained that I didn't go and visit them as often as I should. "Mother, it's your mistake I don't visit very often." My mother was shocked and thought she had upset me in some way. She asked what kind of mistake. I smiled. "It's your mistake that you married me to this man I love so much."

At this my mother started laughing. I remember how happy my mother was to see me so content with my family. That's what every mother wishes for her daughter, isn't it? I would love my own daughters to be as happy in their marriages as I've been in mine. I can't forget what a kind and caring person my husband was from the first time I met him on my wedding day. Every memory of him brings joy to me, except the time when sorrow came to my heart and my world turned black. From that day onward I have felt incomplete.

I can recall every detail of that day. I woke up early that morning to find my husband sitting on the mattress and quietly drinking tea. It seemed odd to me. I got up and sat next to him.

"My dear, why didn't you wake me up? I would have made your tea for you?"

"Mahgul," he said softly, "why would I wake you? I didn't want to disturb you." He smiled and joked, "You were fast asleep and looked like you were having some sweet dreams."

"No, I had a frightening dream that woke me up. I didn't like it at all!"

He asked me in his kind voice, "What was the dream that scared my strong wife? Tell me about it."

"It was so frightening that I couldn't move. It felt as if I was frozen on the spot. I dreamt some kind of animal that I'd never seen before was chasing after us. You were trying to save me from this sort of dragon. We were holding hands and trying to escape but it was very windy and that made it harder for us to run. You were holding my hand tightly and pulling me along but the dragon was catching up, and then I felt you let go of my hand. I turned around and there was fire coming out of the dragon's mouth and it took you away from me. At that point I was so frightened and I tried to shout out. Then I woke up. Oh my God, *toba* (have mercy), it was so horrible! I recited all my *kalemas* (verses from the Quran) but when I saw you sleeping beside me I felt better and went back to sleep."

He listened to my dream with such care and attentiveness that I felt a rush of affection. He stared at me like a young lover gazing into his girlfriend's eyes. I hugged him and he hugged me back tightly.

"Well, I'm not very good at interpreting dreams, but I guess it's just a dream. What else can I say?"

I released myself from his embrace. "I feel a bit better now that I've told you, but I'm still worried."

He got up, took his *pakol* (Afghan hat), glanced in the mirror, and then told me to follow him to the front door. As he put on his shoes and walked toward the main door of the house he suddenly stopped in his tracks.

"Mahgul, wait a minute."

I asked what the matter was but he didn't reply. He went back into the corridor, slipped off his shoes, and went to the room where our children were sleeping. He leaned down and kissed all four of them on their foreheads.

As he got up I told him that he'd kissed the children as if he was never going to see them again. "I know you love them but you're getting late for work. Hurry up!"

He approached me, his arms outstretched. "Yes, you're right. I just wanted to kiss them, and now I want to do the same to their mother. You never know when I'll see you again."

And with that he kissed me on the forehead too, then we walked to the front door together and said good-bye. He went to his taxi which, as usual, was parked in front of our house. As he started the engine we kept looking at each other as if we were not going to see each other ever again. I had this strange feeling—a voice was telling me to stop him leaving—but I ignored it and waved my hand as he left.

I went back inside and started my daily work. I made breakfast for my children. Only the two older children went to school then. I went to wake them up. The younger ones would wake anyway and enjoy watching their brother and sister get ready for school. We had breakfast all together around the small square *desterkhan*. I looked at their faces and felt frightened. I didn't know why, but I was filled with a sense of loss. I sipped my tea and tried to calm down.

"God have mercy on me," I said to myself as I handed my two children their school bags and waved them off. Then I locked the door behind them and began sweeping clean the rooms and tidying where the children had been sleeping whilst my two youngest ones played in the sunshine in our garden.

I was just thinking about what to cook for my husband's dinner that evening when I heard a loud bang at the door. My young son ran toward it but I shouted after him, "Wait, my child, I want to open the door. Who can this be?"

It was a strange time for visitors to be calling because most people are busy midmorning. As I got nearer to the door I could hear the sound of a woman crying. Before I had reached the door I shouted out, "Mother, what's wrong? Why are you crying?"

I opened the door to find my mother with her head buried in her burqa. She looked up and hugged me.

"Oh, my daughter, you've become a pot without a top and your children are now so lonely."

"What are you talking about? Please don't talk nonsense. What's the matter?"

My children ran to me and held on to my legs.

"Mother, please tell me, is Father all right?" My father was getting old and often in poor health so I thought something must have happened to him. My mother began shouting and I noticed that other family women had followed her—and behind them I saw my father and brother. They were all crying and my children were crying too. I was still too shocked and frightened to know what to do. In the midst of all that crying and shouting, I'd forgotten how to cry.

My mother sat on the dusty ground and called to my children. "Come to me, my children. You've lost your father, he's dead!"

When I heard these words I began slapping my face and beating myself. I shouted to my mother in disbelief. How could it be true when I could still feel the warmth of his hands? I began to curse everyone; I even cursed God.

My children were shouting, *"Padar jan,* dear Father, is dead!"

I think I must have collapsed—someone carried me back into the house. After a few hours relatives and neighbors started arriving and gathered in my house to mourn but I kept asking for my husband; I wanted him brought to me. I saw that my two older children were sitting beside me. My brother had gone to fetch them home from school. They too were crying and shouting. My world had come crashing down. I was devastated, and I now knew that those premonitions I'd had in the morning had come true.

A short while later they brought my husband's body home. It was already in a coffin. My brother had organized everything for the body. I can't describe what my feelings were at this time; all I remember is that I sat near his head and my children sat around the rest of the coffin. We could only see his face; it had a few bruises but we still didn't know the cause of his death. His face looked as if he was smiling at us, and his eyes were open. I spoke to my darling's dead body.

"Who took you from us? Look at us! Who will take care of us now? You were the one always talking about being with the family and living together forever. You're the unfaithful one, leaving me halfway through our lifetime. Get up! Look at us! You can't leave us alone!"

The children were crying and calling on their dear father. Even if our worst enemy or the cruellest person in the world had seen my children and me clustered around that coffin, their hearts would have melted. Our lives had shattered in one day. My brother came up to me with tears in his eyes and said it was time for them to take the body.

I screamed. It was as if they wanted to cut out my heart and put it into the coffin where it would have no feelings or life. When they covered the coffin I became hysterical. I held on to it tightly and wouldn't let it go. My scarf came loose from my head as I struggled to follow the coffin outside. Our yard was full of men but I didn't care. I fell to the ground and my dress and *shalwar* got covered in dust and dirt. My children ran after me as I tried to stop them taking my husband away. My mother and other women tried to hold me back. It was a terrible scene. Eventually, my father caught me and held me tightly in his arms so I couldn't follow the coffin anymore. I wanted to be dead too. I had lost everything. I cried and cried until no more tears would fall, my voice wouldn't come out and my lips were cracked and bleeding.

I had lost my direction in life; I couldn't even think what to give my children to eat so my mother had to look after them. I had no appetite. It began to get dark; women were sitting around me and some were dampening my forehead with water to refresh me when I suddenly realized that I didn't know how he had died. I called out for my father and brother and then got up and ran to the men's room. My brother saw me and led me outside.

"What are you doing in here, Mahgul? Control yourself. What will happen to your children if you go mad?"

I began crying. "Brother, I've just come to ask you what happened. I need to know how he died."

My brother started to weep. "He was in his taxi taking some passengers to Pul-e-Khumri. He'd just reached the main road when a tank hit his taxi. It drove straight over the top of it. As the tank drove over his car, it crushed his chest against the steering wheel. He died there. When I got to the scene, I saw his smashed car but the tank had gone. I don't know which group the tank belonged to. One of the passenger's sons told me what had happened. The passengers were saved but your husband died."

My brother and I both wept. I went back to my room and looked at my four children huddled close to my mother. They were devastated. I remembered how in the morning he had kissed each one of them. He was right; it was the last time he was going to see all of us. My nightmare had come true. The tank that had killed him had been the monster in my dream.

Days and weeks passed, and the number of guests who visited us diminished. In our culture, relatives and close friends cook food for a bereaved family for forty days after the death. So, for forty days, my family and friends brought me food and kept me company. At the time, I felt the huge loss but I didn't fully realize the challenge ahead. I didn't appreciate the responsibilities for me now as a widow and mother.

For a while I was able to pay for my children to continue in school with the money that my husband and I had saved, but this was coming to an end. I also had to repay a large amount of money to my brother for the cost of the funeral. My family was kind and refused to accept all the money I owed them, saying I would need it for my life ahead as a widow with four young children. I had no income and so inevitably the day came when I ran out of money. I had to borrow from my parents and brother just so we could eat. We all started to grow pale and weak. Our faces looked as if the dust had settled into them. I kept borrowing money as I had no other choice.

Every day I felt my husband's loss more and more. I had lost my partner with whom I shared every detail of my life, I had lost a close friend who would make me angry but could also make me laugh, and I had lost my love. On top of all that, we had lost the person who provided for us.

My family started to get impatient with me borrowing money from them all the time. I don't blame them because they were not very rich themselves, but it hurt my feelings when they got angry with me. Eventually they stopped lending me money altogether. Yet I was too proud to borrow from strangers like my husband's friends or neighbors.

One evening my children and I were walking home—empty-handed—from my parents' home. My mother had told me: "My daughter, your brother only earns enough to fill our stomachs and those of his children. You have borrowed from us a hundred times with no sign of paying anything back. Please don't ask us again. Go and do something. You're still a young woman; go and marry another man because it's getting too much for us. From the day your husband died we have had to look after five more hungry mouths."

I was digesting my mother's words, even though they were painful. I tried to work out what she really meant. In my culture, it's usual for widows to marry again, often to a brother-in-law, but in my case I didn't have any. The only other alternative was to beg on the streets.

I had no money to buy food for my children. When we reached home I told them to go to bed early because there was nothing to eat. They didn't say anything, but my youngest daughter cried all night.

Early the next morning I took my *burqa*, left my children at home, and went out in search of work. I only told my oldest son what I was doing and that I would be back soon. I knocked on the door of every house, asking if anyone needed a servant. One woman whose husband was rich gave me some clothes to wash, and after a while I became popular in the neighborhood for washing and cleaning. I had no education so this was the only work I could do. Some families were kind and gave me enough money to buy food; others took advantage of my situation and gave me a very small amount of money or just food in exchange for a whole day's work. I was desperate, though, and would accept anything to feed my children.

One afternoon when I was on my way home from cleaning and washing at a house in the village, I noticed some young boys running around and creating clouds of dust. They were looking up at the sky and shouting, "*Azadi! Azadi!*"

They each wanted the honor of catching the free-flying kite. It was autumn, the season for kite-flying, when the winds are just right. We call it *Gudiparan Bazi*, which means "flying doll." The kite looked beautiful, like an exotic bird swooping and soaring in the sky. I got such pleasure from seeing the excitement in the children's faces and their hunger for these pieces of colored paper and bamboo, which together made the *azadi*.

Every autumn in Mazar, boys and sometimes men would form teams and start a kite-flying competition. Two groups would have two large kites and two people would fly each one. One would be the leader, the person who actually flies the kite, and the other would be the *charkha gir* (the person who holds the wire). The kite is controlled by the *tar*—the wire—which is wound onto the *charkha* (wooden spool for the kite wire). My father used to love kite-flying, and I knew that special attention has to be paid to the tar. It takes hours to prepare it for fighting. A *sheesha* (a paste used to coat the wire) is made using glass ground up and mixed with crushed rice. The wires or strings of a kite are found in many different colors and sometimes match the kite. The kite whose string cuts another kite is the winner.

Kite-flying is a traditional game for Afghan men and boys. No one is sure when it started but it's been played for more than a hundred years. It may have come from China where kite-flying is believed to have originated. The Taliban banned kite-flying, claiming it was un-Islamic, but since their fall it has become legal and popular again. It can be dangerous, though—some people are injured when they are chasing kites across the roof tops and fall or they are so distracted that they run into the road and are hit by a car.

Girls aren't allowed out to fly kites but my father would tell me how much he loved it. He used to make kites for my older brother. I was allowed to help with the cutting and pasting of the paper around the two sticks that hold the kite together. As I watched the *azadi* scene an idea came to my head and a smile to my face. When I got home I found my eldest son trying to mend his own small kite. I asked him if he thought he could repair it.

"Yes, of course, Mother; I can even make a kite."

In that moment he looked and sounded so much like his father it made my heart cry. I went up to hug him.

"Look, my son, I have an idea. I don't want you to stop going to school just because we're now very poor. I'll make sure we fulfill your father's wishes. I will start kite-making."

I could tell he didn't believe me but he came with me to the local shop to ask where we could get material to make kites. The shopkeeper suggested we visit the main bazaar. So, I took all the money I'd earned from that day's washing and cleaning and spent it on different colored paper, wooden sticks, drums, and wire for the kites. My son and I were both excited as we carried home all the parts. On the way back, we stopped off at the local shopkeeper to ask him if he would buy our kites from us. He was very enthusiastic: "Now the Taliban have gone, kites are selling well. If they're any good I'll buy them from you."

When we got home, I told the other children that we were going to start a kite-making business. My children and I didn't really have a clear idea of how we would do this, but we were determined to make it work. My son was confident he knew about kites and could make them. To begin with we made lots of mistakes, which was very upsetting because if we made a cut in the wrong place or damaged the materials it was an expensive waste. The paper has to be assembled correctly or the kite won't fly properly. Afghan children are experts and won't buy a kite that isn't made well. I used to get so angry if anyone made a mistake and reminded them that we couldn't afford to buy more material. My youngest daughter cried a lot because she was told off the most for getting it wrong. In the end we learned how to make really good kites by going to the main kite shops and looking in detail at how they were put together. We then applied this knowledge to our own kites.

From that day onward my children and I began working. My eldest son would sell the kites to the local shopkeeper after school and my eldest daughter was skillful at creating new designs. We all know what sort of designs the boys in the village like and what sort they will buy with their pocket money. It's like a factory; I cut pieces of colored paper into triangles, squares, and circles and my daughters attach sticks to them and then glue on a tiny flower or star to the corners. We are all involved in the family business. Eventually my younger children reached school age, and we had enough money to send them to school too.

For a while after my husband's death I had lost the will to live. If I closed my eyes, though, I could see his kind face and hear his voice telling me never to lose hope. I vowed to myself that I would become the breadwinner, that I would be the mother whose children went to school and became teachers and doctors.

I see myself and my children as being magicians for other children. With a few pieces of wood, some sheets of colored paper, and wire we can make a doll dance in the sky. I like to think that in those kites are carried the dreams and hopes of Afghan children, soaring and swooping in the sky, freely. Our handmade kites are much sought after in the bazaar in Mazar in the north of Afghanistan.

Fareshta, my youngest daughter once told me, "Mother, when I put this flower on the kite it makes me happy. I can see the bright color of the flower high in the sky when it's flying and feel like I'm flying too because I've made it."

My family is now famous as kite-makers. Sometimes children even call at our house asking for the latest model—but it's painstaking and tiring work. Concentration is needed to get the details right. If we make a mistake in the cutting of the paper then the kite can't be put together. The boys complain about the work. They want to be out playing with other boys, not selling kites in the streets, but I tell them that it's necessary for them to do their job because it makes money that buys them an education. I remind them of their father's dream for them to become teachers, doctors, and engineers.

I'm pleased I've created a successful business. I've gained the skills and so have my children. In the spring, autumn, and summer, we sell more kites, but in the winter no one wants to buy them so we have to survive on the savings we've made during the rest of the year.

Kite-making gives hope to me and it gives hope to my children too. I also like to think that our kites bring joy to the men and boys who play with them.

From what Mahgul told us on *Afghan Woman's Hour*, and also from what I have experienced here in the UK, it is clear to me that having independence is very important in Afghan women's lives. Mahgul, a widow who once thought her life had ended when her husband died, has proved it is possible to take control and secure a happy and economically independent life, even for an illiterate woman. She used her skill and imagination and started living a new life with her children.

During my work on the program, I realized how important economic independence was for me and for other Afghan women. Having a good job, earning my own money, and not being a financial burden on my family has proved crucial to me. It has enabled me to make very difficult decisions in life and it has allowed me to become a free and independent individual who can choose the life she wants to live.

When I think about how much hardship I could have faced if I wasn't able to be independent and work, I am thankful for the luck that's come my way. I consider myself a very fortunate woman to have had the opportunity of having an education, being able to get a job, and use my talent in a positive way, just like Mahgul.

12

Bakhtawara's Story

THE BOY-GIRL

$\mathcal{A}$S Bakhtawara strode along the road, her steps created a trail of dust in her wake. It was starting to get dark, and people were hurrying home. Bakhtawara took long strides, her gun slung over her shoulder, as she hurried home as quickly as possible. Along the way, a few male villagers waved to her, shouting that they wouldn't be late for tomorrow's meeting of the village elders.

Bakhtawara lived in Gurbuz in Khost Province, in southeastern Afghanistan. It's a harsh place to live: the winters are freezing cold and the summers scorching hot. The Khosties are known to be tall, broad-shouldered, and good-looking. They are renowned for being hardworking people who enjoy dancing and music. A Khosti friend of mine, who loves his dancing and drumming, once told me that even the Taliban couldn't prevent Khosties from celebrating by dance and *dohl* (drum). Every special occasion in a Khosti family is marked with their local dance called *attan*, where the men in the family dance, dressed in their local *shalwar kamiz* and a turban with a high *shamla* (the part of the turban which fans out like a peacock's tail). The women dance together in circles, sweeping their long embroidered dresses along the floor. The Khosties also have a reputation for being particularly wealthy compared to other tribes in Afghanistan. And they speak Pashtu with a strong dialect difficult for someone like me, who speaks Pashtu from eastern Afghanistan, to understand.

Afghans are, in general, very hospitable but Pashtuns are considered the most generous and welcoming to strangers. If you find yourself in a village in Afghanistan late at night you will almost certainly be offered somewhere to stay. Your hosts will share whatever food they have with you—they will tear a piece of bread they have for themselves and offer it to you. Pashtuns believe in respecting guests and honoring the person who chooses to take shelter in their home. My mother used to tell me tales of growing up in Kunar Province and how they would often have more than ten guests to stay every night. Most of them were people who'd met my grandfather in the fields and were on their way to Pakistan, but needed to break their journey and rest. My grandfather, a farmer, would bring all the guests home and tell the women in the family to cook for them. My mother said it didn't matter to him if those people remembered him or not; he was just happy to have helped them. My grandmother used to complain that these strangers were eating all their food and leaving her children hungry, but my grandfather would just shrug his shoulders and say he was a Pashtun man and it was part of the code. Like many thousands of Pashtun village men, he believed that a guest is a friend of God and must be treated well.

Pashtuns are mainly farmers, which means most of their disputes are over water or land. Throughout history there have been bitter fights. People have been killed and families have been divided because of these disputes. In this mountainous province people solve their daily problems by calling a *jirgah*, or meeting, of the local elders. If a family has a money quarrel or a family argument over land, they won't go to the government but instead will summon the *jirgah*.

⤝

GURBUZ, BAKHTAWARA'S BIRTHPLACE, IS one of the twelve districts of Khost Province and is located in an area near South Waziristan on the border with Pakistan. Gurbuz is made up of many small villages, and the tribal culture and traditions have strong roots there; but the land is dry and mountainous, which makes it difficult to cultivate for farming. Many young men travel to Pakistan, the United Arab Emirates, or Saudi Arabia in search of work, not just from Gurbuz but from all over Khost province. Most of these men are illiterate, from very poor families, and the trend of going abroad has come into Afghanistan from neighboring Pakistan. It is why many families are wealthy, because their men are working abroad. Their wives and children are often left behind for long periods of time. Some of these women have said that they would prefer to be poor rather than live apart from their husbands and sons for so long, but the lure of big money is too much for some men to resist. As a result, many women have a great deal of responsibility within the family. They do everything that the man of the family would usually do. They take care of the farm work and provide for the remaining family—almost treated as if they were men.

Bakhtawara was one such woman. Her story was brought to us by Fawzia Khosti, an *Afghan Woman's Hour* reporter who was herself from Khost province. Fawzia was a medical student and had attended one of the training workshops we run for women at the BBC's Kabul office. She grabbed our attention on the first day of training with descriptions of life in her province. She told us about the women in her village, their wedding outfits, and about fascinating local characters like Bakhtawara. Fawzia was a regular listener to the program and knew her compelling stories would appeal to us. Although I had heard about women from Pashtun villages who had been forced to act like men, we had never had a woman like this on our radio program, so Bakhtawara's story was particularly special.

As part of her training, Fawzia spent two weeks learning how to collect and record stories. We lent her some recording equipment and she promised us reports on child mortality, the traditions and culture of Khosties, and, of course, Bakhtawara's life story. I wanted to go to Khost and meet Bakhtawara for myself but the security situation there was too dangerous at the time. Instead, I had to be content with hearing Bakhtawara's voice through my headphones back in London. I asked Fawzia for a fuller picture of Bakhtawara: what she wore, how she walked, what she ate. As I listened to Bakhtawara speak, she struck me as a woman whose feelings had been stolen from her long ago, and then imprisoned in a place even she couldn't access. The society she lives in has taken away her right to live as a woman; yet on the other hand she has gained a kind of freedom no other Afghan woman could ever hope to attain.

❦

AFTER A LONG DUSTY walk, Bakhtawara reached home and the children rushed out to greet her. She handed her gun to Shah Mahmoud, her young nephew, to put away safely, and took off her dusty leather shoes. She wore *chapli*, a sort of sandal imported from Khyber Pakhtunkhwa in Pakistan. One of her nieces poured water over Bakhtawara's shoes and feet. Each of the children had a different chore.

Bakhtawara walked into the house and the women and girls greeted her. Her sister-in-law stood up and offered her seat to Bakhtawara as a mark of respect. She sat on the thin mattress near the window in the room, took off her large black turban, heavy with the scent of fresh sweat, and put it on the window shelf. In its place Bakhtawara wore a white-embroidered cap, although the dust and dirt had given it a yellow tinge. The children gathered around their aunt, eagerly waiting for her to hand out sweets, as she often did when she got home. They giggled around Bakhtawara, their hands delving into the pockets of her black waistcoat, which she wore over her *shalwar kamiz*.

The family gathered around the *desterkhan*, and plates and bowls of food were placed on it. A mouthwatering aroma of meaty soup rose from the bowls. Bakhtawara tore a large chunk of bread and dipped it into one of the bowls. The children were also tearing up the bread—everyone was throwing it into the soup! They tore up the bread until the bowl was full and Bakhtawara told them to stop.

"That's enough! It will be very dry if we put in anymore."

Bakhtawara's hands were rough and dry after years spent work-ing in the fields. Her sister-in-law brought out the meat on a separate plate with some onions and fiery fresh green chillies on a side plate. The meat was put in front of Bakhtawara. As head of the family she was expected to distribute it fairly amongst everyone. After the family had finished eating, Shah Mahmoud brought water for the family to clean their hands. It was offered first to Bakhtawara and then to the rest of the family. Bakhtawara would usually tell everyone what she had been up to that day; the women would listen carefully to every word.

"Tomorrow, I have to get up early as the *jirgah* hasn't finished hearing the dispute between the two families."

Her sister-in-law asked, "Tell me, *Hajiani*, what does Khan Mohammad's family want?"

Bakhtawara sipped green tea from the cup before speaking.

"Khan Mohammad wants his brother to divide the house equally, but his brother wants more than he has been allocated."

"Why does one brother want more? Surely they should both inherit the same amount of land from their parents?" Bakhtawara's sister-in-law asked.

"The brother wants more land because he has done more work on the house than Khan Mohammad and he also has a bigger family."

"So what does the *jirgah* suggest?"

Bakhtawara cleared her throat. "Well, we have suggested that they should divide it equally. The older brother must accept that Khan Mohammad has to share the same amount of land on which the house is built. But they also need to build a wall to separate the two sides. We have suggested that Khan Mohammad pay a sum of money to the older brother."

Bakhtawara's sister-in-law got the feeling from the way Bakhtawara responded that she had been asked enough questions and was tired after a long day working hard on the land and trying to resolve other people's problems. So she quietly said, "*Hajiani*, may God give you strength and blessing for doing all this and looking after my family too. I will let you rest and sleep now."

Bakhtawara said to her sister-in-law, "You are my family. If I don't look after you and the children God won't forgive me. When Father died he gave me this responsibility. He asked me to promise that I would stand shoulder to shoulder with my only brother and help my family in any way possible, and I am obeying my father's wishes."

Bakhtawara put her cup on the floor and got up to get some much-needed rest. Alone in her room, she took off her cap and her long brown hair fell onto her shoulders. She then took off her waistcoat and *shalwar kamiz*. As she stood near the open window a cool breeze brushed her skin; the body of an untouched woman was emerging from her male clothing.

Bakhtawara's parents had transformed her appearance from female to male by dressing her as a boy, even as a baby. To dress baby girls as boys in childhood is a common practice among some families all across Afghanistan. Having a son is vital for every Afghan family. A son represents the future prosperity of a family; he perpetuates the family name, and he is the one that his parents will eventually rely on to look after them in their old age. Girls are looked on as temporary guests in the family because when they grow up and marry they will make a family for someone else's son and take their skills to another family.

Bakhtawara looked at her reflection in the small mirror hanging by the door. Her green eyes felt like those of a woman and yet they looked back at her with the unswerving determination and stoicism of a man. She stroked her cheeks and lips, which felt like those of a normal woman but her hands were rough where her skin had been burned after working long days outside in the sun. Like any other woman, Bakhtawara craved love. She looked in the mirror at her broad shoulders and stocky body and sighed. She was tired of always caring for others and wanted someone to care for her. She wanted a dashing young man to hold her hand; she wanted to be the special person on her wedding day. Bakhtawara would often conjure up her own wedding scene in her head. The man of her dreams would come to her family to ask for her hand and her parents would demand a lot of money for her because she was so valuable. In her fantasies her suitor wants to marry Bakhtawara so badly that he doesn't care how much he has to pay. Then she thinks about children: her first child would be a baby boy, then the next child would be a girl, and the girl would be dressed and treated like a girl by the whole family. Bakhtawara smiled as she enjoyed the dream world she had conjured up. She only thought about this imaginary life alone in her room, unseen by others.

Bakhtawara was thirty-five years old but her skin was lined and tanned like that of the older men in her village. So many times she had wished to put on mascara, or yearned to decorate her hands with henna and dress her hair with different colored clips, or wear glass bangles like other girls in her family. On a few rare nights, Bakhtawara would allow herself to feel like a woman. She would begin by slowly touching her face and her neck, moving her hands to her breasts; she would feel a heat build up inside her body and her breath quicken, but as soon as she looked down at her feet the feelings would stop. The sight of her dirty toenails and burned skin would remind her that her life was the life of a man, not a woman, and she would feel ashamed and embarrassed. She would take a deep breath again, recite her *kalema*, and suppress her feelings.

Bakhtawara shook her head and told herself she had a lot of work to do the next day. Her *charpoie* was covered with a white sheet that had been hand-embroidered especially for her by one of her nieces. It had been done in a typical Pashtun style—large flowers in red, purple, and pink with long leaves connected to each other from both sides of the sheet. Bakhtawara pulled the long narrow duvet over her legs and suppressed all her feminine feelings. Tiredness soon overcame her and she fell asleep.

It was the cat meowing that woke up Bakhtawara at sunrise. In the mornings, she felt less like a woman than she did at night. The call of her daily duties meant she had to focus on being *Haji* Bakhtawara, whose life was to do with performing daily prayers, meeting the elders, and working on the land. She fastened her hair on top of her head and fitted her hat on tightly. The rest of the household was still asleep as she went out to wash in the bathroom. She did the *awdas* (ablutions) just as the Mullah began calling the faithful to prayer with the *Azan*.

After washing, Bakhtawara stood out in the yard for a minute, breathing in the fresh morning air, which filled her body with energy.

She then went back in the house where her sister-in-law was getting up to instruct her daughter to get water ready for *Hajiani* to wash. Bakhtawara explained that the cat had woken her up early so she had already washed. It was usually the teenager's job to prepare the water for Bakhtawara, after which they would pray and have breakfast all together.

Before breakfast, Bakhtawara went into her room, fetched her gun, and began cleaning it. She knew every part of the weapon—how to take it apart, clean it, oil it, and load it. Once it was clean, assembled, and loaded, Bakhtawara left it on the bed with her bullet belt and joined the family for breakfast. Bakhtawara's eldest niece Durkhani was fifteen years old. She had attended school until the age of eleven, but after she reached puberty, like most other girls in the village, her parents forbade her to go. In Gurbuz many girls never went to school at all; Durkhani had at least been to school for a few years because Bakhtawara had per-suaded her parents to let her attend. Bakhtawara loved her nephews and nieces but not as an aunt, rather as an uncle who would buy them presents and treat them kindly.

Durkhani poured the *shedo chai* into a cup for Bakhtawara and set it down in front of her, together with some freshly fried *parathas*—round loaves of bread baked on a *tava* (shallow frying pan) in boiling oil. The smell of Durkhani's delicious *parathas* would waft through the house and even reached the neighbors. Bakhtawara greedily ate the *parathas* and sipped the milky fresh tea.

While Durkhani was still busy cooking, her eyes watering from the smoke of the woodfire, she said, "*Hajiani*, I wanted to ask you for a notebook. Would you be able to bring me one today?"

Bakhtawara knew how much her niece missed going to school. She stroked the girl's hair and said, "Of course, my child. While your *Hajiani* is alive, don't worry. I couldn't persuade your family to let you finish school but I will make sure you have the books and notebooks you need at home so you can carry on reading and writing."

Durkhani smiled. "*Hajiani*, if we didn't have you, I'd have forgot-ten what I learned in school a long time ago. Father is never here for me to ask him but thank God you are here with us."

Bakhtawara knew what the life of a woman was in her village. They were allowed to walk in the mountains collecting firewood, but if they were unwell and needed to go to hospital a man would have to accompany them. Girls could be married as young as twelve years old and would often face violence in their in-laws' homes. Some are beaten by their husbands or in-laws if they do not do their chores properly, some are treated as slave labor. They have no right to question what the men in their family do, yet they can do nothing without permission. Bakhtawara knew this all too well. She was well aware of the difficulties her niece and sister-in-law would face without a man to look after them. Bakhtawara's brother was abroad most of the time and it wouldn't be easy for the family to live in the village without a man to support and protect them. Once the tea was drunk and the *parathas* eaten, Bakhtawara rose from the table. The women of the family stood up with her—Durkhani rushed to the window shelf and fetched Bakhtawara's black turban. Shah Mahmoud was ready for school; he waited in front of the door, holding the gun in his hands ready to give it to Bakhtawara. Bakhatawara strapped her ammunition belt around her body, slung her gun over her shoulder, and slipped on her *chaplis*. She said good-bye to everyone and then left the house with Shah Mahmoud, the only male in the household, who would walk to school with Bakhtawara. Every day they would walk holding hands as they passed through the neighborhood. Boys from Shah Mahmoud's school sometimes called out, "*Narkhazak! Narkhazak!*" (eunuch).

Bakhtawara was used to hearing these words and ignored them but Shah Mahmoud found it hard to dismiss their cries. "*Hajiani*, these boys are always telling me that you're a *narkhazak*. Is it true? Are you not a man and not a woman?"

"Don't take any notice of them, my child. What do you think I am?"

Shah Mahmoud, who was only seven, looked up at Bakhtawara.

"I know you're a man, but sometimes I can see you have big breasts like a woman, so I get confused."

The children in Bakhatawara's family had not been told about her gender and did not realize she was a woman until they worked it out for themselves.

Bakhtawara smiled. "Your *Hajiani* is a strong man—you've seen pictures of sportsmen, haven't you? Well, they all have big muscly chests because they're so strong. This is why I have breasts—it's because I'm strong. Let these boys say what they want."

Shah Mahmoud thought for a moment and then said, "Of course, it's because you're so strong and you have a gun too!" With that he laughed, said good-bye to Bakhtawara, and ran into school.

Being called names by adults as well as children in the village was something Bakhtawara had got used to since she was a teenager. In those days Bakhtawara had genuinely believed she was male. She would wear boy's clothes, play with boys, and tease girls. She had a large dog, which she trained for dog fights. She could even beat the other boys in most of the games. One particular game involved holding the left leg with one hand and then fighting another person doing the same thing. The first one to fall down was the loser. If a boy or girl had called her names in those days she would beat them up.

When Shah Mahmoud asked her if she was a man or a woman Bakhtawara was reminded of the day she reached puberty. When Bakhtawara was born, her family only had one older son—her brother—and after her birth, two other babies were born which didn't survive. Bakhtawara's parents owned a lot of land in the village which they were anxious to protect. They were worried that with just one son they would not be able to survive in a tough tribal land like Gurbuz. Jealous cousins and others around them might take advantage.

Finally, after two stillbirths, Bakhtawara's mother gave birth to a daughter. Her father was worried about only having one son but an idea came to him. When Bakhtawara was three years old she started being brought up as a boy. This meant the family now had the security of two sons and one daughter, instead of one son and two daughters. Her parents didn't stop to consider what harm this might do to their child; they just started to treat her as their second son. Bakhtawara was dressed as a boy and taken to the men's gatherings. She had her hair cut short and wore male *shalwar kamiz*. She would play with her brother and everyone in the family treated her as a boy. At Eid she would get new clothes just like her brother; her father taught her to use his old gun; she was never expected to wash dishes or cook with her mother and sister; instead, she attended *jirgas* with her father. She was respected as a boy but no one ever thought to tell her what changes to expect in her body.

When Bakhtawara's brother was sixteen years old and she was ten, he was sent to Dubai to work. Now Bakhtawara was the second man in the house. After her brother had been away for a few years, and as her parents were starting to get older and frailer, Bakhtawara began to feel the burden of responsibility on her shoulders. It was also at this time that she began to develop a woman's body. One morning as she was washing, Bakhtawara noticed that her breasts felt swollen and were getting larger. She was frightened and ran into her room. She tore up an old white scarf and tied it tightly around her chest. She took her father's waistcoat and wore it over her *shalwar kamiz* to conceal her changing body. She had no idea why this was happening to her. Before long, her elderly parents' health began to fail, so her father decided to give her part of the land. Her brother had married a girl in the village and returned to Dubai for work and her sister was now married. It left Bakhtawara with all the responsibility of looking after her parents. As her father's health worsened he called her to his bedside.

"My child, my life is near its end. You're still very young but I want to hand you your responsibilities."

"Father, I'm your son; it doesn't matter if I'm young or old, I'm ready to take on my duties."

Bakhtawara's father put his hand on her head and said, "You must take care of your sister-in-law; she's the young bride of our house. Her husband is away and I don't want anyone to start gossiping about her."

He asked her to fetch him his gun and bullet belt. When she brought them to him, he asked her to stand. He put the belt around her waist and handed her the gun. "From now on, my child, this belongs to you."

Bakhtawara understood this gesture. In Afghan culture when a gun is handed to you it means the whole pride and dignity of the family now rests in your hands.

"If you look after the family well," her father said, "our honor will remain and you will keep my name alive."

Bakhtawara promised her father that she would look after every member of the family, just as he had done. She would do as she had learned from him and follow in his steps. She would protect and uphold the dignity of the family, just as he had done.

Bakhtawara stopped thinking about her childhood when she reached the house of Malik, the head of the village. She entered the house, took off her sandals, and the male villagers all greeted her. In Afghan villages everyone knows about everyone else. All the adults would have known about Bakhtawara's life and identity, and known and accepted how she had been brought up as a boy. She was respected for fulfilling her parents' wishes and taking on the responsibility of the head of the family. Her name became a byword for strength in the village and she was upheld as a role model.

Bakhtawara sat on one of the *charpoies*. Khan Mohammad and his brother—the two men at the center of the dispute—sat opposite each other.

Malik opened the *jirga*: "In the name of Allah, the *jirga* is resumed," he said.

Then he began to explain to Khan Mohammad's brother why everyone in the room believed the brothers' house should be divided equally between them.

Bakhtawara interrupted and said, "Malik saab, I agree that the two brothers should do as our religion dictates and inherit an equal share of what their father left. However, we should also consider the work that Khan Jan's family has already put into the building and compensate him for this."

Many of the men who were present in the *jirga* agreed with *Hajiani* Bakhtawara's suggestion. The *jirga* therefore ruled that Khan Mohammad should pay a sum of sixty thousand rupees to his older brother to build another room for his larger family, and Khan Jan agreed to abide by the *jirga*'s decision.

The deal was sealed with green tea and sweets. There was relief that the *jirga*, which had already lasted for several days, had come to an easy and amicable solution, and Bakhtawara was praised for her leading role and for her fair treatment of both brothers.

It was harvest time and Bakhtawara was anxious to get back to her farm and asked Malik if she could be excused to leave after tea. Before she left, Khan Mohammad invited her and the other elders to dinner to show his gratitude and respect for the *jirga*'s decision. Bakhtawara accepted the invitation, shook hands with all the elders, and headed back to the fields.

She chatted with one of the other elders whom she had agreed to share the farm work with as they made their way back to their farms. Once she reached her land she removed her turban and gun and hung them on the branches of a tree. She rolled up her *shalwar* to her knees and set to work. Bakhtawara didn't acknowledge her tiredness; she just continued to dig in the hot sun. She wanted to do some work on the land before her nephew brought her lunch. She ignored her hunger and thirst as she tried to make the land softer for further cultivation. She took the *bailcha* (spade). She took the bail and drove it deeper into the ground. With every push she panted and sweated. Bakhtawara was proud that she could work as hard as any man. Her sister-in-law and nephews and nieces all respected her efforts, but her brother who was working in Dubai wanted to spare his sister this exhausting work. He promised her that once he had made a lot of money he would hire a farmer to look after their land so that Bakhtawara would not have to do it. But Bakhtawara had insisted that she wanted to work and that it was important for her to keep her promise to her father to look after the family for as long as she could.

Bakhtawara was still busy working when she heard her little nephew calling, "*Hajiani, Hajiani*, look, I've come with food."

She pushed the *bailcha* into the ground and walked toward the tree where she had hung her turban and gun. Shah Mahmoud greeted her, put the food on the ground, and went to fetch the water pot. He first poured it over Bakhtawara's hands and then washed his own. This was one of Shah Mahmoud's daily chores: after school he had to bring food for Bakhtawara, which they would share under the shade of a tree. Bakhtawara unwrapped the food and found potatoes and hot bread, which her sister-in-law had cooked on the griddle pan. She took the onion, pressed it down with her hand until it split, and gave some to Shah Mahmoud.

"Did anyone tease you at school today?" she asked him.

"Yes, the boys are still calling you a *narkhazak*."

The mention of this word again set Bakhtawara's mind back to the time when she'd become a woman. As she ate, she remembered the day it had happened. She had been playing marbles with the boys in the village—they all thought she was another boy and treated her like one. Suddenly she felt an ache in her back, then as she got up to chase the marbles, she felt a pain in her legs and stomach but ignored it. She kept playing and running, and was on the verge of winning the game. She squatted down as she pushed her marbles into the little hole, making her the winner, and then stood up in triumph. As she did so, she felt some liquid escape between her legs and thought that perhaps she had wet herself. She ran home to change, but when she looked down at her cream-colored *shalwar* she noticed it was stained with blood. Bakhtawara ran toward the washroom, shouting to her sister-in-law that she had been shot and was bleeding. When her sister-in-law saw where the blood was on Bakhtawara's *shalwar*, she guessed it was her monthly period. Bakhtawara was still checking her legs to see where she had been shot. Her sister-in-law told her not to worry and that this sort of bleeding happened when girls became women. It was the first time Bakhtawara had heard such things; she was embarrassed and upset. She went into her room and wept.

She wanted to be like the other boys but nature had shown her otherwise. Alone in her room, Bakhtawara unwrapped her breasts and looked at them. She hated her body and hated being a woman. She wanted to play marbles with the boys and be free like a man.

Bakhtawara went to speak to her mother who was now old and weak. She told Bakhtawara that as her father had given her all the responsibilities it was impossible for her to return to being a normal girl. She had no choice but to accept living like a man. So Bakhtawara started to wear baggy clothes and a waistcoat to hide her female form.

Shah Mahmoud interrupted Bakhtawara's memories. *"Hajiani,* should I go now?"

Bakhtawara told him to take the pots back to the house immediately and not to get involved in fights with other boys. Then she said her prayers and returned to work.

After several more hours' work, Bakhtawara picked up her gun and turban and headed home. It was getting dark but she noticed that the small shop in the village was still open. She went inside to buy sweets for the children and a notebook for Durkhani. This was a typical day for Bakhtawara: working in the fields, sorting out problems in the village, and providing for her family.

Back at home, Bakhtawara ate with the family and told them how tired she was and how she would be going to sleep early. Once she was alone in her room she tried to work out why so many past memories had come back to her today. She realized it was the word *narkhazak* that had reminded her of her past life. Bakhtawara had long accepted this was her fate but there had been one occasion when she had bitterly regretted it. A couple of years ago there had been a wedding for a close family member of her sister-in-law. Her sister-in-law's family knew that Bakhtawara was really a woman but there were some women from the more remote areas of the community who didn't know this. This wedding was to be a grand affair because the family was rich.

In Khost a man might pay several thousand dollars for a wife. The man's family is responsible for all the wedding expenses but sometimes the cost of the bride's jewelry and items for the couple's new home would be shared. In rich families the event can last for three or four days. The groom's family will start their celebrations a month in advance of the actual wedding. Women in the groom's family will be bought several new outfits—the more expensive the clothes the happier they are. On the day that the bride arrives at the groom's home, food is served to hundreds of people. Rich people will slaughter cows and sheep for the wedding feast. Women and men are kept in separate areas: the men usually gather outside in the courtyard and are entertained with professional musicians; the women are given a large room inside the house where there is singing and drum playing.

In Afghan weddings, especially Pashtun ones, the groom's sisters and female family members will all dance. The women in the bride's family will also wear new and expensive clothes—a sign that they are upset that their daughter is leaving. Sometimes the mother will be too upset to wear new clothes since she does not know if the new in-laws will treat her daughter well.

Bakhtawara's sister-in-law had persuaded her to go to this wedding so that she could see what a rich bride's wedding was like and enjoy the lavish celebration. Bakhtawara would usually go to village weddings as a man and attend the male parties. Occasionally, at close family weddings, she was allowed to go to the women's party but this was the first time that she would be attending a larger wedding as a woman.

Bakhtawara wore a new white *shalwar kamiz* and her niece had polished her leather *chapli* until they shone like new. She felt happy and carefree when she left the house with her family. All the women were wearing brightly colored and glittery Pashtun dresses and lots of makeup. Bakhtawara walked ahead of them with Shah Mahmoud. When they arrived at the house, they found the garden had been decorated with bright plastic flowers. Bakhtawara followed her sister-in-law into the part of the house where the women were gathering. As she got closer she heard the women giggling.

"Oh, I see you've come with your *narkhazak*," they teased her sister-in-law. "What does this *narkhazak* carry in her trousers? A *kus* or a *khota*?" And they dissolved into peals of laughter.

Her sister-in-law warned the women that if they didn't keep quiet Bakhtawara would get angry and attack them. At this, the women quietened down. Meanwhile Bakhtawara went to sit by herself in a corner of the room. She pretended that she hadn't heard any of this exchange because she knew her sister-in-law would be embarrassed at her family's behavior. Bakhtawara felt helpless. With men she had the strength and skill to fight them, but she had no idea how to defend herself against the mockery of these giggling women. For the first time Bakhtawara recognized she had less power and confidence amongst women than she did amongst men. On that day too, she realized exactly what she had lost with the denial of her womanhood and she felt a grief almost as profound as when her parents had died. Her physical strength, her gun and turban all helped her gain respect from men, but she had nothing in her armory to defend herself against the maliciousness of women.

Bakhtawara sat silently with Shah Mahmoud at her side. Delicious plates of food were brought in but Bakhtawara had no appetite. Her heart felt heavy and broken. Bakhtawara's sister-in-law could see she was upset and came to ask if she needed anything more, but Bakhtawara shook her head and with that her sister-in-law fled, ashamed by her family's attitude toward Bakhtawara. Bakhtawara wanted to cry but she was so used to being strong and manly that she couldn't. Her parents had taught her that only weak men cry and that if she were seen to be weak people would take advantage of her. Tears may not have fallen down her face but her stony expression couldn't mask the fact that Bakhtawara was shattered.

After all the guests had eaten, a young girl went around the room with a water pot, offering it to the guests to wash their hands. Bakhtawara moved her hands toward the girl so that she could pour water on them but the young girl couldn't stop laughing. After Bakhtawara finished washing she asked, "What's so funny? Have you heard a good joke?"

The little girl stepped back and said, "*Hajiani*, my friends and I think you are the joke!"

The girl burst into giggles again, and other young girls joined in the laughter.

"You shameless girls," Bakhtawara said, her anger rising. "What's so funny about me? Is there a joke written on my forehead?"

The girls ran to each other and shouted, "Yes, the joke is that you're a man with no beard. You look funny, like a cartoon. You pretend to be a man but you're really a *narkhazak*, aren't you?" And with that they laughed and went away.

Bakhtawara didn't want to make a fuss and spoil the wedding for her sister-in-law, so she told herself that she must say nothing and suffer in silence. A crowd of women were singing as they walked in procession with the bride. They were leading the bride to her place in the corner of the room. Bakhtawara gazed at the bride in her red glittery dress, green shawl, and gold jewelry. She looked so young and happy. As Bakhtawara joined in the clapping for the bride, she again felt that yearning to be a woman, a mother, and a bride. How she wished that she was standing in the bride's place. Surely she deserved all this, too, but she remembered that she was over thirty years old and that no one had ever praised her for her beauty, no one had ever knocked on her door to ask for her hand in marriage. She knew, however, that people would soon come and ask her for her niece Durkhani's hand. It wasn't the first time that Bakhtawara had felt this hunger to be cared for and loved as a woman. Whenever she saw her brother behaving attentively toward his wife she felt this pang of envy, and whenever her sister came to the house with her children she wished she could have a family too, but she never spoke to anyone about these feelings.

She stopped clapping and went back to sit in the corner with Shah Mahmoud. She felt suffocated surrounded by all these bitchy women and wished she were at the men's party where they respected her for behaving like a man. She was considering making an excuse and leaving when the groom's family entered the room singing. They hadn't met Bakhtawara before and didn't know the truth behind her masculine exterior. When some of the women spotted Bakhtawara sitting in the corner watching them, they assumed she was a man and suddenly stopped singing and covered their faces with their scarves. The mother could hear that the singing had stopped abruptly.

"What's happened? Why have you all stopped?"

One of the women stepped forward. "We have all our female relatives here. Yet there's a man here who keeps staring at us. It's very shameful and disrespectful to be treated in this way."

Another joined in: "You know, we came to your house with trust.

All our men have gone to the men's room. Why is this one still here sitting and watching us? It's an insult."

The mother of the bride saw Bakhtawara and smiled. "That is our *Hajiani*. She's not a man. Come, let's carry on singing."

But the women were not so easily reassured or diverted. "No, I'm going to call for the family men to come here and look at him. If he's not a man then I'm a man!"

The bride's mother said, "Bakhtawara is a *narkhazak*. She's neither a man nor a woman. Don't worry, we know how to keep the respect of our guests. Come on, let's carry on singing."

When Bakhtawara heard the bride's mother refer to her as *narkhazak* she got very upset. She stood up and went over to face the women.

"Do you have a question about me and my gender? I'll tell you what I am. I've got the same things as you have, I have the same breasts and the same hair and what's more I've got the same feelings as you. It's just that I've been unlucky, I've been brought up as a man—my parents raised me as a boy because they needed a son. I'm going to leave now. I just want you to be careful not to do what my mother did to me. Never change your daughters into sons because no one can change the feelings God has given us. You can change a person's clothes, you can change the way they walk and talk, but you can't change their feelings. I may look and act like a man but my feelings are the same as yours!"

Finally, Bakhtawara pointed to her sister-in-law and said, "She will go home with Shah Mahmoud."

That night Bakhtawara cried until the early hours of the morning. Her dress, her sheets, and her pillow were all wet from her tears. She would never go to another women's party at a wedding again.

❧

THE DAYS WERE USUALLY easier for Bakhtawara because she didn't meet many women and she was busy with her work. She also knew that in many ways she was freer than other women. She didn't have to stay at home, didn't have to suffer domestic violence; she could meet men in public and they respected her. She was in charge of her own life. There was no one to tell her what to do. She worked hard and had money of her own, which she could spend as she liked. If she needed to see a doctor, she just went. No one would gossip about her if she were seen talking to a strange man. She was given respect in the home and in the village.

But at night she felt tired, lonely, and unloved and it was hard to forget she was a woman. She wished she could have a family of her own. It hurt her that no one had asked for her hand in marriage and she was frightened of becoming old and frail. She worried that she would be abandoned when she no longer had the strength to farm the land, attend the *jirga*, and provide for the family.

Each day on her way to the fields, Bakhtawara would pass men in the village. She would shake hands with them and stand chatting for a few minutes with each of them. The men would talk to her as they would to any other man but they would not greet her with a kiss or embrace, as they would with other men, because they knew she was really a woman. Bakhtawara was a powerful figure in the village. She was influential and enjoyed the respect and attention she got from men in her community. She felt comfortable in their company; they didn't call her spiteful names; she was just considered a good Muslim and a hardworking person. Men judged her less, and so for a long time Bakhtawara stopped mixing with women.

As they had promised, Khan Mohammad and his brother hosted a dinner to thank the *jirga*. It was held at Malik's house. After a day in the fields, Bakhtawara got ready to go to the dinner. When she arrived at the house, the villagers stood up out of respect and shook her hand. The atmosphere was easy and friendly. No one called her names because they respected the fact that she could farm as well as them, shoot her gun as accurately as them, debate with the same reason and eloquence as them, provide for her family as they did; in all, she acted the same as them. Even though Bakhtawara felt comfortable with the men, she sometimes missed washing up a cup instead of digging the land, and sometimes she longed to bake bread instead of growing wheat. Even cooking the meat instead of just bringing it home from the shops seemed appealing.

After the meal was over, Bakhatawara walked home. Everyone in her house was already asleep. She went straight to her room where she took off her gun and turban and laid them on the table. Once again she stood in front of the mirror; she stroked her greasy and unwashed hair, and saw that her face was full of wrinkles. She looked closely at her reflection and realized she couldn't change her appearance to become more feminine. The time for that had passed. Now cooking for the family was more of a challenge to her than digging a field; sewing a pattern was a bigger test than oiling her gun.

Bakhtawara thought about the practicalities of her life and accepted her lot without shedding a tear. She had come to terms with the fact that her parents and local traditions had forced her to become a man. She had learned over the years how to suppress her femininity but there were times when she found it difficult to hold back her feelings. It was impossible for her to throw away her dreams completely. Bakhtawara knew the harsh realities of both worlds: the world of the man and the feelings of the woman—she had experienced both. Her parents had altered the course of her life in order to make the family more secure. Bakhtawara's advice to the listeners of *Afghan Woman's Hour* was simple: "Please, never change the fact that God has given you a girl. You might be able to change her appearance or the way she lives but you'll never be able to change the natural feelings God has given her."

◆

As a child I often wished I had been born a boy rather than a girl. I am sure many girls still wish the same when they see the significance that is attached to having a son. Girls are brought up to give priority to their brothers. Until I heard Bakhtawara's story, I wasn't aware of the lengths to which some families would go to produce a son. While researching this book I discovered several stories similar to Bakhtawara's. I found that dressing a girl as a boy was very common in families that didn't have a son, or sometimes only had one son and many daughters, but very few would carry on with this into adulthood. The girl would be allowed to resume a female identity once she reached puberty. Until then the girls would be dressed as boys, play with boys, and do all the activities that boys were allowed to do. The adults were aware of the girls' real sex but the children often were not.

I also heard the story of Berond, another woman living a man's life. She was born into a strict tribal Pashtun family in Ghazi Abad village of Kunar Province in east Afghanistan, close to the Hindu Kush mountains. This is an area renowned for disputes over land and other family matters. Berond was a tall, broad-shouldered woman with dark skin who usually hid her long hair in her turban. She had worn men's clothes since childhood and the male villagers showed her the same respect as they would show to any other male villager. She used to take part in *jirgas*, worked as a man on the land, and was the breadwinner for her family. She was brought up as a boy because her father and brother were in prison due to some land dispute and there were no other men in the family. Berond suddenly had to be transformed into the man of the family.

Women like Berond and Bakhtawara are much respected amongst villagers. They are praised for their bravery and for taking responsibility for their families. They are accorded the same respect as a man. In an Afghan family, when they want to praise their daughter, they say she's like a son, and when they want to praise a woman, they say she's strong and brave, just like a man.

In Khost, Bakhtawara's province, I heard of two other women— Mangala and Senzila—who had also lived as men, but this was many years earlier. Fawzia, our reporter there, told me that she thought perhaps Bakhtawara had been made into a man as a result of the popularity of these two women in their communities.

13

Ghutama's Story

A LOVE STORY

G HUTAMA WAS UNLIKE ANY OTHER WOMAN I'VE EVER MET. SHE WAS a strong and free-spirited Kuchi or nomad. The Kuchis travel all over Afghanistan and to neighboring countries to graze their animals. There are approximately six million Kuchis living in Afghanistan (out of a population of twenty-five million) and they are mainly Pashtun and Baloch nomads. They have their own unique lifestyle. A Kuchi woman once told me that they cannot bear having to live under a roof in a large building. She said that for Kuchis to be surrounded by four walls would be like living in a prison. So wherever they go, wherever they graze their sheep and build their tents, there in the middle of God's land is their home.

You'll find Kuchis in any part of Afghanistan that has water and fertile ground. They have a reputation for hard work, with both men and women taking care of the animals: sheep, goats, cows, and camels. They make cheese, ghee, and different kinds of yogurt from their cows' and goats' milk, and they use the wool from sheep and goats to make cashmere and carpets. These are then sold in markets or by going door to door to people's houses. According to the UN High Commission for Refugees, before the last thirty years of war, Kuchis owned thirty percent of the country's sheep and goats and most of the camels. They were also responsible for slaughtering animals and spinning wool, as well making dairy products.

Family ties amongst Kuchis are very strong. Kuchi women are renowned for being particularly beautiful—tall, tanned, with generous lips, high cheekbones, and mesmerizing eyes. They would not look out of place on a European catwalk, such is their grace and elegance. Kuchi men are no different—tall, broad-shouldered, and handsome, their renowned bravery makes them attractive to most Afghan women. However, Kuchis only marry within their own tribe.

Kuchis have suffered along with everyone else from the decades of war in Afghanistan. In some ways they have endured more because they have had to stay put and look after their animals without the opportunity to flee if they needed to. The UN has identified them as being one of the most vulnerable groups of people in the country. They have been especially harmed by land mines because they often travel to remote areas where land mines have not been cleared. They are also vulnerable to natural disasters like floods, droughts, and heavy snow. Their nomadic way of life means that they have limited access to hospitals, schools, and clean water, and the lack of security means they sometimes can't travel to better grazing land.

⌒≋⌒

I MET GHUTAMA EARLY in 2001 while I was in Peshawar working for a BBC radio education project for Afghan children. I used to visit the refugee camps in Pakistan every week and record interviews with the women and children there. Ghutama's life story was one that I'll never forget. I can still remember her face and how she talked very clearly. I had seen some Kuchi women before but I'd never had the chance to talk to them and find out about their way of life. Previously I had only seen them from the window of our apartment in Kabul. It was a breathtaking sight to see the caravan as it passed by our house: the women, men, and children walking in a long line with their animals.

Like me, Ghutama was a refugee in Pakistan but our lifestyles were very different. I was a city girl while Ghutama was a child of nature.

Life for Afghan refugees wasn't easy, as most lived in extreme poverty. Those who had fled Afghanistan in the Soviet era tended to live in better conditions because they had built houses and settled down in Pakistan. Their mud houses were far superior to the plastic tents of the Afghan refugees who had fled the Mujahedeen and Taliban. Only refugees who had jobs like my dad and those who had family members in the West and Europe were able to rent places in the cities like Peshawar, Islamabad, and Rawalpindi. Many thousands more spent their lives in those basic tents with no clean water and no money.

Ghutama had been a refugee for many years. Her family had fled Afghanistan during the years of the Soviet-supported communist government. Her story stayed in my mind all that time. Almost every woman and man in Shadalan refugee camp knew who Ghutama was. In the last few years there wasn't a woman who hadn't shared their life stories and secrets of the heart with her, and there wasn't a man who hadn't been captivated by the sound of Ghutama's jewelry. Wherever she went, there would be the sweet sound of bells ringing as she walked through the village. Equally famous were the ornaments she made, carefully crafted with her long feminine fingers. Almost every villager owned at least one of her handicrafts.

Many boys were in love with Ghutama. She stole their hearts with her free nomadic spirit and her songs. When they saw her approaching, the boys would even break into song themselves:

> Your golden nose ring looks so beautiful
> The leader of Kuchis, you walk with lavender in your hair
> Among the happy, playful girls,
> You are the leader of Kuchis with the flowers in your hair,
> The boys are mad for you, crazy girl!

Ghutama's beauty was irresistible. She had large, mesmerizing black eyes, her dark brown skin had a golden glow, and her smile was framed by high cheekbones. She wore a long *kochani kamiz*, a traditional nomad dress. Its sleeves were flared at her wrists, and whenever she raised her hands they would fall open to reveal her arms and her glowing skin. Like all other Afghan Muslim women, she wore a head scarf, but her hair refused to be contained and flowed down her shoulders and back. When Ghutama walked in the green hills of Shadalan camp wearing her nomad *shalwar* and her long flowing skirt, the fabric would sway from side to side as she walked. Nomadic women would only make two or three dresses in their lifetime but these dresses had so much time and effort poured into them that a typical Afghan woman would have been able to make a dozen or more dresses in the same amount of time. Ghutama's dress appeared to be deep red but on closer inspection it was made up of a patchwork of fabrics, all cut into different shapes and carefully sewn together, their colors shimmering. Across the chest Ghutama had created a Kuchi-style of *charma kari* (golden lace) onto which were sewn real silver rupees. Ghutama liked to hang a lot of jewelry on this part of her dress, and so wherever she went the sound of tinkling bells would announce her arrival to villagers. She also wore two *taveez* (amulets), which would hang around her neck to ward off evil. Ghutama said they had been made by a mullah and given to her mother a long time ago.

Shadalan is a mountainous region in Tal district in the North-West Frontier region of Pakistan, bordering Afghanistan. Alongside the Pashtuns from this area, there were many Afghans who had fled the conflict and made this new region their home. It was a fertile area with fresh breezes passing through its mountains every morning. The small villages of Tal were spread out from one another along the mountainside. Here the Afghan refugees built small clay houses for themselves and began farming. They lived alongside the Afghan Kuchis who pitched their tents and grazed their animals here too.

Ghutama's father's name was Warishmeen. His wife, Ghutama's mother, had died while giving birth to Ghutama's youngest brother. This is the fate of many Kuchi women—giving birth in their tents far away from doctors and hospitals there is no one to help if something goes wrong. Ghutama's mother had left behind her daughter, husband, and two young sons. Warishmeen wasn't a typical Kuchi man: he didn't work hard to provide for his family but spent most of his time in his tent resting. He had long hair, a messy beard, and a gray moustache. Ghutama knew that her father's laziness had lost them many sheep and now they were left with only ten. They also owned one adult camel and two baby camels, which Kuchis call *jongi*.

After his wife's death, Warishmeen had become even more ineffectual. Ghutama was forced to become the breadwinner and head of the family because she was the only one who earned any money. Every day she would get up early and take their animals to the hillside to graze. When she left her tent in the morning, people in nearby tents would know it was Ghutama because of the jingle of the bells on her anklet. Her animals also made noises as they moved up the hillside. The little group was like a mobile alarm clock for those in the tents they passed, but the strange thing was that no one seemed to mind. In fact, most young men in Shadalan camp would wake up to the sound of her jewelry and their hearts would beat a little harder and a little faster in anticipation of seeing Ghutama. Ghutama walked with confident strides and in one hand carried a long stick. It was said she had the elegance of a giraffe. She would call to her flock of sheep and sing a traditional Kuchi song as she herded the animals up to pasture. When Ghutama reached an area that was green she would stop so the animals could graze. Then she would find a large stone to rest on and start her other job. In an embroidered bag that she wore on her shoulder, she carried her sewing kit. She would embroider Kuchi designs on clothes for men and women; she was particularly good at the delicate embroidery on the front of dresses. But Ghutama also made small Kuchi jewelry: covers for small mirrors, key rings, necklaces, and bracelets from small colorful beads. It was a lot of work, but she had little choice: she had lost her mother and needed to earn money to feed her brothers and her aging father.

At around eleven o'clock she would return with her flock to her tent. Warishmeen would usually be up by then and would have made breakfast for himself and his two sons, saving some food for Ghutama. But on some occasions Ghutama would return to the tent and find she had to make breakfast for the whole family. After breakfast was finished, Ghutama would sew dresses for village girls. She used an old sewing machine to make the golden lace for dresses for girls who were about to marry or who were attending a wedding party. She would sew until late in the afternoon when it was time to take the flock out again onto the hills. She would stay out until dusk, and then as it started to get dark she would once again lead the animals back to the tent. Warishmeen and his two sons would know when Ghutama was returning home from the sound of her jewelry.

The Afghan refugees in Shadalan camp did not live as close to each other as they did in other camps in Pakistan; yet even though their homes were spread out, these refugees still had a sense of community and of supporting each other during difficult times. There was a mosque where the men would go for prayers, and after prayers they would stay behind to chat. Warishmeen wasn't that companionable and didn't have many friends, but Ghutama's popularity made up for his lack of sociability. Ghutama would maintain contact with people by being kind and helpful. She was good at numbers and counting money, which most of the women in the village found hard, and so she would help them make business deals with men. Men respected her for her bravery and her trading skills. Many boys in the village were desperate to find any excuse to talk to Ghutama. They wanted to gaze longingly at her beauty, but her confidence prevented them from showing her insufficient respect.

Ghutama's excellent animal husbandry skills meant that her sheep produced lambs that she could sell at the local market, and her handicrafts were so popular that word quickly spread of her talents. Her crafts had an artistry and skill that only a daughter of the hills and deserts would know how to make; only someone well acquainted with nature could work with such purity and delicacy, people said. Some even paid in advance for Ghutama's handicrafts. And what she couldn't sell in the village, she would sell to a shopkeeper she knew in the main bazaar, or she would go with her father and sell her pieces of art there herself. With the money she earned Ghutama was able to care for her lazy father and her two younger brothers. Sometimes she would even help some of the poor refugees in the village. Ghutama didn't hide her face like the Afghan refugee women in the village would do. She did the same jobs as men and that took her out into the village, into the hills, and the marketplace.

One night a fierce storm hit Shadalan camp, the wind blew down their tent and tore the sheets, and the rain scattered their possessions. Ghutama woke to find their home damaged and their belongings in disarray. Warishmeen sat on a stone in the corner of their plot complaining to Ghutama. She knew her brothers were too young to do the heavy work of rebuilding the tent so she rolled up her sleeves and said to her father, "You just sit there and relax. I know it's upsetting to see your home ruined, but I'll see what I can do."

Ghutama knew exactly what she was doing because she had helped her mother make the tent on numerous occasions before. She told her father to take the sheep and camels to the nearest grazing ground, while she set about mending and reconstructing the tent, which she managed to do by the end of the day.

⁂

WHEN SHE WASN'T EARNING a living and caring for her family, Ghutama's heart was also beating for a Kuchi man called Babray, for whom she had made a specially embroidered handkerchief. They would meet when she went to fetch water or when she took her animals to graze on the green hillsides, and would spend hours talking to one another, exchanging stories and jokes. It was a very pure and simple love.

However, Ghutama's beauty had also been spotted by Malang, a young man who had just returned to the camp after several years working in Dubai. He had earned quite a sum of money in Dubai and had come back to Shadalan camp to look for a bride. One day as Malang walked through the village's green hillsides, he saw Ghutama and was immediately drawn to her beauty, her confidence, and her love of life.

Malang's family called on Warishmeen's tent several times to ask for Ghutama's hand, but Warishmeen knew that if he gave his daughter to Malang he would lose both the breadwinner and the carer of his household. He was also aware that his daughter was unlike other Afghan girls in the village; she had the power to say who she wanted to marry and who she didn't want to spend her life with.

When Ghutama refused to accept Malang as her husband, rumors started circulating about her—mostly spread by Malang's friends. People gossiped about Babray and his relationship with Ghutama, and criticized Ghutama for rejecting a rich young man like Malang. So Malang tried to win over Warishmeen by offering him large amounts of money for his daughter. He finally persuaded him that if his daughter married a poor Kuchi she would leave her father without an income and he and his two sons would be left hungry and poor. He promised enough money for Warishmeen and his sons to secure their future.

One evening, those with tents near Ghutama and her father could hear raised and angry voices. Warishmeen had been convinced by what Malang had told him and was willing to give his daughter to him. Ghutama wanted nothing of it and shouted back at her father. Their noisy argument gave her a bad reputation in the village, and the next morning when Ghutama left the tent to take the animals out to graze, people gave her black looks, and some boys even shouted out after her, "Ghutama doesn't want a rich husband; she wants a poor Kuchi man."

Ghutama was upset by the change in people's attitude toward her. That day she was quiet, she didn't sing or smile, and she didn't touch her handicrafts. She knew a major decision was being made, one that would change her entire future, and it might go in her favor or against her. She decided to return home in the early evening even though she would have preferred to stay out on the hillside in the fresh air, alone with her thoughts. She knew she couldn't stay out any longer or more gossip and bad looks would come her way. She was being judged for falling in love.

As Ghutama walked toward her tent, she recalled the time when she had had an argument with her mother about making a dress. Ghutama loved her sleeves to be big and wide but her mother would protest, saying it was not right for a young girl to show her arms. Ghutama remembered the words her mother used to say when she was angry with her: "May you marry a village man." By this she meant: "I curse you to marry a man who lives in a house in a city." For Kuchis this was a terrible fate, as every Kuchi girl wanted to be free in the green hills with her family and animals and not tethered to a brick house. For the first time since her mother had died, Ghutama cried. It was as if her mother's curse was coming true. She was afraid that her father would make her marry Malang—a city man with money. The thought of living in a city was like being sent to prison for Ghutama, but she was also thinking about the loss of her love, Babray.

That evening Warishmeen was so angry with his daughter that he wouldn't speak to her. He made the boys eat separately from her and didn't care whether she ate or not. Her father's attitude just served to make Ghutama angrier still. She accused him of trying to blackmail her and said she would never marry Malang and that if he forced her then she would be forced to take a more drastic step. Warishmeen accused her of being selfish and said if she agreed to the marriage he and his two sons would have a better and happier life. Ghutama's anger rose.

It was just before the call for evening prayers. As usual, Warishmeen didn't go to the mosque. Ghutama was determined to resolve the issue. She left their tent and ran toward the mosque; as usual the sound of her jewelry rang out across the camp but she didn't pay any heed to this. Warishmeen assumed Ghutama had run out to weep by herself. Ghutama ran and ran, each step faster and more urgent than the last. She wanted to reach the mosque before the evening prayers were finished. When she reached the mosque, she knew that almost every man in the village would be there, including the rich Malang and her love, Babray.

She stood in front of the mosque as the village men came out one by one after their evening prayers. Ghutama was still so angry she didn't care what people thought or said about her. When she saw Babray among the other men, and with Malang not far behind, she walked up to him and stood in front of him. All the men were surprised to see Ghutama in front of the mosque and stared at her. Had she gone mad to stand in front of a man and hold his arm? They were shocked by what was going on and waited to see what would happen next. Babray was also surprised and fearful.

"Ghutama, what's happening? What's gone wrong? Why are you behaving so strangely?"

Malang watched Ghutama closely. He suspected she was here to tell Babray that she was leaving him and that she would now accept his own proposal because of all the money he had offered her father. However, Ghutama's words took everyone by surprise.

Taking Babray's hand, she announced in a loud clear voice, "Babray, you are the love of my life and I want to be your wife."

Then, still holding his hand tightly, she waited for his answer.

Babray was in shock but his love for Ghutama gave him the courage to speak.

"I'd be happy to be your husband!"

The news spread rapidly that Ghutama, a Kuchi woman, had chosen a husband for herself. It was considered a massive taboo amongst all the tribes in Afghanistan. Malang accused Ghutama of being shameless and it wasn't long before the gossip reached Warishmeen's tent. When Ghutama returned, her father was at a loss for words and just stared at his daughter.

But Ghutama said, "Well, Father, if you had acted with more kindness and hadn't forced my hand I needn't have done this. Now according to our Kuchi and Pashtun culture no one can take me away from Babray. Tomorrow you are called to the mosque where the Mullah will make a decision about us."

Warishmeen had no choice but to go to the mosque with Babray for the village meeting. According to Pashtun culture, once a woman calls on a man to be her husband, the man cannot leave her, so the *jirga* decided that Babray should become Ghutama's husband. Ghutama was called in and the Mullah performed their *Nikkah* there and then.

Ghutama was the first young woman to choose her husband in front of everyone. She was lucky because she called on a man who loved her and in the village she was very popular. At first Ghutama went to live with Babray but after a few weeks she persuaded him to move to her tent and live with her father and two younger brothers. So Babray and his old mother moved in with them and they began living as an extended family. She looked after the family and animals with Babray and eventually Warishmeen forgot how wounded he had felt. Ghutama and Babray were liked and respected in the village for being kind and helpful. Malang returned to Dubai to earn more money while Ghutama and her love lived a long and happy life in the village with their animals.

⌘

FOR A WOMAN TO go to a man's house or to ask a man in public to marry him is considered a hugely shameful act. Such a woman brings dishonor to her family and that kind of dishonor never fades—if she has children, people will still remind them of how their mother once called on so and so. These women are shown no respect in the family unless they are fortunate enough to be loved by their husbands. It often happens to women and men who have a love affair like Ghutama. There are stories of widows who have called on their brothers-in-law or men they liked. It becomes the responsibility of the man because the man is involved in the affair. For an Afghan woman, having a love affair with a man is still a big taboo. Obviously in Ghutama's case she didn't care about what people said.

I'm not sure that I would be strong enough to take such a step. On the other hand, I do know that I'm not one of those Afghan women who would judge Ghutama or girls like her. So much has changed for me over the past few years since I divorced my husband. Sometimes I think about how much I enjoy the free spirit I have now—I really do appreciate it immensely. I believe this kind of freedom is the basic right of every human being, but you need confidence to achieve it. Some people, like Ghutama, are braver and can seek out what they want early in life; sometimes you need to learn how to gain your freedom and get the confidence to speak out, thanks to the experiences you have gone through.

⌘

I SPENT MORE THAN three years married to Javed. During this time, I discovered I wasn't the only one who had accepted family and cultural pressures and married an unwilling partner—Javed was in exactly the same position. We were like two birds who didn't care for each other but had been put together in a cage. In Afghan culture, you brew up a revolution if you try to push against the system and force open your cage. One of us had to be brave and break down the door.

Even though I was very unhappy, the thought of divorce didn't cross my mind. It wasn't until I began working on the life stories section of *Afghan Woman's Hour* that I realized I could break my silence. These stories gave me the confidence to start my own revolution. I decided I had to tell my family how unhappy I was in my marriage.

Initially I was a much-praised daughter-in-law. Javed's family complimented me for accepting this marriage and for looking after Javed, even though he was lazy and clearly didn't love me. But the moment I decided to leave him and he lost his right to live in my flat, they turned against me. I was cursed and called a prostitute. I felt very alone and abandoned by those closest to me, even by my own family. I was denied a family home and denied the right to call someone my mother or father.

The program I worked on was blamed for turning me into a feminist. I was accused of being a shameless woman who didn't care about the dignity of her family. No one asked me what I was feeling. Instead, I was told to keep up appearances by taking Javed back and not bringing the shame of divorce on the family. I was told that a Pashtun woman should suffer in silence. No one in my family or my community supported me through my divorce. Islam says that the family is the base for society, but if two people cannot make a happy family, then divorce is agreed to be the final solution. But if being a Pashtun woman means being treated as a second-class citizen and not fighting for my rights, then I am no longer a Pashtun woman.

I spent so much time crying, especially on the Central Line going to and from work. My emotions were very mixed. I was angry that I had to pay a substantial amount of my hard-earned money to end a marriage that I never wanted in the first place. With that money, Javed bought himself a nineteen-year-old bride from Kabul. Yet in all this darkness there was light, and this light was the kindness of my friends in London, who are mainly not Afghan. They were friends I chose and with whom I decided to share my life. They didn't judge me for being a divorced woman. My friends taught me how to love and to accept being loved. It hurts less when I remember the women in my country and their bravery.

When I took the decision to end the marriage and leave Javed I knew I would be going against the will of my family. It was the hardest thing I've done in my life, and with that decision I lost my blind faith in Afghan traditions and culture. It made me the center of gossip amongst Afghans in London and back in Afghanistan. I felt lonely and vulnerable but every judgment made against me made me more determined. Every hurtful comment made me stronger. It enabled me to understand the pain of others better. This one action empowered me and made me kinder to other women whom I might have judged more harshly had I been the same old Zarghuna.

~

GROWING UP IN A country like Afghanistan has given me the benefits I have today: I have an understanding of the languages and traditional culture, and I work with Afghan people, yet I can travel around London as freely as the woman sitting next to me on the tube—this is all a privilege. It's a big advantage to know and understand two different cultures. My heritage has given me so much and I love it when friends who are not Afghan enjoy the Afghan music I introduce them to. Equally, I enjoy it when they introduce me to ABBA or Madonna.

Of one thing I'm certain: the pain I went through in my childhood and early adulthood have made me the Zarghuna I am today. As one of my friends pointed out, I'm the Zarghuna who is ready to fight for every scrap of her rights. I've found that in life there is always someone or something that helps you make difficult decisions. For me, it was the example of the Afghan women that I came into contact with through

Afghan Woman's Hour. Their lives and their strength helped me make this, the hardest decision of my life. Women like Anesa, Sharifa, Shereenjan, Wazma, Layla, and Ghutama; they have all given me the power to make changes in my life. They made me realize that I didn't have to embrace the traditional views of people around me and accept being humiliated as a woman.

The stories of these Afghan women have given me the courage to write my own life story and share it with you. They made it clear to me that telling the truth is important, accepting the truth requires strength, and dealing with difficulties is what adults do in a civilized society. These Afghan women enabled me to write about my life openly to millions of readers across the world so I would like to give them a big thank-you for empowering me.

It is forbidden in traditional culture in Afghanistan for a girl to fall in love with a boy before marriage. However, if a boy sees a girl in his village and falls in love with her it is accepted and encouraged. Usually, his family will do what they can to try to get the girl for him, but any girl found to have feelings for a boy will be condemned and her reputation stained forever. Ghutama was brave enough to stand up for what she wanted and decide her own future. When I look at her example I'm forced to ask myself if one day I will ever find the courage to tell my parents that there is someone that I am in love with, but, after all the upheaval of the last few years of my life, am I prepared to cause another revolution so soon?

Epilogue

IN AUTUMN 2001, AFGHAN AND COALITION FORCES OUSTED THE
Taliban from power and an interim government was set up with
assistance from the international community. The expectations of
Afghan people were raised, with the hope that at long last their country might find some peace and even prosperity. Women and men felt
liberated. Men shaved off the beards they had been forced to grow by
the Taliban and many women in cities swapped their *burqas* for a head
scarf. Women once again could leave their homes to go to work or
study. Now, a decade on, there is still the freedom for them to do this,
but the question remains: How far have the lives of women improved
since 2001? After all the lives which have been lost fighting against the
Taliban and Al-Qaeda, and all the millions of dollars that have been
spent on international aid, has the situation got much better for women?

There are undoubtedly advances: there are more than sixty women
members of parliament and many women in powerful positions in
local government, the judiciary, and media, but this is a country that
is still deeply religious and intensely traditional. At the beginning of
2009, a law was introduced by the Shia Mullah of Afghanistan—Shias
make up a minority section of Muslims in Afghanistan, the majority
are Sunni—and signed by President Karzai himself, which limited the

rights of Shia women. The government argued that the law was being introduced to provide more protection for Shia women within the family, but others saw it as directly responsible for limiting the rights of women. For example, it gave a husband the right to starve his wife if she refused to have sex with him. She could only deny him this if she was ill. It also forbade a wife from leaving the house without the permission of her husband unless it was an emergency.

This new law became a major discussion point amongst my colleagues in the Afghan service at the BBC in London. I found myself arguing fiercely against male colleagues who believed that a wife should ask her husband's permission before leaving the house. One day one of my colleagues said to me, "Zarghuna, you wouldn't be arguing like this if you were still living in Afghanistan." I thought hard about his comment and realized he was right. Living in a country like Britain has made it much easier for me to stand up for women's rights. Many women activists in Afghanistan also raised their voices against the law, but making any progress in a fight against society is difficult even for women who are lawyers or members of parliament. I realized I certainly wouldn't have been able to leave my husband and face the shame it would bring upon my family had I still been living in Afghanistan. When I think back to the days when I was trapped in an unhappy marriage, I can still feel every moment of the pain I endured. At the time my future seemed very bleak, but I found the strength to fight and defend my rights even though it meant confronting my own community.

⟳

THE WOMEN IN THIS book, the women who have trusted me with their stories, have had far more strength and courage than me. They have stood up for their rights in much harsher conditions than I have ever known. Women like Janpary, who was denied her right of inheritance but nevertheless went to court to try to claim it, or Nasreen, whose crime was to fall in love with the boy next door; these women were not afraid to follow what they felt was right in spite of their family. Others like Shereenjan, who experienced cruelty almost beyond belief, or Anesa, whose marriage was for the benefit of appearance: these women were brave enough to tell us their stories.

When I put on the headphones and heard the words, "Dear Zari," my heart would pound with expectation and emotion. I knew the voice wasn't just speaking to me but to the thousands of women it would touch with its story of pain, courage, and hope. This is what these stories do. It doesn't matter if you are Zarghuna in London or Gulalai listening in Kabul, they have the power to change lives for the better. Fatima from Pul-e-Khumri told us: "Dear Zari, I have been listening to *Afghan Woman's Hour* for almost four years. I have benefited from it so much. In my village women get together to listen to the program. They finish their chores quickly so they have time to listen to the friendly words and interesting stories. I have learned about other women's lives. I heard the story about the woman who was given away to settle a dispute and from listening to the program I realized there are other ways to end a disagreement, like giving animals or money. In my village, a local family had decided to give away their daughter to settle a dispute but after listening to your program decided to offer the other family money instead. This is a big step that we women have made to stand up for our rights and understand that, even though we have suffered, there's no reason for our daughters to have to go through the same experience. We can prevent it."

THE POLITICAL CHANGES IN Afghanistan now mean that women's voices are heard in parliament through female members of parliament and politicians. Women are nominating themselves in elections. Many that I've spoken to tell me that the first thing they will do if elected is give equal rights to women.

In some ways it's easy for me to stand up for my rights because I work full time in a well-paid job and live in a country that has equal rights legislation, which is enforced. However, all this doesn't protect you from gossip, judgmental comments, and disapproving looks. Other Afghans would be critical of me for divorcing my husband. It was I who was always blamed for the marriage not working, not him. People would criticize me if they saw me enjoying myself and they would accuse me of becoming a Western woman and forgetting my own culture. These remarks hurt less now, but going through all this did enable me to identify more strongly with women like Layla.

In January 2010, the British government decided not to fund *Afghan Woman's Hour* any longer and have turned their attention to other broadcasting projects. However, the program has had a lasting effect on my life and I know it has changed the lives of other Afghan women and men. Suraya Parlika, an Afghan woman's rights activist in Kabul who appeared on our program several times, sent us this message:

Dear Zari,

Afghan Woman's Hour *has been very successful in exploring human rights in our country. I went into a village and saw some women working; I asked then how they had learned to do this and they said they had been taught to work by listening to* Afghan Woman's Hour. *For the last six years this program has had a positive impact on the lives of women. The stories have been very popular and enabled Afghans to learn about their own culture. The program made it clear there should be respect for both women and men.*

Another listener, from Khost, the same province as Bakhtawara, said that the program was so popular people remembered the wavelength and the time of broadcast by heart. When *Afghan Woman's Hour* ended, many people contacted us to thank the program for the contribution it had made to their lives. I too want to thank the program and the listeners but most of all I want to pay tribute to those who said "Dear Zari" and told us their stories.

Glossary

AAYAT—verses from the Quran

AEENA MISAF—the part of an Afghan wedding ceremony when the bride and groom see each other for the first time in a mirror

ATTAN—local Khosti or Pashtun dance

AWDAS—ablutions

AZADI—a kite flying free from its string

AZAN—mullah's call to prayer

BACHA BE REESH—"boys without beards" (i.e., male prostitutes)

BAILCHA—spade

BURQA—full-length robe worn by some Muslim women to cover their bodies in public places

CHADOR—big scarf

CHALAK—clever

CHAPLI—sandal imported from Khyber Pakhtunkhwa in Pakistan

CHARKHA—wooden spool used for kite wire

CHARKHA GIR—person who holds the wire of a kite

CHARMA KARI—golden lace

CHARPOIE—daybed

CHIRAGHS—lights

DAIRA—tambourine

DEGADAAN—wood-burning stove made of clay

DESTERKHAN—large plastic tablecloth

DOHL—drum

DUKHMANY—the practice of using girls and women to settle disputes by offering them as brides

EID—three-day Muslim festival that marks the end of Ramadan

FAHISHA—whore

GAHWARA—cradle

GELIM—carpet

HAJIANI—a woman who's been on a hajj (pilgrimage)

HAMAM—steam bath

HARAM—something which is forbidden in Islam

HIJAB—head scarf

INSHALLAH—"God willing"

JIRGAH—gathering of leaders, or tribal or local elders

JONGI—baby camel

KALEMA—verses from the Quran

KARGAH—loom

KHEENA PAICH—a triangle-shaped cloth made from glittery material used especially for weddings (usually green and silver), which is wrapped around a bride's hands after henna has been applied

KHOSTI—people from the Khost province in the southeast of Afghanistan

KHOTA—cock

KHUDA HAFIZ—"May God be your guardian"

KOZA—water jug

KUCHI—nomadic Afghan tribes people

KUNI—homosexual

KUNJED—local sweet from the Balkh province

KUS—cunt

MAHRAM—someone legally related to a woman, e.g., brother, husband, father, or uncle

MAST—high on drugs or drunk

MEERAS—inheritance

NARKHAZAK—eunuch

NIKKAH CEREMONY—official Islamic wedding ceremony

NOOR—grace

NOWROOZ—Afghan New Year

PAKA—a paddle-shaped fan

PAKOL—Afghan hat

ROZ AFZA—a sweet, perfumed drink

SALAMALIKUM—"Peace be with you"

SHAH SALAMI—ritual where a groom goes to see his bride's family the morning after their wedding to show the sign proving she was a virgin, and he is proud to have married her

SHALWAR KAMIZ—an outfit of loose trousers and dress or top

SHAMLA—the part of an Afghan turban which fans out like a peacock's tail

SHEESHA—paste used to coat kite wires

SHORBA—meat stew

SHROMBI—fresh sour yogurt

TABLA—percussion instrument

TALAQ—divorce

TANOOR—oven

TAR—kite wire

TAVA—shallow frying pan

TAVEEZ—amulets

TOBA—repentance; also used as an exclamation in speech, "Have mercy!" or "Never ever again!"

TOJAR—trader

Acknowledgements

IT IS HARD TO believe that my once scattered notes and scattered feelings have become *Dear Zari*. If it wasn't for the letter Elizabeth Foley wrote to me a few years ago, and her listening patiently to my story, I wouldn't have this book in my hands today. Thanks to Liz for having the imagination to see the potential for a book in my life and these stories.

A special thanks goes to Imran Ali, the person who has stood by me all the way through and helped me with my first draft. Imran is the man I have been able to trust with my story; I knew he would read the draft with care and correct the confusing words I had used in English, as my mind works better in Pashtu and Dari.

Thanks to my editors, Poppy Hampson and Juliet Brooke. Their creative ideas and guidance have been invaluable and I have learned many things from them. Their experience has added to my knowledge.

My SPECIAL THANKS TO all those Afghan women whose real life stories gave me such support and inspiration in my own life. These women have encouraged me to become a courageous woman and today I feel I can face the world.

I am grateful to all of the reporters on *Afghan Woman's Hour*, whose names I have already mentioned in the book. I really appreciate their help and some of these stories are the direct result of their hard work.

Last but not least, I would like to thank Naomi Goldsmith, who has had a key role in *Dear Zari*. Naomi has worked with me on the project right from the beginning, from writing the synopsis to finding a publisher, right up to the final stages of checking proofs. She has been helpful and understanding, and her knowledge has been a key component of the book. Naomi's friendship and teamwork has been wonderful and the support she has given me will stay with me all my life.

About the Author

ZARGHUNA KARGAR, AN AFGHAN woman now living in London, grew up in war-torn Kabul before she and her family fled to Pakistan shortly before the Taliban took power. In 2001, Zarghuna moved to the UK to begin a new life. Working on the BBC World Service program *Afghan Woman's Hour*, Zarghuna was part of an influential project that gave support, education, and encouragement to millions of women across Afghanistan. For ten years, *Afghan Woman's Hour* aired discussions covering difficult—often taboo—subjects, and Zarghuna heard from hundreds of women eager to share their stories. It is these life stories which have inspired her to write this book.